JASON MORGAN enlisted int[...]trained to become a combat weatherman. The combat weather team is a small elite unit in the Air Force Special Operations Command. In June of 1999, Jason was deployed to South America on a counter-narcotics mission while attached to the 160th SOAR (Special Operations Aviation Regiment), called the Night Stalkers.

An operational accident left Jason in a coma. He awoke two months later, lucky to be alive but paralysed from the waist down. Soon after his injury, Morgan's marriage ended and he then raised his three young boys almost entirely by himself – with the help of a service dog from Canine Companions for Independence.

DAMIEN LEWIS has written a dozen non-fiction books and thrillers, topping bestseller lists worldwide. His books include the Sunday Times No. 1 bestseller *Zero Six Bravo*, as well as *Judy: A Dog in a Million*. He has raised tens of thousands of pounds for services-related charities, and several of his books are being produced as feature films.

# A DOG CALLED HOPE

*The wounded warrior and*
*the dog who dared to love him*

Jason Morgan
&
Damien Lewis

Quercus

First published in Great Britain in 2016 by Quercus Editions Ltd.
This paperback edition published in 2017 by

Quercus Editions Ltd
Carmelite House
50 Victoria Embankment
London EC4Y 0DZ

An Hachette UK company

A CIP catalogue record for this book is available
from the British Library

PB ISBN 978 1 78429 716 9
EBOOK ISBN 978 1 78429 547 9

10 9 8 7 6

Text designed and typeset by CC Book Production
Printed and Bound in Great Britain by Clays Ltd, St Ives plc

For Napal

# AUTHOR'S NOTE

This book is written from what memories and recollections I still have of the fateful events that took place over a decade ago. My story begins in the South American jungle and most of what took place there I have only ever relived in my dreams, well after the memories were wiped from my mind by my injuries. It was a long time – many months, years even – after my injuries that I started to recollect anything at all and the memories started to bleed through.

Those official military reports that I have seen state that my injuries were sustained in a car wreck – which they were – but my dreams and my nightmares speak of so much more. Did these things really happen? I believe they did. In my flashbacks this is the way I remember it. It all makes sense, both to me and my buddies and to other survivors of that mission. I will probably never know the full truth, but in a sense I have stopped worrying about that. The end result is the same: injuries, paralysis, life in a wheelchair. A life that I have had to learn to lead. I have reconciled myself to never really fully knowing.

We had been sent to the South American jungle to train the Ecuadorian special forces to combat the scourge of drug trafficking in their country and those of their neighbours. Believe me, the local special forces needed some serious improvement; they could not be compared even to an average NATO infantry airborne unit. And it was not as if they were operating in a classroom environment. Far from it. To train the Ecuadorian special forces we had to go with them on active operations. My injuries were sustained in the course of one of those.

My memory and my sense of time and place has been affected permanently by my injuries. I have no doubt about that. What is written in these pages comes therefore with that one caveat: *it is as I remember it*. One final point. Due to the respect and love that I feel for my family I have not plumbed the depths of the reasons for my divorce from the mother of my three children. I am sure readers will understand why.

*Jason Morgan, McKinney,*
*Texas, Spring 2015*

# ACKNOWLEDGEMENTS

We wish to thank our literary agent, Annabel Merullo, and all at agency Peters Frazer Dunlop for helping us bring this book to fruition. Likewise, film agent Luke Speed, at Curtis Brown, for bringing the early manuscript of this book to the attention of Safran Films, whose enthusiasm for this story was so evident from the very first.

We'd like to thank our editorial team at UK publishers, Quercus – Richard Milner, Charlotte Fry, Ben Brock, Fiona Murphy et al. – plus Josh Ireland, for your staunch support and insight throughout the editorial process, and likewise our American publisher, Atria, and the editorial team there.

Very special thanks to Wounded Warriors Family Support Group, both for the sponsorship to attend the Marine Corps Marathon and for supporting the Morgan family on a very special vacation to Disney World. Many thanks also to the HALO for Freedom Foundation, for the support which enabled that first parachute jump so many years after the fateful military jump in Ecuador. Huge thanks also to Jim Siegfried, for enabling us to tell his and Napal's amazing story from the early years. Thanks also to Greg Hardesty, for assisting so capably in that storytelling process, and to Tean Roberts, for transcribing the tape-recorded interviews. And of course thanks to John Libonati, for helping us to tell his side of this story.

Finally, we'd like to thank our families – wives, sons, daughters, siblings, parents et al. – for supporting us so wholeheartedly throughout the process of writing this book in all the many ways that they did.

*Jason Morgan and Damien Lewis,*
*November 2015*

# PROLOGUE: AIRBORNE AGAIN

My name is Jason Mark Morgan. Or Goshman for short. I'll explain why Goshman later. There are parts of this story I cannot tell simply because I wasn't there. Others will have to step in to do so.

Otherwise, I'm here for you, the reader, all the way.

We roll out to the waiting aircraft.

It's just after dawn.

A crisp winter's sun with just a hint of spring brightens up the scene. I'm dressed in a military-style shirt, with both my US Air Force and Army special forces patches proudly on display.

Paul, the tandem master who's going to jump with me, sticks close to my side. He's a tall, muscled, tough-looking guy with cropped hair and mirrored shades, but I've quickly come to realize that he's got a heart of gold. As we near the plane he bends to have a word in my ear. He has to shout above the noise of the roaring turbines.

'When I pull the chute, you good to do some real tight turns? We'll fall real fast. More speed – less time in the air. You good with that?'

I smile. 'Sure, I'm good. Sounds like fun! Let's do it!'

He grins, his shades sparkling in the fine winter sunlight. 'OK, buddy! Good to go!'

Paul and the other guys help manoeuvre me onto the plane, getting me strapped in for the flight. Already I can feel the blood rushing to my head, my pulse pumping like a machine gun with the adrenalin. It's always like this when you ready yourself for the greatest rush of all – free-falling from the heavens.

The aircraft hauls itself into the skies and we begin the ascent to around 10,000 feet. The climb towards the roof of the world is a long and noisy one, and it's too loud to talk much. We're all of us 100 per cent focused, zoning into the jump.

In truth, I'm feeling pretty relaxed about this one. I figure there won't be any shooters lurking in some badass jungle below, preparing to open fire on us as soon as we bail out of the aircraft. And at least today we're not leaping into the depths of the empty night, faces blacked up, going in under the cover of darkness. I was trained to feel at one with the night. To welcome it. To see darkness as my friend. I was trained to embrace what others fear because that would enable me to outwit, outfight and defeat my enemy.

But today, on this jump, there's no need for any of that.

We reach altitude and the jumpmaster gives us the hand signal. Five fingers flashed twice before our eyes – we're ten minutes away from hurling ourselves out of the plane's open door.

Paul steps across to me. He manhandles me into a position where he can strap me to the front of his jump rig, with both of us facing the same way. Like that we'll free-fall from the burning blue and drift to earth under the one chute, in what is known as a tandem jump.

The two most dangerous moments when making a parachute jump are exiting the aircraft, and – most of all – landing. As my military parachute instructor used to tell me, 'It's not the jump that kills you, it's the ground when it hits!'

Paul and I pause at the open door of the aircraft. Outside it's a wind-whipped howling void. He inches us closer to the exit, until I'm right on the very brink. The last thing he does is grab my legs and strap them into the specially designed harness that'll hold them up so they won't smash into the ground.

I peer ahead into the stark rectangle of the doorway. Outside the aircraft it's a snarling whirlwind. I can feel the wind tearing at my helmet and trying to rip the goggles from my face.

Paul flashes the jumpmaster a thumbs up. 'We're good!'

I glance at the jump light, positioned to one side of the open doorway. It begins flashing red: *Get ready.*

I get my head down and steel myself for the dive forward into nothingness. Out of the corner of my eye I see the red jump light switch to green.

The jumpmaster drops one arm in a chopping motion. 'GO! GO! GO! GO! GO!'

I scrunch my hands tight into a ball so they won't snag on anything, as Paul thrusts forward, driving me ahead of him . . . and moments later we're falling into thin air.

As one we plunge into the emptiness. We're sucked through the churning vortex of the aircraft's slipstream, the violent turbulence tearing at us ferociously, before we're spat out the far side and begin the free fall, a crazed plummet towards earth.

I flip my arms out into a star shape so they'll act like air anchors and stabilize the fall. Behind me, Paul does likewise. So begins our 8,000-foot death ride at pushing 300 mph, and – not for the first time – I'm experiencing the greatest adrenalin rush of all.

Paul pulls the chute at 3,000 feet. It's like hitting a brick wall. All of a sudden my world changes from the roaring rush of the free fall to one of total calmness and serenity, as we drift beneath a billowing expanse of silk the size of a yacht's mainsail.

He taps me on the shoulder. 'You wanna do those tight turns? Some spirals? Real tight?'

'Hell yeah!' I yell a reply. 'I'm up for anything right now! Let's do it!'

Paul pulls down on the left steering toggle, raises the one on the right, and we go into a spin, turning and dropping like a crazy top. The centrifugal force of the turns throws my legs out almost at right angles. We must be pulling nearly three Gs – approaching the kind of gravitational pressure fighter pilots put themselves under when training for combat.

It's insane – and I love it.

But all too soon the ground is rushing up to meet us. Paul executes a final corkscrew turn, and it's then that I feel the straps give way – the ones that hold my legs clear.

I shout out a warning: 'Man, the straps just broke! They broke!'

I try to grab my trousers and yank my thighs up higher, but there's nothing much I can do right now, for it's touchdown time. As for Paul, he's 100 per cent concentrated on the landing. *It's not the jump that kills you, it's the ground when it hits . . .*

We hit. *Bam!*

It goes without saying that Paul's a total pro. He takes the impact with his feet and his legs for both of us. My lower limbs seem just fine despite them having broken free at the last moment. Or at least there's no damage that I can see.

Paul hauls us to our feet and we both kind of take a bow as best we can when strapped together as one. The crowd standing to either side of us goes wild. As for me, I feel as if I'm walking on clouds. Everybody's cheering, but I've only got eyes for one spectator right now . . .

I search him out, scanning the crowd at around knee height. Finally I spot what I'm looking for – a glistening black muzzle poking out from behind some legs. The next moment there he is, dashing across to greet me.

*My best buddy – my dog!*

He can sense my every mood, and he hates – *he absolutely hates* – being parted from me. It's OK if he can still see me. If he's got eyes-on me he's good. But at 10,000 feet I was well out of even my handsome-as-hell black Labrador's range of super-laser-vision.

He bounds up to me. I greet him and pet him and tell him he's a good boy, and how glad I am to see him again. If he could speak human – and trust me, sometimes I almost believe that my dog can – he'd be telling me the same things right now: that I'm a good boy and how glad he is to see me again.

I can read as much in his loving eyes.

A helper rolls up with an all-terrain wheelchair – one that runs on caterpillar tracks so that it can negotiate grassy terrain like the landing strip. Paul unstraps me from the tandem and helps lower me into the chair. I lift my legs onto the footrests, but before I can get moving, my dog intervenes. He gets his front legs up in my lap, and he congratulates me on making the jump as only he knows how – with a big slobbery dog kiss. He can sense that this is it – the absolute zenith of what I've always wanted to achieve ever since the day of the 'accident' that put me in a wheelchair.

I gaze into my dog's beautiful, trusting amber gaze. 'We did it, boy! We did it!'

He speaks back to me, his eyes glowing like fire, and it's as if I can hear the words ringing through my head: *We did, Dad. We did. With me by your side you can do anything!*

And you know something? He's dead right.

For this special moment a dog kiss is just not enough. My dog rises higher, gets his paws on my shoulders and gives me the longest-ever doggie hug, his graying muzzle nestled against my cheek. The crowd goes ecstatic. They're cheering and yelling and some even seem close to tears.

Having worked his magic he drops down and gets into position, falling into step beside the chair as I set the tracks turning. But as we cross the dew-misted grass, I notice that my dog's not moving with the same easy fluidity or energy that I'm used to.

Back in our hotel room he seems utterly exhausted. He flops down and I can barely get him to eat his food. It's been a hectic few days at this wounded-warrior event, so maybe he's just exhausted, but still I'm worried for my best buddy, my dog. A couple of weeks back I took him to the vet due to a cough that just wouldn't seem to go away, so he's had a full check-up. But I tell myself that if he's not back to his old self by the time we get home we'll go and get a second opinion.

As I groom him and pet him he drifts into a deep sleep, his paws twitching and his throat emitting little yelps as he chases squirrels in his dreams. And as my dog rests, so my mind flips back to the last time I ever made a parachute jump.

It was almost two decades ago, and I was a whole world away from who and what and I am now.

# CHAPTER 1

The air was slick with moisture, yet burning hot all at the same time.

Suffocating.

As I waited for the C-130 Hercules transport aircraft to fire up its giant turbines, I ran my eye along the column of brother warriors lined up on this sun-baked tropical runway – each American, like me, dressed in unmarked combat fatigues. For a mission such as this, you never wear any mark of unit or rank, or anything that might betray your identity, just in case things go wrong. If taken prisoner, you don't want anything on your person that might distinguish you as being anything particularly *special*.

As with my fellow warriors, I'd sanitized myself completely: removing all patches from my clothing and not carrying a single piece of ID or family memento, anything that might link me to my nationality or my unit. Carrying even a photo of my wife and three infant boys was a strict no-no.

Such precautions have to be taken utterly seriously when involved in this kind of war against this kind of an adversary. We were in Ecuador, training that country's special forces to fight FARC – the Revolutionary Armed Forces of Colombia – a notorious rebel group that finances its operations from kidnap and ransom, illegal mining and, most of all, from drugs.

FARC's narcotics-smuggling network stretches from the South American jungle as far north as the USA and east across the Atlantic into Europe. With an income of some $300 million a year and tens of thousands of armed fighters under its command, FARC is a well armed battle-hardened force constrained by none of the normal rules of war. They have gained a reputation for horrific brutality, and are the last people you'd ever want to mess with.

I checked my watch. We were twenty minutes to getting airborne.

I glanced at my two jump buddies, Will and Travis, sleeves rolled up, shirts unbuttoned at the neck, looking easy and relaxed. Hailing from the Special Operation Aviation Regiment (SOAR), a renowned US Army special forces unit, you'd have thought they were stepping out for a practice jump over Florida and not heading into a jungle full of the world's foremost narco-rebels. It was the late 1990s, and the SOAR – also known as the 160th, the Night Stalkers – had taken casualties on previous missions here. What we were stepping into was a deadly serious business. But for Will and Travis it was just another day of doing what they loved. And, truth be told, it was getting to feel that way for me too.

Being an air force special forces guy, it had taken a good while for the SOAR to come to accept me. The competition between army and air force is merciless, and we'd never want it any other way – the intense rivalry serves to sharpen both arms of the military – but I'd been with the SOAR for months now and I was getting to feel like very much one of the boys.

We were here to train the Ecuadorian special forces – the 9th Special Forces Brigade, better known as PATRIA – to combat FARC and put a stop to the illegal drugs trade. But practically speaking we could never train these guys if our remit only ever kept us in the rear with the gear. The only way to do this properly was to go out into the field alongside them. The Ecuadorians were lined up with us, but they were a long way from being sanitized. Each wore the distinctive PATRIA badge on his left sleeve, a skull flanked by daggers, with a cobra twined through its empty eye sockets. The way they saw it, if they were captured by FARC they'd face a horrific death anyway, so why bother disguising what unit they were from?

The enmity between the narco-rebels and the armed forces here ran very deep, and neither side was inclined to show much mercy. We were about to fly north into the remote and lawless Cordillera Central, a spine of jungle-clad mountains snaking into neighbouring Colombia. Intelligence reports suggested that FARC was using the rivers there to traffic drugs from the heart of the rainforest to the outside world, with America most likely as their end destination. The PATRIA boys planned to stake out one of those rivers, put a stop to any narcotics operations, and take prisoners from whom further intelligence could be garnered to help break the drug-trafficking network.

Our role was to train them to prosecute these kinds of missions more effectively, and this was the type of tasking that we could wholeheartedly believe in. We were fighting the good fight against entirely the right kind of enemy, and despite their lack of experience and expertise – or maybe because of it – we'd grown close to the PATRIA guys. They were ideal trainees, like the proverbial sponges – ready to suck up all that we could throw at them. And boy, did they have a lot to learn.

From behind me I heard a high-pitched whine as the starter motors on the Hercules fired the aircraft's engines up. Gradually the massive hook-bladed propellers spooled up to speed, the avgas burning fierce and heady in the hot sludgy air.

As I turned to mount up the aircraft, Jim offered me a high five.

'Looks like we're on! Way to go, Goshman!'

My SOAR teammates called me Goshman because I never cuss much, and especially not around my parents or anyone in authority. That was just the way my folks had raised me. The most I ever managed was a 'gosh', hence the nickname. But that hadn't stopped the 160th from making me one of their own. Recently I'd been pulled aside by our unit commander. He'd told me that as I was serving with the SOAR I'd get to wear the Night Stalkers flash as well my air force special operations badge. I had the Night Stalkers badge on my right shoulder and my air force special operations badge on my left chest pocket. It was highly unusual to wear both, and I felt hugely honoured to do so.

We mounted up the aircraft; I pulled on my helmet and fastened the strap beneath my chin, settling into the fold-down canvas seat. We took to the skies. The aircraft executed a short climb, then thundered low and fast across the treetops, keeping below any radar. Going low also reduced the threat of ground fire because you'd flash past in a matter of seconds and be gone.

I was seated in the plane's tail section, next to a massive

heap of rucksacks secured to the floor by netting. Through the partially open ramp I could see the jungle speeding by. It felt close enough almost to reach out and touch the highest treetops. The pilot sure knew his stuff. If he took the Hercules any lower its propellers would be shaving the topmost branches.

We sped onwards across the carpet of green, the wind noise and the throbbing roar of the turbines killing the chance of any chat. Now and again there was a break in the forest canopy, marking a river, a narrow trail or a jungle village. But 99 per cent of what we were flying over was pure wilderness.

As with so many previous flights, I bore a special responsibility for this one getting airborne. I just hoped and prayed that I'd called it right this time. As I gazed out over the jungle, I reflected on just what had brought me to this position – an air force guy embedded within an elite army unit. I hailed from a tiny, little-known outfit – the 10th Combat Weather Squadron, part of Air Force Special Operations Command. The 10th was a seventy-two-strong unit when I was a part of it. Only sixty of us were jump-trained and mission-qualified and thus able to undertake the kind of task I was now on.

Combat weathermen do pretty much what you'd guess: we draw up the weather picture for combat operations. As such, we need to be first in on any mission, predicting the weather at the target – and above the target, if it's an airborne mission – so helping determine if it can go ahead.

Air Force Weather School is one of the hardest military courses there is. It's not just predicting when it's going to be 'partly cloudy' so folks can better plan their barbecues. It's about anticipating what type of cloud formations will be present at what altitudes, what the visibility will be for aircraft heading through those clouds, and when exactly they'll hit the heart of a thunderstorm. It's learning how a hailstone forms with concentric rings, like a tree, and what makes it burst out of the top of a cloud like popcorn and plummet to earth in a dark curtain of ice. It's getting to know local weather, and predicting when storms may occur, and what the conditions will be like when they do. It's working out how to read the weather, so as to make snap decisions on the ground.

Mission-critical decisions.

When I went through weather school we started as sixteen, and only three from our original class made it all the way. We had to score 80 per cent or higher on all tests to move to the next section. Weather school took about a year with over 1,500 hours of classroom instruction.

Combat weathermen have to pass air force special operations selection *and* combat weather school. Having done so, I felt as if I'd truly made it. My first assignment with the 10th Combat Weather was on attachment to the army's 3rd Special Forces Group at Fort Bragg, North Carolina. Life was good ... apart from one thing. My job – briefing pilots on weather conditions – didn't really do it for me.

I stuck at it for about two years, until word went around that the SOAR was seeking volunteers. When you have guys going deep behind enemy lines, as the SOAR do, it's vital that they know what weather's coming. Only air force guys can become combat weathermen. The SOAR is an iconic regiment, and my commander personally asked me if I'd be willing to join them.

I talked it through with my wife, Carla. She'd always been

supportive of everything I'd ever done, but for once she asked me not to follow my dream. We both knew that operations with the SOAR were dangerous. Carla told me that she had had a dark premonition, a really bad feeling about this one. She had a sense that something terrible was going to happen to me if I transferred to the SOAR.

But my commander stressed how much they needed me and I sure wanted to go. In due course I transferred from Fort Bragg to Hunter Army Airfield, the headquarters of the 3rd Battalion of the 160th Night Stalkers, and moved my family up there too. Carla and I had three boys below the age of four, so ours was one busy household. We purchased a modest one-storey house with a wraparound porch, room enough for the boys to bounce around in.

At Hunter I was introduced to the 'Skiff' – a hyper-secure underground vault protected by a series of massive code-activated doors. The Skiff was the nerve centre of SOAR operations, and it was from there that I would study the weather as it affected their missions around the world. I threw myself into my new task, striving to prove that an air force guy could be as good as any army man. I was at the front of all the training runs. I had to be. If I slipped back, I'd get all the usual abuse about being a 'pansy-assed air force guy'. And, like many a Morgan before me, I thrilled to the challenge.

I grew to feel at home among these army aviators.

Despite Carla's warnings, I thrived.

I worked my weather data like a magician. I conjured statistics to predict how storms would impact upon visibility or communications, or how wind speeds at the different altitudes of a parachute jump might enable a squad of paratroopers to hit a landing zone pretty much simultaneously. I sought current and tidal data, so we could do airborne insertions into water: I knew that if the current was more than one mile an hour, when swimming our guys would not be able to make headway against it. If we aimed to hit a beach, I needed to know the high and low tide times so I could advise on the best time of landing. Because sound travels more clearly through water than air, in damp, humid conditions I had to warn our guys that the enemy would hear us coming from much further away.

I tried to use the weather to our advantage, while warning how it might hinder operations. After prolonged rain a river might be rendered too hazardous to cross, making our planned exit from a target unworkable. If it was a sniper mission, I needed to predict how crosswinds might hamper the shot. If it was a night operation, I needed to know what lunar illumination we should expect. There might well be a full moon, but if there was heavy cloud cover, little light would filter through. Conversely, there might be too much light, causing human forms to cast shadows – making us visible and vulnerable to ambush.

If I ever felt the weather picture made a mission look undoable, I'd make that known to my commanders. My final call – the weather call – would be made four to six hours ahead of the mission start time, which was just what I'd done today, here in Ecuador. Prior to the mission I'd studied the local weather patterns for weeks on end. Our area of operations sat right on the equatorial trough, a tropical storm corridor running along the equator. Weatherwise, it's a hugely volatile region.

I'd already inserted two combat weather guys around a

hundred kilometres east of our target. As the weather blew in from that direction, they would be our eyes and ears, warning us of whatever was coming. Trained climatic observers, they'd transmit key data: wind direction and speed, air temperature, cloud types and height, and dew point. The dew point is the temperature at which the air becomes saturated with moisture, so fog or rain will form, impacting on visibility. They'd warn us if cumulus cloud was incoming, since it tends to build rapidly into violent tropical storms.

It was largely by using their data that I'd been able to green-light today's mission. But once we were on the ground I'd carry on monitoring the weather every step of the way. Stuffed into my rucksack were the specialist tools of my trade, chiefly a portable combat weather laptop, via which I could acquire my own data on the weather above us or download stats from the Skiff. The area we were flying into was heavily mountainous. We had hundreds of millions of dollars' worth of equipment in the air with us, plus several dozen men-at-arms. There were thunderstorms every day over the Cordillera Central, and a bad downdraught could cause an aircraft to fall out of the sky or scatter injured parachutists across a wide swathe of terrain.

That's why I bore such a heavy responsibility for the present mission.

By now, the SOAR guys had pretty much come to trust my decisions. A while back we'd been on a training exercise in Kentucky. I was on the ground with an advance force of SOAR operators, preparing to call in the main drop. But the area was hit by a series of tornadoes and for a while it looked as if the exercise was a no-go. Then a narrow weather window had opened and I'd called the aircraft in. We'd driven out to mark the landing zone, so the parachutists would know exactly where to put down. We were halfway to the LZ when the heavens opened – massive hailstones. The inbound aircraft were close now, and unless I called it off we risked having parachutists jumping out of the skies into a hellish hailstorm.

As the hailstones pounded onto the roof of our vehicle I could feel the SOAR guys staring at me. I knew what they were thinking: *How the hell could he have got it so wrong?* And, no doubt about it, I was sweating it big time. But I stuck with my gut instinct. The weather window was coming.

The jump remained on.

Sure enough, the hail stopped, we got the parachutists in, and the last set of boots had barely hit the ground when the weather window closed again. It had all been down to some good judgement, coupled with a great deal of luck and split-second timing. On the drive out the SOAR guys told me they were amazed at what I'd just done.

'Shoot, we'll believe anything you say now.'

'Goshman, you tell us you're God, you got it.'

But I knew for sure that I wasn't God. And on this mission into the Cordillera Central – as with every one before it – I was praying that I'd called the weather right.

I'd brought with me a small disposable camera and I asked my buddy Travis to take a photo of me perched at the aircraft's open ramp, my hand on my M4 assault rifle and my eyes gazing out over the rolling green canopy of jungle. It was the summer of 1999, and I looked young, full of spunk and unstoppable – like I was ready to take on the world.

Shortly after that photo was taken we piled off the C-130's open ramp, a string of stick-like figures tumbling into the void. We made a low-level jump, an elite-forces parachuting technique that enables you to get fast and unseen onto the target.

We landed in a wide forest clearing thick with dense waist-high jungle grass. It was mid-morning by now, and out in the open it was furnace hot. Within seconds my combats were plastered to my body and drenched with sweat. But the big upside was this: not a shot had been fired at us, and there was zero sign that FARC had detected our presence. We'd just inserted a covert force of elite operators into their very backyard. And, a massive bonus for me personally, *the weather had held real good*.

I gathered in my camouflaged silk chute, feeling unbeatable. Invincible even. I loved what I did. I thrilled to the intellectual rigour of the combat weatherman's craft, plus I welcomed the physical challenge and the buzz of jumping into missions with the SOAR. I was in the prime of my life and the fittest and the most highly trained and capable that I'd ever been.

We cached our chutes, hiding them in a specific place so we could return and retrieve them later. Then we began the long trek towards our end destination – a fast and angry river that snaked and boiled through the jungle. If our intelligence was accurate, the narco-traffickers would be heading downstream using open boats stuffed with bales of drugs and gunmen. All we had to do was to lie undiscovered in the thick bush and wait.

But for months after this mission that would be my last conscious memory – trekking through the thick, suffocating jungle. The next thing I knew, I was in a military hospital fighting for my life with zero idea of how I'd even got there.

# CHAPTER 2

Jim Siegfried hunches over the wheel of his Chrysler minivan, making steady progress up the Ocean Road. Spring in California is a beautiful time of year, especially when driving north beside the Pacific Ocean, and today promises to be a very special day. He rolls down his window and settles back to enjoy the warm sea breeze, mulling over what the next few hours will mean to him – and how for the best part of two years they will completely change his life.

Puppies. What was it about puppies?

A dog lover all his life, Jim never had been able to resist falling head over heels for a puppy. And the one he is going to collect today promises to be real special. Napal. Napal II – the second – to give him his full name. Napal II, the son of Terence, who was without doubt the most awesome dog that Jim had ever had the good fortune to raise.

Jim had reared Terence from a puppy until he was two years old, serving as a volunteer puppy raiser for Canine Companions for Independence (CCI) – a not-for-profit organization which provides service and assistance dogs to US military veterans and the disabled.

It wasn't cheap rearing a CCI dog: Jim figured it cost him a few thousand bucks to raise Terence, what with the vet's bills and everything. And it wasn't until he attended his first CCI graduation that he had really started to understand why it was all so totally worthwhile. Prior to that Jim had figured he was raising a CCI puppy for the obvious reasons: the companionship and the unquestioning loyalty that a dog brings. But you could get that from having your own pet, and that way you didn't have to endure the heartbreak of handing the dog back to CCI after two glorious, lovestruck years. It was only at that first graduation that Jim had truly got his answer as to why.

Jim had watched as a little boy with autism and cerebral palsy had got his first CCI assistance dog. At the front of the graduation hall the animal and its new owner had been brought onto a stage to be joined together for life. Jim had watched the boy take the leash of his assistance dog, and for the first time he saw that kid smile.

But it was more than that.

It was so much more than just the smile.

For the first time the boy had seemed truly to come alive.

His entire facial expression had changed. He'd been lit up as if by magic. It was like the child had met an angel, and that's how Jim had come to view assistance dogs: as angels on four paws. The change in the boy's features and his body language – his pure, simple, newfound joy in life, knowing that he had a companion who would stick by his side, no matter what – had been life-transforming for both the child and all in the audience. That was when it had really hit home. *This is why I raised the dog. I didn't do it for myself. I raised it to help the person for whom the dog was destined to become a life companion.*

For that disabled kid, having the dog was going to be like having an angel permanently on his shoulder, and what could be better than helping give someone that?

Raising Terence had been such a joy (with, admittedly, real pain at their parting) that Jim had asked immediately for another CCI puppy to rear. But he'd made a very special request: he'd asked if he could get the first of Terence's offspring. And so it is that today Jim turns his minivan east onto Route 76, making for CCI's Oceanside facility, to collect a six-week-old bundle of fun and mischief called Napal.

Jim had raised Terence in the hope that he'd make it as a CCI assistance dog. But, on balance, the odds were against it. The demands upon the puppies are so great that only 34 per cent who enter CCI's intensive training programme make it through. The rest 'wash out': they fail to graduate and are rehomed as domestic pets.

The main reason a dog washes out is 'distractibility'. Picture this: you're that little boy with autism and cerebral palsy and you're in the park with your assistance dog. But he spies a flock of ducks and immediately takes off, making them scatter. Normal doggie behaviour, right? It sure is. But that distractibility – a dog's inability to focus 100 per cent on the person he or she is there to help – doesn't make for a good CCI assistance dog.

CCI dogs have to be able to tune out everything else in their environment – squawking ducks included – to focus on the one person they're there to help. The dogs that can't wash out.

The other main reason that dogs fail to graduate is that old chestnut – food. A dog with a high food drive will want to eat all the time, and dogs like that make up a significant percentage of those that fail.

When Jim handed Terence back to CCI he'd had no idea if the eighteen-month-old dog would make it or not. He knew what Terence faced. The CCI trainers would put him through weeks of rigorous tests. They'd have someone hide and then jump out on him, to try to scare him, checking how long Terence would take to get on task again. They'd run a squirrel toy on a string through the training ground, to find out whether Terence could resist doing what comes naturally to a dog and chase that fun-looking thing. They'd introduce Terence to cats, to make sure he could stand firm against the urge to chase them. The same with live rabbits and a lot of other household pets that dogs tend to find irresistible.

Three weeks after he'd handed the young dog in, he'd got a call from one of the CCI trainers. 'Well, Jim, we've got some news,' he'd announced.

Jim had presumed he was calling to let him know that Terence had failed to make the grade. 'When do you want me to come and pick him up?' Jim ventured.

The trainer laughed. 'Oh, no, no, no . . . it's good news. He's going to be sent up to Santa Rosa to become a CCI breeder dog.'

Terence had been judged one of the best of the best, a dog destined to make fine CCI breeding material. The rare animals that demonstrate all the traits that CCI are looking for get put through to CCI's own breeding programme, from which puppies are provided to raisers all across the USA.

Napal, the firstborn of Terence's first litter of puppies, sure promises to be one hell of a dog.

Terence's breeder-caretaker – a volunteer who raises litters for CCI – is Gayle Keane, daughter of Bil Keane, the author of the famous comic strip *The Family Circus*. The character Dotty in the series was actually based upon Gayle. She lives in the beautiful Napa Valley, and Jim knows that Terence has had the best of all homes.

A few days back Gayle sent Jim a picture of Terence and Alexa II's first litter of puppies. The photo showed four shiny jet-black balls of fluffy mischief seated in a row on a chequered blanket, the foreground a confusion of floppy puppy forelegs and big clumsy puppy paws. On the far left of the photo sat Nelson, Napal's brother, his head turned to the right and his gaze full of inquisitive curiosity. On the right of the photo sat Naya and Nella, Napal's sisters, one clearly a cute bundle of trouble and the other – the smallest of the litter – with a gaze somehow tinged with anxiety.

Centre left was Napal.

And the thing about Napal was this: he was the only one sitting bolt upright, head erect and staring directly into the camera, those extraordinary eyes already displaying an arresting, penetrating vision. Even at eight weeks old the love and the devotion and the desire to serve shone out of Napal – or at least that's what the look had communicated to Jim.

The gaze said, *I'm here for you. I'm right here and I'm ready to open my heart.*

Jim leaves Route 76 via the Mission Avenue turn-off, and noses the Chrysler left onto Rancho Del Oro Drive. He pulls into a parking lot. He's arrived at CCI's Oceanside facility, set just a few blocks back from the sun-washed waters of the Pacific Ocean. The grand, pillared entrance lies before him, and somewhere behind the white stucco walls and the lush palm trees is his new charge-in-waiting.

He parks and presses a lever in the armrest. It releases the seat, and Jim is able to swivel it round to face the rear of the Chrysler. He slides open the vehicle's side door and presses a button, at which there is a high-pitched electrical whine. A metal ramp drops from the side of the van, sliding out until it makes contact with the ground. Next, Jim reaches for a folded-up device strapped into the rear of the minivan. He unties it, folds it out and manoeuvres it into a position where it's side on to his seat. Using both of his hands, he levers himself up out of his sitting position and lowers himself into the seat beside him.

He turns round and rolls down the ramp, exiting the vehicle in his wheelchair. He locks the Chrysler, turns the chair to face the CCI entranceway and, using the circular bars that run around the wheel rims, rolls himself towards the start of a new chapter in his life.

Jim Siegfried is forty-four years old, and he's been in a chair since the age of nineteen, when he suffered a road accident. It hasn't stopped him from doing what he wants to in life or, crucially, from giving back. In fact, it's very likely Jim's experience of life in a wheelchair that has given him such an ability to empathize with others with disabilities.

Jim knows exactly what it's like.

Over the last two decades he's never once stopped giving back. Today is just the first page in another chapter in that story. But, first things first: even a veteran puppy raiser like Jim needs to join the new recruits for a stern talking-to. He heads for one of the training rooms, where the CCI head trainer – today's puppy programme leader – is preparing to brief the assembled throng on their forthcoming responsibilities.

'These are the dos and don'ts,' he begins. 'You do have to remember these are not your dogs. They are your charges. You are responsible for their feeding, their vet bills, their daily structure and their training till they're eighteen months old. And then . . . you have to hand them back to us.

'You will learn as you go the dos and don'ts, as you attend your local puppy classes. Those classes will happen every two weeks. For those of you who've raised puppies before, we have a few new rules, so just take a moment to familiarize yourselves with them. Rule number one . . .'

He holds up a packet of Eukanuba. 'We recommend you use this type of dog food. It contains everything a dog needs. It's precisely formulated to help keep them healthy, which is why the manufacturers are our chosen supplier. You can feed them other food if you have to, but we need you to get them back on to Eukanuba before you hand them in . . .'

By the time the lecture's done, Jim is bursting with curiosity to meet his new charge. The puppy raisers get taken out to a patch of beautiful, pristine grass. Before Jim there are four tiny glistening bundles of fur tottering and scampering about, constrained by a portable puppy fence. They've been weaned, checked by the CCI vets, bathed and groomed meticulously in readiness for today's handover.

Each dog is pretty much identical to the other and equally captivating.

In short, they look perfect.

Jim scans the four, trying to figure out which is Napal. One dog draws his eye right away. He sits, a long-suffering, pained expression on his features while another – one of his siblings – chews on his ear. Napal has one brother and two sisters. Jim figures the puppy doing the ear-chewing has to be one of the girls. And somehow he just knows that the puppy with the absolutely riveting stare, the one that cries out to be loved, is Napal.

It's hard to roll a standard wheelchair on grass. The thin wheels – designed to move on hard surfaces – tend to sink in and get stuck. Jim waits patiently in his chair, one hand held out beckoningly to Napal. The puppy totters over, his big paws seemingly too large and ungainly for such a tiny ball of magic.

Jim reaches down from his chair and ruffles the dog where he figures he'll most like it – in the velvety-soft folds of puppy flesh right behind his ears. Man and dog's eyes meet.

'Your daddy's going to be real proud of you, you know that? Real proud.'

The bare stub of Napal's tail twitches to and fro. He gazes up into his new companion's eyes with a look that is 100 per cent irresistible.

For Jim the experience is uncanny. He feels as if he's staring into a gaze that he already knows so well, Napal being the spitting image of his father. Physically, mentally, in terms of his mannerisms – the tiny ten-ounce puppy is an exact replica of Terence.

*Wow. There's almost no telling them apart.*

As Jim makes his farewells and leads his new charge across to the parking lot, he figures the next eighteen months will be a rerun of the incredible experience of raising Terence. He can't wait to get started.

Upon arrival at the Chrysler, Jim rolls around to the passenger door. He opens up and with whispered words of reassurance lifts Napal and places him gently inside a travel kennel lying on the seat. The kennel is strapped in, so he knows for sure Napal will have a safe ride during the drive back to his new home in Santee, some thirty miles south of where they are now.

Jim moves around to the side door, lowers the ramp and, using his powerful shoulder and arm muscles, pulls his wheelchair up inside. He lifts himself and swings round to the driver's seat. The vehicle is operated by hand controls, so all the functions normally carried out by the feet – braking, accelerating, shifting gear – are performed via a series of buttons positioned on the steering wheel. He part-folds the chair and straps it in, then, with a reassuring glance at Napal, Jim backs the Chrysler out of the parking lot and turns onto Rancho Del Oro Drive once more. As he sets off on the journey home he feels a burst of happiness at the prospect of getting to raise a second Terence.

But little does he know that with this dog he'll be pulled so much closer than he's ever been before.

# CHAPTER 3

It was eight o'clock in the morning in Heatherdale, a suburb of Dallas, Texas, and the call came from out of the blue.

Patti Morgan was readying herself for a normal day at work. The phone in the five-bedroom house trilled, and Patti presumed at this time of day it had to be to do with her job. She picked up and answered. It wasn't anything about work at all; it was a call from one of her son's commanding officers.

'Ma'am, I have to tell you your son's been hurt in a car wreck. He was on active duty in South America and I have to warn you that he's suffered serious injuries.'

Patti's hand went to her mouth in shock. 'Oh my goodness. Oh my goodness. No . . .'

She and her husband Mike hadn't even known their son was on a mission. Over the years they'd got used to Jason being away in mysterious locations on exercises or operations, but they'd never know if a mission was live or not. For obvious security reasons Jason wasn't inclined to let on.

'Ma'am, you need to understand,' the voice repeated, 'he's very badly hurt. This could be life-threatening. He's in Quito,

Ecuador right now, but we're doing everything we can to get him home. Ma'am, we'll keep you posted.'

The last of the caller's words were lost to Patti, as the shock realization of how serious this was began to set in. After the caller rang off, Patti did the only thing she could think of, she phoned Mike.

'Jason's been in a terrible accident with the military,' she blurted out as soon as he answered. 'The caller said it's real bad and could even be life-threatening. Mike, what are we gonna do?'

Mike was at his downtown Dallas office, from where he and his partner Jim Lake Senior ran their own business – a commercial real estate company. It had never crossed his mind that something like this might happen to their son. This was pre-9/11, and back then the world was a more peaceable place, and America wasn't involved in any major conflicts.

'Where is he right now?' Mike asked, his voice an archetypal gravelly Texan rumble.

'They say he's in some place called Quito, in Ecuador.'

'Right. I'm coming home. And I'm going to Quito, wherever the heck that is – that's what any father would do.'

The next call Patti made was to Julie, Jason's twin sister. Born just a few minutes apart, the twin thing was really powerful between the two of them. She repeated what she'd told her husband, only to have Julie somehow confirm the worst.

'Oh, Mom . . . You know, I didn't sleep at all well last night. I had this bad, bad feeling. Kind of like a premonition. I tossed and turned all night long.'

Julie said she was leaving the office and driving straight over. But for Patti having her daughter reveal that she'd spent such a sleepless night somehow made things even more daunting. Patti had no idea how bad things were with Jason right then, but Julie wouldn't have felt what she had without reason.

Patti was in total shock. She felt as if her world was falling apart. She knew Jason was badly hurt, but that was all. He was a long way from home in a foreign country, one completely unknown to them all. She felt waves of anxiety wash over her, and as she said her first prayers she felt utterly helpless.

What was she supposed to do – wait by the telephone, hoping it would ring? Patti also ran her own business. She had a private practice working as a speech and language pathologist, mostly with the disabled. She made the snap decision to call in at the office where she worked and warn them that she might be about to disappear for some time. And from there she would ring around her clients and give the same kind of warning. At the very least, it would give her something to occupy her mind.

By the time Patti was done and had returned home, Mike was already there. He'd packed his bags and was checking flights to Quito, the capital of Ecuador. Mike put his arms around his diminutive blonde-haired wife, enveloping her in a tight hug.

'Honey, I know this is just such a massive shock right now. Such a massive, massive unknown. But it's our son we're talking about here. And I just know somehow or other that I've got to be there with him. He needs that right now.'

Barely had he said those words when the phone rang. Mike answered, trying to put the kind of steely certainty into his voice that he was a whole world away from feeling right then.

'This is Mike Morgan.'

'Mr Morgan, it's Colonel Funk, commander of the 10th

Combat Weather Squadron. I presume your wife has told you about your son's accident. The trouble is we're having some issues getting him flown out of there right now. But I want you to know that General Peter Schoomaker, chief of army special ops, is making it a top priority, and we're locating an aircraft that can accept a mobile ICU.'

ICU stands for intensive care unit. Funk was talking about a life support system that could be slotted into an aircraft. Mike understood that much from his own days serving with the US military.

He did his best to steady his voice. 'Colonel, you need to know I'm ex-air force myself. I understand. I know how difficult it can be. I've got my bags packed and I want to head out there to Quito, to be with my son.'

'Mr Morgan, sit tight,' the colonel advised. 'Don't go anywhere. We're getting him medevacked. They want to operate on him out there, but we're not going to let that happen. We're going to get him back first. We have military people with him, and, trust me, we're taking care of it. We'll get your son home.'

'We're getting two doctors and three nurses and a full colonel on board the medevac aircraft,' he continued. 'It'll have two air-crews, so it can fly non-stop to Quito, re-gas when it gets there and fly back to Kelly Air Force Base, with Wilford Hall Medical Center right next door. We're going in to get your son, and no one's going to ask any questions or stop us. So stay right where you are. We're making a no-holds-barred effort to get this done.'

Mike thanked the colonel. He replaced the receiver, figuring that even if he did fly out to Ecuador, the medevac aircraft would very likely beat him to it. He might even pass his son in mid-air, which would mean he'd only lose precious time. There was nothing for it but to stay put and wait.

The trouble was, how on earth were he and his wife, plus Julie – not to mention Jason's older brother John, who'd also got a warning call from Patti – going to fill the hours until they got any meaningful kind of an update?

The call came in the middle of that sleepless night.

They'd managed to get Jason airborne, and he was scheduled to arrive at Kelly AFB at 0600 hours. He was jetting in on an unmarked plane and would be rushed direct to ICU in Wilford Hall. That left Mike, Patti and Julie six hours to make the drive from Dallas to Kelly, lying on the eastern side of San Antonio, 300 miles straight down the I35. If they set off right away, they should just make it.

Thankfully, the military was sorting flights to get Jason's wife and kids to the hospital, so everyone who needed to be there for him would be.

Julie had brought her infant son Connor with her. The Morgans threw a few things into suitcases, carried the sleeping Connor out to the Chevy Suburban, loaded up and set off into the night. The drive was tense and deathly quiet. The phrase the military was now using to describe Jason's condition was 'severe, with massive internal injuries'. In truth, they didn't even know if he would be alive by the time they got to see him.

The shock was really starting to grip now. As Mike – a big, gruff, mustachioed born 'n' bred Texan – crouched over the Suburban's steering wheel, he reflected upon the one ace he had up his sleeve. When serving with the air force he'd been stationed at Lackland, a training base adjacent to Kelly AFB. He figured he knew his way around the place better than most. They should be able to get the Suburban into Lackland, from where you could get right up to the runway at Kelly. And that meant they should be able to meet Jason pretty much directly off the plane.

Sure enough, just as Mike pulled the big Chevy into Lackland, Patti spotted an unmarked white Gulfstream jet making its final approach to the airfield. Mike pulled to a halt at the perimeter fence, and through the wire mesh they watched it land. Two military ambulances raced out to meet it. The three watching figures could only presume that this had to be the jet carrying Jason.

They saw the ambulances rendezvous with the aircraft. It seemed to take an age to get whoever was on the plane linked up to some kind of a mobile breathing apparatus, but finally Mike spotted two stretcher-borne figures being transferred – one into each ambulance – although the family was too distant to make out who they might be.

As the ambulances set off, lights flashing and sirens blaring, Mike powered up the Suburban and gave chase. He managed to get the bulky SUV to the entrance of Wilford Hall Medical Center just as the two ambulances screeched to a halt.

None of the family was prepared for what they were about to see.

Mike, Patti and Julie jumped out of their vehicle just as a stretcher was lifted from the first ambulance. A figure was strapped to it. He was covered in blood, his neck was in a brace, and his face sprouted a forest of breathing tubes.

He seemed completely motionless, and they could hear the eerie suck and blow of the breathing machine, which was all that seemed to be keeping his lungs pumping.

That figure was Jason.

Patti practically fainted on the spot. She had a school friend who'd had a medical ventilator called an iron lung. As she listened to her son's artificially maintained breathing, it reminded her so much of that. Jason was so much worse than she'd ever feared. She was in such pain, the panic and anxiety overwhelming her.

As they rushed the figure towards intensive care, Mike shouted to him: 'Jason! JAY-SON!'

There wasn't a flicker of a response.

Then Patti issued one strangled, agonized cry: 'Jason!'

Somehow it must have filtered through.

Incredibly, they saw the prone figure raise one finger in an attempt at a response . . . and then he was gone, whisked through the double doors and out of their sight. That was pretty much the only sign that they had that Jason was still alive.

Mike, Patti and Julie were shepherded into the ICU waiting room. Wilford Hall is a military establishment, but the staff wear the kind of white medical gowns and headgear you see in a normal civilian hospital. Mike grabbed the nearest orderly and made it clear that he needed to see his son.

'Sorry, sir, but you just can't do that right now. As soon as we have him evaluated and stabilized you can see him. But not yet. Help yourself to coffee and food and anything—'

'Food!' Mike exploded. 'That's the last thing on my cotton-pickin' mind right now.'

Normally when Mike Morgan was nervous he tended to eat. Comfort food, he called it. Patti was the opposite. If she got worried, she'd stop eating. But now Mike couldn't stomach the thought of food. He felt zapped. Emotionally upended. He could only focus on one thing right now – his son.

The wait turned from minutes into hours. Mike and Patti had been emotionally exhausted even before they'd reached the hospital. It was going to be a long day at the start of a very long summer.

Meanwhile their daughter-in-law Carla was embarking upon an epic journey to get to the hospital, together with her and Jason's three infant boys. The air force was making an apartment available for them right on the base. Mike killed time by trying to help sort Carla's travel arrangements, but with three boys all below the age of four to manage, she had to be having one hell of a time of it.

Two hours stretched into four, and still no one had told them anything. All they'd seen was Jason being carried out of the ambulance, and the only reason they believed him still to be alive was that one miraculous lift of the finger. This was sheer torture. But each time Mike tried to ask, he got the same answer: Jason had so many injuries it was taking an abnormally long time to stabilize him.

Finally, the chief surgeon came out. He gathered Mike, Patti and Julie together in the hall adjacent to the ICU waiting room.

'Mr and Mrs Morgan, your son has suffered very extensive injuries. His back is broken and there is extensive nerve damage. We know he has a collapsed lung and that a percentage of the other lung is barely functioning. His spleen is ruptured, and he has been so severely damaged that we do not know the full extent of his other injuries. We don't know if there might be brain damage or not.'

'But . . . when can we see him?' Patti gasped.

The surgeon shook his head. 'Not yet. He's very severely injured. We're still doing our stabilization and evaluations. There are more X-rays, scans and tests to do.'

'How bad is it?' Patti whispered. 'His back?'

The surgeon dropped his eyes to the floor. 'I'm just so sorry to have to tell you, but your son will never walk again.'

At that Patti let out a strangled wail. It was only Mike holding her up that kept her off the floor. All the pent-up emotions of the last few hours had suddenly broken forth. In her job as a speech pathologist she'd spent hours working with those paralyzed due to spinal injuries, so she knew what the future might hold for her son.

'He has a broken back and the break is complete,' the surgeon continued, though by now Patti was lost to his words. 'The spinal cord is totally severed. Incomplete would mean he'd still have some movement below the injury. Complete means there's no continuity of the spinal cord at all. I'm afraid he'll never walk again, and there may well be other injuries we've not yet detected . . .'

Mike buried his head in his wife's hair. In his darkest moments he'd never once imagined this.

'We will only address the injuries that are life-threatening right now,' the surgeon continued. 'That's the priority – to keep him alive.'

'Can we at least see him?' Mike asked for the umpteenth time.

The surgeon shook his head. 'Not yet. As soon as it's possible, we'll get you all in.'

It felt as if the wait went on for ever.

Finally, they were allowed to see Jason. They walked into the ICU room as if in a daze, to find a figure strapped to numerous tubes, drips and a mass of complicated machinery. Clearly, there would be no raising of a finger now.

'He's in a coma, and we fear he may have brain damage,' one of the medical staff began to explain. 'It's been hard to get any kind of a response. We ask him questions and he doesn't respond. We squeeze his hand and he doesn't respond . . .'

All that night Mike, Patti and Julie dozed fitfully in the waiting room. Come dawn, they gathered for a conference outside. The early-morning sun was strong, but it did little to warm their hearts. This was the blackest of days.

By now Patti had recovered her senses enough to know what she had to do. No matter how long it might take, she had to remain at her son's side. There and then she made one of the most difficult decisions of her life, but one that was also so easy and so obvious in light of all that had happened. She was going to have to give up her medical practice and hand her clients over to other therapists.

She worked with children and adults with severe disabilities, and she loved what she did. She collaborated with counsellors, nurses, physiotherapists and doctors. But now it was Jason who needed her. She would not leave him until she was able to bring him home, and that meant her forty-year-old business was done.

She explained to Mike what was on her mind.

Reaching this decision was even more difficult than it might sound. At that point in their lives Mike and Patti had no other income other than what Patti earned. Since the 1987 Texas real estate crash, Mike and Jim Lake Senior had ploughed every cent earned back into their business, and that had meant not taking a penny for themselves. Yet without a moment's hesitation Mike agreed to Patti's suggestion. Neither of them had any idea how they were going to live – they just knew this was what they had to do.

After a torturous and sleepless night with their son lying battered and broken in a coma, Mike took a call from Jim Lake Senior. Jim was also in hospital, waiting for a heart transplant operation, which made Mike the key man at the company right then. But word had filtered through to Jim about Jason's accident, and he'd decided to make the call.

'Mike, I just want you to know we at the office will take care of everything,' Jim announced, his voice halting and breathless. 'I want you to stay there with Patti and take the time you need to get it sorted. Prioritize your son and take the time you need. And that's an order!'

Mike was tearing up. Who was Jim right now to be issuing orders? But if ever there was a time when they had need of such a true and constant friend, it was now.

# CHAPTER 4

Jim Siegfried pulls his Chrysler into the condominium complex where he lives: 144 pretty much identical units overlooking rugged scenery. It's very, very rural out here. All around are the hills and woodlands and climbing trails of Sycamore Canyon County Park. *It's out in the sticks*, Jim would say. And it's the kind of environment he just knows Napal will love.

Jim's yard is somewhat different to most residents'. It's a twelve-by-twelve metre set-up, and it's mostly concrete and ramps. The ramps are there to provide access. Jim can't get from his van to the house if there are steps, for the simple reason that he can't negotiate them in a chair.

First things first. Jim shows Napal around his new home. It's not a big place, so it doesn't take long for the ten-ounce bundle of curiosity to see the sights. Jim figures he doesn't need a lot of space. He lives alone. Or at least he *did* live alone. Not any more. Now it's two: Jim Siegfried and Napal II. But he's well aware that he's going to be raising his third CCI dog – there was one before Terence – all on his own.

Sightseeing done, Jim shows Napal his chow and drinking area – set just inside the back door, the same place where he fed and watered his two previous charges. There are no other pets in the Siegfried household – not that Napal is going to be a pet, of course. There just isn't the room for a menagerie of squawking, chirping, squeaking, mewling, barking four-footed things. And anyhow, what with the coyotes, rabbits and bobcats that inhabit the area, there's plenty of that right outside the door.

Jim manoeuvres his chair into the pantry and grabs a packet of Eukanuba. He places it in his lap and rolls across to a kitchen cabinet. He pulls open a drawer, retrieves some scissors and slices open the packaging, the rich meaty scent of the dog biscuits wafting up to him.

He glances at Napal. 'So, little buddy, it's chow time.' He taps the packet in his lap. 'Eukanuba. Eu-ka-nu-ba. Got it? This is Napal food.' He points at himself. 'Me, Big Jim. I never get to eat it. And for you, rule number one – no human food. Oh no. Never. That's a big no-no, OK?'

Napal is perched on his haunches, gazing up at Jim with that incredibly focused, big-eyed, you've-just-gotta-love-and-cherish-me look. He twitches his ears forwards, as if to say, *Hey, big buddy, run that by me one more time.*

'No human food,' Jim repeats. He reaches into the fridge and pulls out a packet of sausage. 'None of this, OK? Human food is all a big no-no.'

Jim gets the feeling that Napal has given a nod of understanding. *OK. I got it. No worries. Eu-ka-nu-ba is just fine!* It's starting to feel as if he's known this darned dog for a lifetime, not just a few short hours.

The no-human-food rule is a deal-breaker as far as CCI is concerned. If a trainee puppy gets to hang around the fridge begging for scraps, it's a dead cert that the dog will wash out.

Jim pours some dog biscuits into a metal bowl, the little rounded nodules of dried food beating out a rhythm. The bowl – a hand-me-down from Terence – is spotless. It was lovingly cleaned and polished that very morning. Jim will wash and sanitize it after each meal to stop Napal picking up any infections. Just as a human wouldn't want to eat off a dirty plate, so the puppy raisers are taught that a dog shouldn't have to either.

Jim watches Napal like a hawk as he sniffs at his first bowl of chow. This is the litmus test. If Napal is feeling sad or unsettled in his new environment then he'll be off his food. Jim sees him lift a crunchy nodule in his delicate mouth and bite down on it, his tiny head bobbing up and down as he chews and . . . swallows.

Ever since weaning, Napal will have been fed nothing but Eukanuba, so the smell and the taste will have become associated with life and love and home – and *feeding time*. As far as Jim can tell, there's nothing much bothering Napal right now. For the first time in his short life the puppy has been separated from his siblings. He's alone in a strange place with a guy who wheels himself around in a chair, but it doesn't seem to have unsettled Napal greatly.

When he's done eating, Jim offers Napal his first reward – a Charlee Bear low-calorie dog treat. The 'low-calorie' bit is important. Jim keeps a handful of Bear Crunch treats in his pocket at all times, the reason being that you only ever teach a CCI dog anything via positive reinforcement. You congratulate the dog using your high-pitched 'praise' voice, and you offer him a treat.

With a CCI puppy, the training begins from the moment you get him, and it's a 24/7 process. Jim might give Napal a dozen or more Bear Crunch treats in one day. Each Charlee Bear is like a buttermilk cookie for dogs, the difference being that it has only three calories. Jim can keep giving them to Napal without any worries of the dog getting overweight. Being a CCI assistance dog is hard work, and the young animals have to be in peak condition.

Jim takes a Bear Crunch in his hand and reaches down to Napal. 'Good dog. Good boy. Here, have your treat.'

Napal hesitates for just the barest instant. Jim wears Valeo Meshback fingerless gloves, which are more commonly used for fitness and weight training. Every single time Jim wants to move anywhere – unless he's in his van – he has to grasp the metal rims attached to his wheels and power himself with his hands. The gloves are there to prevent him from getting blisters.

Napal sniffs at the proffered glove. He's clearly not used to a human wearing such things on his hands. But the alluring scent of the Bear Crunch is irresistible. He reaches out his front left paw, hooks a tiny claw into the mesh of the glove to hold Jim's hand steady, and with a sideways wriggle of his head he slips the treat into his jaws.

Jim laughs. He feels like they've just shaken hands – him and his new dog. No doubt about it, this is the cutest puppy that's ever put a paw through his door. He reaches down to give Napal a good scratch behind the ears. But Napal kind of wriggles Jim's hand around until it's on the exact spot where he loves to be scratched and petted most – right beneath his chin and directly under the jaw.

Jim laughs again. 'Uh-huh, I get it. So, little buddy, that's where you like it, huh?'

Napal doesn't reply and he's not going anywhere. With his Bear Crunch and those fingers working away on his lower jaw, he's in seventh heaven right now.

Treat finished, Jim figures it's grooming time. He rolls himself across the kitchen and grabs his de-shedding tool, a robust plastic handle with a metal-toothed comb set at right angles to it. He holds it up to Napal.

'Furminator. Fur-mi-na-tor.' He grins and runs a hand across his balding head. 'Sounds like something I might need . . . you know, with the way I'm kind of losing my hair!'

Jim goes out to the backyard, taking Napal with him on a light lead. The puppy wears a blue collar with two metal tags attached to it. They clink and chime as he moves. One is Napal's official CCI dog tag. On one side is his CCI number, 001456. On the other is stamped, 'California Assistance Dog'. The other is a bone-shaped metal tag with 'Napal II' and Jim's telephone number stamped beneath it. Because he's Napal II, there must have been a previous Napal raised as a CCI dog. Often a benefactor gets to name a new dog, and 'Napal' is likely a favoured name of one of CCI's donors, but no one seems to know exactly what the inspiration is behind the name.

Jim reaches down and lifts Napal into his lap. He takes the Furminator and pulls it gently through his coat, moving from his shoulder to his tail, dragging out little glossy puffs of hair. By the way Napal wriggles and shivers, Jim can sense that he loves the feel of those long gentle strokes. Furminating done, Jim gives Napal a good brush. By the time he's finished, Napal's coat feels as smooth and glossy as dark silk. Then Jim takes a kind of toothbrush on a finger puppet, and with a squirt of toothpaste he starts on the next task, cleaning Napal's teeth.

As far as Jim is concerned how often you groom your dog is a crucial sign of how good a puppy raiser you are. A good raiser puts in the extra 5 per cent that's required to forge man and dog into a world-beating team. Grooming is a big part of that 5 per cent. If a dog isn't regularly groomed his fur will matt, and he'll keep licking himself to try to clear it, which will give him hairballs. But, mostly, grooming is part of the physical closeness you need to forge with your dog. It's also a part of keeping your animal in peak condition. It goes hand in hand with cleaning their teeth and ears or clipping their nails so they don't get caught in cracks in the sidewalk and rip out. Every puppy raiser loves to do the fun stuff with their dog. Regular grooming is the more mundane side, but it's one that keeps an animal in top form at all times.

A dog like Napal will have cost some $50,000 by the time he's ready to graduate – that's if he graduates. By then he'll be one of the most highly trained animals on the planet. And Jim is absolutely determined that Napal will graduate and go on to achieve that most precious of things: changing a life.

Jim set himself a specific goal recently. He's decided to raise five CCI dogs – Napal being the third – and then to apply for a service dog himself. Jim's a paraplegic, paralyzed from the waist down. He's wheelchair-bound and lives alone, so if he falls from his chair there's no one around to help him get back in again. He's also a born-and-bred dog lover. On paper he's the perfect candidate for a CCI assistance dog, but Jim figures he'll only apply once he really has the need. With Napal, that's three more dogs to raise, which equates to six years – longer with the waiting times in between. By then Jim will be past fifty. With age his condition will only worsen and his need for a service dog will grow.

But for now, and for as long as he can handle it, Jim is determined to give back.

The little boy with autism and cerebral palsy whose graduation really opened Jim's eyes – he was given what's termed a skilled companion dog. Basically, that's a dog for a kid who needs a friend at their side the whole time. It's sad but inevitable that a child like that will get stared at and ostracized, and it's hard to find friends. But with a CCI skilled companion dog, he'll have a guaranteed best buddy – a four-legged one. With such a dog at his side the attention switches from the boy to the dog. It always does. And if such a gorgeous, smart, mind-blowing dog can love that kid with such devotion, it shows other children that they can too.

Jim's connection to that kid was truly heartfelt. The reasons for that reach far back into his own childhood. Jim's younger brother Danny was born with Down's syndrome. Whenever he was out and about with Danny, Jim had to get used to other kids staring and pointing and saying unkind things, and even poking fun. Or at least he tried to get used to it. He never really managed to: it made his blood boil.

Jim's first CCI dog was Gigi IV, a stunning-looking golden retriever burnished copper-gold in colour. Being a dog lover, Jim thought he knew everything there was to know about raising a dog. In truth, he knew absolutely nothing. He knew how to feed a dog and how to walk a dog. Well, kind of, being in a chair . . . maybe how to roll with a dog was a better way of putting it. But when it came to teaching and training and raising a dog properly, Jim's experiences with Gigi taught him just how much he didn't know. That was a tough awakening, having to relearn from scratch his relationship with dogs. And it was made all the more difficult by the fact that Gigi didn't graduate.

It wasn't anyone's fault; Gigi failed to make it due to distractibility. Like golden retrievers tend to, Gigi just loved to run, and there was no way of breaking that habit. No matter what Jim tried, there was no stopping her, especially when there was anything around to chase. At CCI they did everything they could to get Gigi through, but it was clear at the end she just didn't want to be a service dog. Gigi wanted to run, and that's just how it was.

She went to live with a friend of Jim's, the father of a fellow puppy raiser. He made a $1,000 donation to CCI, and in return he got a wonderful, lovable, fantastically trained and obedient dog – one that loved to run and run. He was one lucky guy. Still, Jim couldn't deny that he was disappointed when his first dog failed to graduate. Yet he wasn't discouraged, as only 30 per cent of dogs make the grade.

Jim got Terence just two weeks after learning that Gigi wouldn't graduate. It could have been a daunting experience, but from the get-go Terence was different. From the start Gigi had always been easily distracted because of her urge to chase and run. By contrast, Terence had a focus and an attentiveness that made Jim think that he would make it. And Terence had more than made it. He'd become a breeder dog with his offspring going to needy kids and adults all across the USA.

And so along had come Napal.

The sun sets on a glorious first day together for Jim and his new dog. The grooming done, Jim figures it's time for bed. He's got a special small kennel in his bedroom, and he places Napal in there for the night, gently closing the door. Then he turns his chair and, in a repeat of the getting-into-the-Chrysler manoeuvre, he parks and lifts himself onto his bed.

He part-folds the chair, leaving it within easy reach. He's got no doubt that he'll have need of it during the dark hours. It's Napal's first night away from his brothers and sisters. It'll be his first spent sleeping alone, without a bundle of warm siblings scrunched up all around him. Jim knows how the dog will be feeling. He'll be lonely, isolated and fearful. He'll very likely cry and whimper, and call for his missing family. *Where are you?*

Jim's more than ready for what is coming. He has to start Napal in his kennel – what CCI terms the dog's crate. This is the first stage of crate training – getting the dog used to where and how he must sleep. Whoever he finally goes to, Napal is going to need to sleep in that person's room, being ready and willing to help as required, but he may never be allowed to get onto their bed, as the person's disability might make that an impossibility. So the dog has got to get used both to staying an arm's length away but being always to hand.

Unsurprisingly, Napal can't sleep. Jim can hear him scratching around and whining, and it tugs at his heartstrings. He leaves the puppy for ten minutes, just to start the crate training – *This is your place* – and then he relents. He leans down from the bed, unhooks the crate door and scoops Napal up, placing the dog beside him.

'So, little buddy, first night away from your family?' he whispers. 'A big deal, huh? But listen, you've got a new family now. Big Jim's here for you and I ain't going anywhere anytime soon. So settle down. Settle down, little buddy. Settle down.'

When Jim senses that Napal is dozing, lulled to sleep by the warm body at his side, he lifts him up and places him gently back in the crate. Every three hours or so Napal wakes, and Jim has to stir with him. Several times he lifts the disoriented, bewildered animal up and places him in his lap, so together they can go out into the yard.

'Time to go potty,' Jim murmurs, as Napal sniffs around to find a place to pee.

With a last look at the beautiful night sky Jim lifts the puppy up again and rolls back inside. Then he places him on his bed and begins the process of coaxing Napal back into his lonely kennel all over again.

CCI's motto is 'Raise a puppy, change a life.' As he settles down to sleep, Jim reflects upon how, with Napal at his side, he's living it.

# CHAPTER 5

After a sleepless night in a military hospital waiting room, neither Mike nor Patti had the faintest idea how they could remain in San Antonio. Hotels were out of the question. So was renting somewhere. Both would be prohibitively expensive.

It was Julie's mother-in-law Gail who came to their rescue. Gail was an executive at a company called Skyline Properties, and it just so happened that they owned a suite of rental apartments in San Antonio. One was empty right now. On the morning of their second day at Wilford Hall, Gail called and offered the family the use of the apartment for as long as they had need of it.

There wasn't a great deal more Mike, Patti or Julie could achieve by staying at the hospital. They'd seen Jason and believed they'd learned the worst. He was alive, and maybe there were things to be thankful for. Right now they needed a wash and a sleep and to recharge their batteries. Somehow, Mike managed to navigate the Suburban across town. He and Patti took one bedroom, Julie and her infant son Connor the other, and they settled down to an exhausted sleep.

Patti woke some time later to the sound of voices filtering through from the balcony. It was a second-floor apartment and looked out over a swimming pool. It was mid-afternoon and Julie was sitting on the balcony with John, the Morgans' eldest son, their conversation all about Jason.

Bits and pieces filtered through to Patti. 'No, he will walk again . . . He'll walk again . . . He absolutely will . . . He will . . . He will . . . He will . . .'

Patti dabbed at her eyes. Of course she believed this too, but no matter how often she kept telling herself, she didn't know if she was really certain in her heart. The surgeon had sounded so absolutely certain: *I'm just so sorry to have tell you, but your son will never walk again.*

They gathered for a family conference. The decision they reached was unanimous. Between the four of them they would keep a 24/7 vigil over Jason. They would sleep at the apartment and eat at the hospital cafeteria, so food and rest shouldn't be too much of an issue. Julie – the Morgan family organizer and enforcer – would draw up a rota. Each of them would have to alternate between the vigil and helping care for Connor, plus Carla and Jason's three infant boys once they arrived.

Julie knew that the rota would need to be rigorously policed. John in particular had a habit of wriggling out of chores. He had a few weeks' vacation right now, and he seemed determined to spend every second of it at his little brother's side. Julie loved him for it, but he really needed to take his share of caring for the kids.

By the time they made it back to Wilford Hall it was late afternoon. If anything, the situation seemed to have worsened. Jason was absolutely motionless, and the doctors explained that they had put him into an induced coma, a deep state of unconsciousness artificially maintained by controlled doses of drugs. There was no sign of life: it was as if the raised finger of yesterday had been some kind of a cruel illusion.

There were two reasons for inducing the coma. Jason had suffered a massive blow to the head, along with countless other injuries. Via a complex medical process it was hoped that the coma might reduce the risk of brain damage. The second reason was to stop Jason moving, so as to give his broken back a fighting chance.

'It's going to be day by day,' the head surgeon warned them. 'Day by day. He's right on the edge. Any further trauma to the back could exacerbate the spinal injuries, plus there's a danger he may catch pneumonia. If he does . . . well, we don't think he'll pull through. And he's certainly in no fit state to have any surgery right now.'

Jason had also somehow managed to breathe so much swamp water into his lungs that he was classified as a 'near-drowning victim'. The big worry was the danger of catching any number of nasty respiratory diseases that the jungle harboured.

The surgeon mapped out what might happen, though nothing was for certain. Just as soon as they could risk moving him they'd get Jason into a bed that tilted this way and that, to stop him from developing sores caused by lying still for too long on the pressure points of the body. He would need to be strapped in to prevent him from falling out, but all of that was some way down the line.

A new figure introduced himself to the family. He was an army captain and a special operations medical officer. He'd been sent to Wilford Hall to be with them until Jason was stabilized and to take care of all of their needs. He was a youngish guy, maybe in his early thirties, and he was wearing full uniform.

'I just want you to know, I will be here before you get here and I will be here when you go to bed,' the captain told them. 'I will be keeping total vigilance. I will have been briefed on your son's night hours, so anything you have missed I will be able to fill you in on. I'm staying right nearby, so I will be always on hand. My only duty is to be here to assist you and to help coordinate whatever you might need.'

Mike smiled tiredly. 'Well, you know, we're really genuinely grateful. We appreciate it, we really do.'

In a moment of unspoken understanding Mike and the captain stepped away from the others, to a place where they could talk with some degree of privacy.

Mike fixed the captain with a very direct look from his steely blue eyes. 'You know, there is one thing you maybe could do for us right now. Y'all able to tell me what happened the day my son got hurt? What happened to cause such injuries?'

The captain hesitated for the barest moment. 'Mr Morgan, I figure you have a right to know. All I've been told officially was that there was a road traffic accident while on operations.' He paused. 'Unofficially, Jason and his guys were in that part of South America ... and they weren't there, if you get my meaning.'

Mike tapped the side of his nose. 'Kind of hush-hush. Yeah, I get it. Jason never did tell us much and we figured that was the reason why. But how exactly did he end up like that – so broken apart and smashed up and with a lungful of swamp water? I mean, what kind of road accident does that?'

The captain stepped a pace closer. 'Way I heard it, Jason was in a four-by-four driving through a ravine. The vehicle hit a corner, was going too fast and went off the edge. It rolled down the mountain. Jason was thrown out; the vehicle rolled over him, and that's what caused the injuries. By the time he was found he was deep in a swamp.'

'Hence the water in the lungs?'

'Hence the water in his lungs.' The captain glanced over his shoulder towards the office in which he'd established his base of operations. 'Wait one, Mr Morgan. I got something you might want to see.'

He was back a minute later with a wad of colour photocopies clutched in his hand. He thrust them at Mike. 'Photos of the vehicle your son was riding in. That's it. Or rather that's what remains of it.'

Mike held the first up before him. It showed a white civilian Chevrolet Blazer in some kind of a wrecker's yard, with jungle and mountains forming the background. Mike had rarely seen a vehicle so beaten up. Every window and light was smashed, the roof was buckled in, and the doors were bent at crazy angles.

'Holy cow, it's a wonder anyone survived.' He glanced at the captain. 'How many were they?'

'Three. All hospitalized. And Mr Morgan, your son, I'm afraid he got it the worst of the three of them.'

Mike flicked through the remainder of the photos. He couldn't work out how his son could have been tossed clear of the vehicle. All the doors were shut, so how could a guy of Jason's size have been thrown out? But as Mike looked closer he realized that the doors had been roped shut with makeshift straps. Whoever had recovered the vehicle must have forced the doors closed and tied them shut, to make it easier to move the wreck.

In his mind's eye Mike had an image of a white Chevy Blazer tumbling down a ravine, cannoning off rocks and trees as each of its doors pinged open under the impacts. It would have left those inside vulnerable to being thrown out, which was what must have happened to his son. He shook his head, trying to clear it. The final image in his mind – of the wrecked Chevy rolling over his son's body – was one he did not want to see. He flicked his eyes down to the vehicle's licence plate. It read E MAULME. ECUADOR. GKM-473.

He glanced at the captain. 'Local plates. Ecuador plates.'

The captain nodded at the photos. 'Like I said, they were there and they weren't there . . .'

The captain finished by telling Mike that just as soon as Jason recovered consciousness he would need to talk to him privately, to 'debrief him'. Mike figured this was to ensure that Jason would say only what he was allowed to say. He had no problem with that. All he wanted was his son back, and he was more than grateful for the captain's honesty and his help.

The day passed.

The highlight that evening was when Carla and the three boys finally made it to Wilford Hall. They were exhausted from the flights. The decision was made right away that there was little point in the boys – Blake, three; Austin, two; and Grant, just six months old – seeing their father in his present state. It might be too much for them. Patti offered to help Carla by staying over at the house that the military had provided, freeing Carla up so she could visit Jason pretty much at will. There was a preschool on the base, and the boys could go there during the day, which would help fill the hours. All agreed that it was best to behave with the youngsters as if everything was pretty much as normal. The watch rota was adjusted to allow for caring for the boys, and to give Carla as much time as possible with Jason.

That evening a young wife sat by her comatose husband's bedside trying to come to terms with the seemingly impossible, while Patti took the boys out to play by the pool. It was a clear night and the stars were gorgeous and bright. They seemed so close that Patti felt as if she could reach out and touch them: in spite of everything she was struck by their awesome beauty. She sat the eldest, Blake, on her knee and pointed, showing him the Big Dipper, the Little Dipper and the North Star, one of the brightest in the sky. Blake was fascinated, gripped by the wonder of the heavens, and for a few precious moments Patti was able to forget about the dark place in which her younger son was trapped. It was a magical moment for grandmother and grandchild, but it was a sadly fleeting one.

The biggest fear was that Jason would catch some kind of disease in his lungs. Overnight that was exactly what happened: Jason developed pneumonia. The medical staff figured that it had been gradually creeping up on him, as his temperature spiked and his pain-racked body tried to fight off infections. The following morning the family returned to their hospital watch to find Jason in a raging fever and mumbling like a crazy man. By now he was in the rotating bed and could somehow sense the straps that bound him. In his delirium he was convinced that the bad guys had got him. Jason was raving that FARC were readying themselves to operate on him and sell his organs. He managed to rip off a strap and start pulling the feeding tubes out of his mouth, before the orderlies rushed in and were able to restrain him.

In the hours that followed Jason begged John and Julie's husband Scott to help him escape. He was in a basement being tortured by FARC, he told them, and he had to get out of there.

'Buddy, you gotta help. Just untie me. Untie me. Untie me and let me get out of that window, and when we escape I promise I'll allow you to tie me back up again and put the tubes back in. Cut my tubes, and I'll go out the window, and then you can hook them back up again.'

John laughed. What else was there to do? If he didn't find humour in this moment, it would surely break him. 'Hook them up to what, little brother? Hook them up to what, Jase? To what?'

Jason kept insisting to anyone who would listen – Julie, John, Mike, Patti, Carla, plus his other visitors – that he'd been captured and that they had to help him escape. Of course no one in the family knew what Jason had been doing in Ecuador. They didn't even know if it had been an active mission, as opposed to a training exercise. It all seemed a little crazy, and they had no idea how bad a place Jason was in right then. But mostly they were just desperate to know if he would make it through alive.

They were less than a week in when John missed his first slot on child watch. He'd overstayed his time by Jason's bedside and forgotten all about his other duties. Julie was not happy. She called a family meeting, and they sat together on the kerb outside the ICU as she gave her big brother a serious dressing-down.

John pretty much took it. Like her mother, Julie was a slight, petite lady, but she could be 'as strong as bulls' knees', as Mike would say.

The very next time John was on Jason watch, his little brother started having a conversation with the oxygen tank that stood in one corner of the room.

'We gotta get out of here,' Jason said to the tank. 'Get the bars off the window and bust out.'

The tank didn't respond.

'You know, everyone's in a mask. The bad guys. Masks. Trying to hide their faces.'

The tank still didn't respond.

'But anyways, where's my mom? You got any idea? Where's my mom?'

No response from the tank.

Jason went on like this for some time before he realized the tank wasn't ever going to say much. Then an amazing thing happened. He turned to John and addressed him by name: 'John, there's not a person over there, is there? That thing, it can't talk.'

John burst into tearful laughter. He reached for Jason's hand. 'No, little brother, it's not. It's not a person. It's an oxygen tank.'

The flash of lucidity was short-lived. Transient. It lasted for no more than the time it took for the two brothers to exchange those few words. Two sentences. Fourteen short words. But it meant so very much. For John it was like a miracle. It was the first indication that his brother might not have lost his mind. He rushed out of the ICU to where Patti, Mike and Carla were sitting having coffee.

'He blipped out!' he cried. 'I was in there and he turned to me and he spoke my name. He said "John". He freakin' said my name! He recognized me!'

John related the entire story – how, for just the briefest of instants, Jason had been conscious and able to recognize someone.

'Yeah, so I'm bragging about it,' John admitted joyfully. 'Why not? I love him like a brother!'

The story struck everyone as somehow so funny. Talking to an oxygen tank about how they were going to bust out of there was just so typical of Jason. The relief and joy of that moment made them all laugh, and, God knows, they had need of laughter right then. The humour was vital. It gave them the strength to endure the seemingly unendurable.

Of course, the laughter quickly turned to tears. The family were crying and laughing, and crying through their laughter, and somehow that was a vital part of the process of pulling through. Jason was in a coma fighting for his life, and his family could find it in themselves to laugh. They say laughter is medicine for the soul. Right then it was like a small slice of normality – bringing the two brothers one step closer to where they once had been. John and Jason had always had that kind of relationship: they were forever making fun of each other and yanking each other's chain.

The surgeon tried to give them some sense of perspective. 'Even though he's talked and he's saying stuff and recognizing people, don't think he's out of the woods. It's touch and go. He's not out of the woods yet.'

Patti shook her head tearfully, her smile shining through. 'He's good. He's coming back.'

John grinned, tears in his eyes. 'Sure, it's an oxygen tank, but at least he's talking! And at least he's not trying to pick the tank up for a date!'

'Hey, he keeps asking for his mom,' Mike complained. He laughed his booming Texan longhorn laugh. 'When's he gonna start asking for his cotton-pickin' dad!'

Jason had been truly smashed up. His body was covered in dark purple-green bruises from head to toe. He was fighting a raging infection from the depths of a coma. Because he couldn't communicate, he couldn't even tell the medics what hurt and what didn't. But there was absolutely nothing wrong with nurturing hope.

Why not let hope flourish in the darkness?

The family wanted hope. They needed hope.

What was wrong with hope?

# CHAPTER 6

On the second day of life-after-getting-Napal, Jim puts him into the sitting position by speaking the 'Sit' command, one that Gayle Keane must have already taught the little dog. Jim then offers the tiny, serious-faced puppy a hand to shake.

From his chair he reaches down. 'Shake.'

Napal gazes at the proffered hand for a moment, then lifts up his left paw and offers it to Jim.

*Wow.*

The two shake hands/paws. They shake the very first time Jim asks him to. That's how fast this dog is at working out what's what.

Jim has booked a couple of weeks' vacation so he can concentrate on settling Napal in. He sits down that morning to type an email to Gayle Keane. The way they'll do these emails, Jim will write as if he is Napal penning a message to his dad Terence – a son writing to his father. And of course they'll read the messages out to the dogs.

Jim types:

Hi Dad,
I finally made it to Jim's place. He came up to Oceanside to

get me. He was an hour early. We had a great drive to his house, my new home for now. Home is good – lots of room to play. I had a couple of accidents – I guess I was excited. Jim didn't seem to mind.

It sure was weird sleeping alone. Jim comforted me until I fell back asleep over and over again. He kept saying something about me snoring and sounding like you, Dad!

I'm going to take a small nap now, and Jim is going to show me where I can do my business.

I'll write real soon and send some pics when I can.

Your son,

Napal

Jim reads the message out to Napal, and when both seem happy with it he presses 'Send'. 'Terence' replies an hour or so later.

Hey there Napal,

We were wondering when we'd get to hear from you. I'm glad to know you finally made it into Jim's arms safe and sound. He's a really good guy and you can depend on him to take good care of you. I've got him all trained up for you. Have you found any of my old toys lying around?

Be a good boy, give Jim your very best enthusiastic puppy kiss and let him get his sleep.

Your daddy, Terence (aka Goofus – I think I deserve a little more respect around here)

PS Gayle says to have Jim give you a cuddle from them. Sheesh! Like he didn't know that already.

Jim's barely a week into life-after-getting-Napal by the time the little puppy has pretty much mastered his crate training. Every night the two of them retire to the bedroom, and Napal automatically makes for his little kennel. By now Napal has also discovered his favourite place in the Siegfried household. It's uncanny, because it's exactly the same spot as Terence chose before him. It's the Hot Tub Lookout, as Jim and Terence had named it back then.

In the centre of Jim's backyard sits a hot tub. It's got wooden side-panels and a plastic cover that rolls over the top. Terence used to sit up there all day long, keeping watch. The hot tub raised him high enough to see over the fence that runs around the yard, making him king of all he surveyed, particularly the parking lot, where he would watch all the comings and goings. He'd never bark and he'd never growl, but he'd never miss a thing either. When Jim had to hand Terence back to CCI, there wasn't a dog looking over his fence any more. Everyone in the neighbourhood commented on it.

'Hey, Jim, where's Terence? You don't have the dog?'

It's funny how quickly you get defined by your dog.

Napal wants to take up where Terence left off. Thing is, he's a little small to jump up onto the Hot Tub Lookout. The plastic cover stands maybe four feet off the ground. He sniffs around the base of it and scrabbles with his forepaws as if trying to scale a mountain. When Jim finally lifts him up, he can tell immediately that the puppy has found his all-time favourite spot.

But with Napal it's a little different on the Hot Tub Lookout. The little dog lifts his head, his gaze scanning the crystal-blue sky, and his eyes are big and wonder-wide as he watches the birds. As they swoop and dive and flash overhead, catching summer insects on the wing, Napal's head zips this way and that, following their wild aerobatics.

One evening Napal is up on the Hot Tub Lookout, Jim beside him in his chair. The sun is sinking towards the western horizon, and the birds are wheeling overhead, catching the last of the day's insects for supper. It's going to be a glorious sunset, and Jim decides to wheel himself inside and fetch a beer. He rejoins Napal, a can of cold Budweiser perched in his lap, and offers the dog a Bear Crunch.

Napal cocks his head to one side and looks at it enquiringly. *What've I done to deserve that?*

Jim shrugs. 'Nothin' specific, little buddy.' He taps his can of beer. 'But I got my treat, so I figure it's only right you got yours.'

Napal takes the dog biscuit gently between his two front teeth, tosses his head back and chews contentedly. He settles down on his belly, legs stretched out in front of him and his head resting on his forepaws. Now and again he flicks his eyes skywards as a lark wheels and cries.

'So, it's just the two of us, kid, you and I,' Jim muses. 'I guess I know all about your short life, but you know diddly squat about mine. So, here goes . . . If you're anything like your dad, you'll be a darn good listener, that's for sure.

'I grew up around dogs. I guess you figured that anyways?' Jim glances at Napal. Feeling his gaze, the puppy's eyebrows twitch as if to say, *Go on, I'm listening.*

'Pretty much ever since I was born I had a dog in my life,' Jim continues. 'I was the kind of kid who'd turn up on the doorstep saying, "Mom, look what followed me home!"' Jim chuckles. 'There were all sorts – everything from a dachshund to a German shepherd. Gretchen was the German shepherd. You know why Gretchen sticks in my mind? It's because she was so smart. I'd say, "Go get to the car." Gretchen went to the car. I mean, she picked up things without me even trying. When I think back over what I've learned with CCI, well, I was lucky to have a dog so naturally smart.

'Gretchen was always there. When I came home she was there; when I left for school she was there. I was big into dogs and I was big into football. I went to Central Elementary, in Baldwin Park. Back then we didn't have anyone to coach us. A bunch of us got together and said, "Well, we don't have a coach so we'll coach ourselves." And you know what, we went on to win the city championships! Get that!'

Jim takes a sip of his beer. 'My position was wide receiver. I was a wide receiver for four years. And, you know, we had a bunch of guys who were *real good*.' Jim laughs. 'That wasn't me. Our quarterback was Paul McDonald – he graduated at USC, and he actually amounted to a star player. But, you know, I was solid. I was solid. Not a star player, which was fine, but I played OK.'

Jim glances at Napal. 'You ever seen a football game? Nope? Guess not. We gotta fix that. Anyhow –' Jim pats the wheel of his chair '– I guess you're wondering how a guy who was solid at football ended up in a chair.'

Jim gazes into the setting sun, reaching back into the memories. 'It was November 4th 1977. Bishop Amat High was playing Servite High for the homecoming. I was nineteen at the time and I'd been gone from Bishop Amat a good year. I graduated in '76, so this was my second homecoming game. My girlfriend at the time was a cheerleader, so I absolutely could not miss the game!'

Napal gives a little yowly yawn and wriggles lower, enjoying the feel of the sun-warmed cover on his belly. He glances at Jim. *Go on. I'm listening. Go on with the story.*

Jim smiles and reaches into his pocket. 'Here you go. You're a fine listener. You deserve a Charlee Bear. So, my girlfriend's name was Catherine. Catherine Attila. She was a cheerleader going to her first homecoming. A big deal. Sadly we lost the game. Final score was 25 to 17. Now the rest gets a bit sketchy here, 'cause you'll understand my memories were knocked out . . .

'We were leaving the game, and a friend drove by in his Volkswagen Beetle. Kind of a cool car. Me and a friend asked for a ride. It was just a short way back to our own car. The guy's car was crammed, but he said we could ride on the running board. So we hopped on, one on either side, and held on to the guttering.

'It was a goofy kind of thing to do, but our car was close, so what was the harm? All was fine and we were approaching our stop, so we yelled at Craig – that was the driver – to slow down. I guess Craig braked too hard or something. Anyhow, the next moment me and my friend were thrown off. He landed on the sidewalk, but I was thrown into the path of an oncoming vehicle.'

Jim pats his lap with one hand and reaches down to caress Napal's head. 'You wanna come up here, little buddy? Or you good there? You're good there? Well, OK. So, the car hit me in the back.' Jim gestures at his left side. 'I guess around about here. The impact broke my back, crushed my sternum and punctured my right lung. And you know something? The car threw me about twenty feet and stopped twelve inches from my head. The front wheel. But I was out cold by then.

'Well, you know, I don't recall anything much from that point on.' Jim glances around. The sun has sunk below the horizon, and the yard is enveloped in a warm and inky darkness. He checks his watch. 'Jeez, is that the time? I guess that's your instalment done for the evening. Time to hit the hay.'

Napal's only response is to wriggle deeper into the plastic cover of the Hot Tub Lookout and to issue a throaty puppy grumble. *Hey, you can't end the story there – on a total cliffhanger. You just can't do that.*

Jim gives in. He talks some more. It's hard to refuse this dog.

'OK, so some time later I came back to consciousness. I was in a hospital. My brother was at my bedside. He said, "Everything's gonna be all right." Of course, he was just trying to keep me calm. And you know something, I was just so darn lucky. I'd just started a job with Jeans West, the clothing store. The day before I'd signed the papers for the company's health insurance. That meant I was insured. I could get the best treatment. But only by a day.

'I'd been wearing a thick Leatherman jacket at the time of the accident, so the leather kind of protected me externally. But internally I was banged up pretty bad. It was the following day when the doctor came to speak to me. He said, "Jim, we've got some good news and some bad news. The good news is you're alive. The bad news is you'll probably never be able to walk again."'

Jim drains the last of his beer. 'Yeah. That's what he said. *Never be able to walk again.* I'd broken my back in two places – T5 and T7. That was the level of the breaks.' Jim leans forward and shows Napal the places the breaks occurred, just below the shoulder blades. 'So, I was left paralyzed from the waist down.'

Jim pauses, then chuckles. 'And you know something? You know my first reaction? I said, "Oh man, can you call my girlfriend? Can you call my girlfriend and tell her that I'm not going to be able to make it to the dance tonight." It was her homecoming ball, and that was my first reaction. Let my girlfriend know.

'And then I kind of sat back and thought about what the doctor had just told me. And I thought, *Oh shit, what did I do? What did I do? How can I live a life if I can't even walk?*'

Jim is silent for a long beat. Napal is silent too. It's one of those special, special moments shared between man and dog.

Finally Jim reaches out and scoops Napal into his lap. 'Hey, no protests. Time to hit the hay.' He holds the puppy up before him, so man and dog are eye to eye. 'And, little buddy, I guess you know anyhow, but I'm not dating right now. There's no one around on that level. With you, I got someone to be here and to help occupy my time. I like to talk. You listen good. You're good company.

'I know the day will come when I gotta give you up. I know that. But let's hold on to this moment and let's remember – you'll go to the very best of causes.'

With that Jim ruffles Napal's ears, turns his chair round and rolls up the ramp that leads into their home.

# CHAPTER 7

That first moment when Jason Morgan recognized his big brother John was only a fleeting beat, a temporary resurfacing. The days grew more surreal – closer to the turmoil Jason was feeling inside. One day John and Scott were asked by Jason to take his testicles – one each – and scrub them clean, because they were soaked in swamp water.

Scott turned to John. 'Hey, sounds like that's a big brother's job to me,' he joked.

John laughed. 'Can't argue with that. You got it.' Although he had no intention of doing what Jason had asked of him.

There were strict rules for visiting the ICU. Supposedly. But in Jason's case the rulebook was torn right up. It was supposed to be only one hour in the morning and one in the evening, two people at a time. But Jason was still touch and go, and often there were half a dozen visitors or more.

One morning Julie got to the ICU early and found herself alone with her twin. For the barest instant Jason knew her. The room had a narrow window set high in one wall. Jason flicked his eyes open and stared at the window. Then he moved his gaze across to his sister.

'Hey, Julie, I think if we pull the bed to the window it's high enough so I can reach up and escape.'

*Oh my God, he's used my name*, thought Julie.

She shook her head and smiled, wiping a tear from her eye. 'Jason, you're good. You're good.'

By now he'd lapsed back into unconsciousness. Julie sat there, staring at her comatose twin. She'd been born seven minutes ahead of him. They'd been at the same school, in the same year and class. Jason used to joke with her classmates: 'I'm a gentleman. I let ladies go first. That's why Julie's seven minutes older than me.'

It struck Julie as being so sad that Jason didn't know he was in a hospital with a whole team of medics trying to save him. It was so sad and so crazy-funny-tragic that he was trying his utmost to escape from those who were trying their utmost to save him. It was soul-destroying yet somehow hilarious all at the same time. Julie didn't have the words to describe such a moment. There were no words.

Fortunately, John – the most constant of the watchers – had prior experience to call upon. A college friend had had a motorcycle accident and ended up in a coma. His friends had made a tape recording of them talking and joking and singing his favourite songs. They'd leave it playing in his hospital room during those hours when no one could be there. A person in a coma can still hear. The words and the love can still filter through.

John applied that experience with Jason. If he was awake and not on child duty, he was in the ICU room talking continually to him. During a quiet moment between Jason's ravings John had gone real close and asked in his ear, 'What is your favourite verse?' The Morgan children had been brought up in a Christian household, and Sunday school had been a big thing. By 'verse', John meant Bible verse.

John had seen Jason's lips move. He'd bent his head closer, fearing Jason was muttering some nonsense about needing to escape from the bad guys. The feeding tubes made it doubly difficult to hear, and John got so close that his ear was practically brushing Jason's lips.

'But those who hope in the Lord will renew their strength,' Jason whispered. 'They will soar on wings like eagles, they will run and not be weary. They will walk and not be faint.'

It was Isaiah 40:31. John cried at hearing those words. His little brother not only still had his mind, it seemed that his memory – or at least fragments of it – was still intact.

It was two weeks into the Morgan family's long vigil when Jason appeared to have stabilized enough for the surgeons to attempt the first, and the most crucial, operation. Jason needed to have a series of titanium rods inserted along his spine, forming a metal sarcophagus to shore up the breaks. In an X-ray this would resemble an oil derrick. The head surgeon declared that he was ready to be operated on the following day and, using a series of charts and diagrams of the human spine, explained the limits of what they hoped to achieve.

'We'll go in there and align the spine as best we can. We won't be able to get it perfect, 'cause there's a lot of swelling still. But at least this will help, and we need to do this now, to start the healing. We'll put in the metal rods. It's not perfect, and he'll doubtless need more surgery, but if he was not in top physical condition he probably wouldn't have made it at all.'

Carla gave her consent for the operation to go ahead, but she was finding it far from easy. A social worker had been allocated to her – a civilian contractor working with the hospital – but even on the eve of Jason's surgery her talk with Carla was gloomy and negative. Not for the first time Carla broke down in front of Patti and Mike.

'She's been telling me all the things that Jason won't be able to do, even after the surgery. She's so negative about what he'll be capable of. He'll never be able to do this, that and the other . . . I mean, is there nothing he'll still be able to manage for himself? Nothing at all?'

Patti comforted her daughter-in-law as best she could: 'We're here for you, Carla. We'll help in any way we can. But we have to remain positive. We have to hope. Without hope there is nothing. And what's so wrong with hope?'

'I know,' Carla sobbed. 'I know. But she just sounds so negative about it all.'

'Without hope there's nothing, Carla,' Patti reiterated. 'There's nothing wrong with keeping our hope.'

It was late by now, and with the surgery scheduled for the following morning there was little point remaining at the hospital. The surgeons planned to sedate Jason heavily, so he could get some proper rest. There would be no blipping up to consciousness between now and then, and there was no reason for anyone to stay.

Carla left to rejoin her boys, while Julie, Mike and Patti ate a dinner in the canteen. They reminded themselves that Wilford

Hall was one of the top military trauma hospitals, and no one doubted that Jason was in good hands. They finished their meal and strolled across to the parking lot. They were almost at the Suburban when Julie stopped dead. She glanced at Mike with one of the most arresting looks he had ever seen. In her eyes was the last thing that he had ever expected to see: *fear*.

'Dad,' she whispered, 'you just got to go back in there and check on Jason. You got to go back in there right now.'

'Julie, we just saw him forty minutes ago,' Mike objected. 'He's sedated for surgery. Julie, he's OK.'

Julie shook her head emphatically. 'No, Dad, you need to go check right now.'

'But Julie, we just saw him and there's no reason to. Trust me, he's fine.'

Julie took a step towards the hospital. 'Dad, if you won't go, then I will. Someone has to go check *right now*.'

Mike held out a hand to stop her. Julie was pretty similar to his wife: he'd learned with them both that it was often easier to go with the flow.

'OK, I'll go. You wait here. Five minutes, that's all it'll take.'

As Mike stepped into the ICU suite he could tell immediately that something serious had happened. It turned out that there had been a car wreck on the base, and the horseshoe of ICU rooms was filling up with the injured. It was chaotic, and Mike had to fight his way through to reach Jason's room.

Just as soon as he threw the door open he practically fainted on the spot. Jason's limbs were rigid with spasms. He'd gone into cardiac arrest, his body convulsing and his blood pressure shooting way off the chart.

Mike screamed, 'HELP! EMERGENCY! HELP!'

A medic rushed in. The instant he laid eyes on Jason he hit the red alarm button. Doctors and nurses charged into the room. They thrust Mike to one side as they went to work on his son. Mike stood back, staring in utter shock as they tried to save Jason's life. The trauma of this moment had sent him into meltdown.

A part of him wondered if he should call Julie, Patti and Carla to warn them that they were losing Jason and to hurry right over. But what good would that do? Who would ever want to see him like this? And by the time they got here it would very likely be over.

Mike felt utterly helpless. This was destroying him. It was then that he sensed a presence at his side. It was Julie. Somehow she'd realized what was happening, and with Jason on the very verge of death she'd come running.

'My God, have we lost him?' Julie sobbed. 'Have we lost him? Dad, have we lost him?'

Mike enveloped his daughter in a bear hug. He couldn't manage any words of comfort right now. Maybe they had lost Jason. Maybe he was leaving them just when they'd begun to dare to hope that he was through the worst.

It took from 8.30 that evening until 4.00 in the morning to stabilize Jason Morgan. It turned out that the blood pressure alarms in his ICU room, which should go off if a patient's blood pressure drops or rises to life-threatening levels, had failed. For eight hours Jason had been balanced on a knife edge. He'd been perched on the very brink between life and death. If Julie had not forced her father to check, Jason would not be with them any more. Just a few more minutes and he would have died.

There would be no surgery the following morning, or for some days to come, the surgeon announced. There was no way that they could risk it. All that remained was for Jason's family to go home and sleep.

As he drove across the night-dark city, Mike felt like a dried-out, shrivelled husk. He was utterly finished. He reflected on how his son had used up most of his nine lives. The first was when the SUV had rolled over him. The second was when he had almost drowned in the swamp. The third was when he was dragged out of the jungle and evacuated to Quito. The fourth was when his lungs had stopped functioning some time during that evacuation. The fifth was when the first ICU aircraft scheduled to evacuate him to the USA suffered engine failure. The sixth was when he'd caught pneumonia, which they had feared would be the death of him. And now the seventh: a cardiac arrest on the eve of his first operation.

Only two lives remained. Was it enough? Mike just didn't know.

# CHAPTER 8

At the Siegfried household vacation time is over – for both Jim and Napal.

Jim works for the Department of Defense's 32nd Street Naval Station in San Diego, as a supply and logistics officer. He has a bare box of an office situated within a block of thirty pretty much identical cubicles. And Napal, of course, has been going with him the few days that Jim has been back at his desk.

Jim turns up each morning, and he and his dog go through the standard routine. Normally, no animals are allowed on base apart from military working dogs, like security K9s or those involved in bomb detection. Jim's had to go through the chain of command to get an exception made for Napal because he is a future CCI service dog.

Napal has been formally appointed Resident Canine Companion in Training, Defense Distribution Depot, San Diego. He's got his own photo ID threaded onto his collar – Napal staring with his big puppy eyes into the camera. Above the photo is the Defense Distribution Center (DDC) badge – an American eagle above crossed arrows, together with the motto 'Visibility. Value.

Velocity.' Under the photo is stamped NAPAL II – EMPLOYEE.
EXPIRY DATE 12/31/2010.

Jim works the graveyard shift from 5.30 a.m. until 2.30 in
the afternoon. He draws up at the front gate of the base in his
Chrysler, and the sentry tries to suppress a sleepy yawn. He
fixes Napal with a supposedly stern look.

'Excuse me, sir, but I just gotta get a look at your ID. That's
right, sir, if you can lean forward a little so I can see.'

Napal's learned to thrust his head and shoulders towards
the window, at which the sentry snaps off a crisp salute, and
the barrier before them rises as if by magic, so Jim can nose
through.

Jim pulls up at the office block, transfers from the Chrysler's
driver seat into his chair, and rolls down the ramp onto the
parking lot. With Napal in his lap, he wheels himself inside.
Only three or four people are there at this early hour. Jim heads
down the corridor, unlocks the door to his office and puts Napal
down on the sky-blue carpet.

'Sit. Stay.'

Napal sits obediently and awaits his next orders, though of
course he knows exactly what is coming. Jim raises the blind,
fires up his computer and settles himself at his desk, before
glancing at Napal with a smile.

'Go on then. Go see Phyllis.'

Napal needs no second urging. Seven doors down is Phyllis's
office. It's become routine that his first big adventure of the day
is to charge down the corridor to get fussed over by Phyllis and
get a delicious doggie treat. Once that's done, he and Jim have
to do the rest of the corridor, greeting the handful of fellow

early-bird workers, for everyone wants their special moment with Jim's dog.

In fact, having a four-legged worker here has proved something of an unexpected hazard due to Napal's extraordinary popularity. A few days back, Jim was rolling along with Napal in his lap, heading for the rest room, which in Napal's case is a patch of ground out the front of the building. It's a long roll to get there – a good hundred feet or more – and at every turn Jim kept getting stopped.

Which was fine, except that he sensed Napal needed to go real soon.

He came across one female worker who just didn't seem able to appreciate the urgency of the moment. She bent over Napal, massaging the folds of puppy fat around his neck and burbling away in that high-pitched baby voice that humans tend to use when talking to puppies.

'Oh, you're such a cutesy puppy-puppy-puppy-puppy-puppy-dog. Oh, you're such a cutesy—'

'Erm, the dog has to go potty,' Jim tried.

'Oh, you're such a cutesy puppy-puppy-puppy—'

'The dog's got to go potty. Like I have to leave now.'

Jim realized it was too late. There was a warm wet feeling in his lap.

It's a challenge when trying to toilet-train a dog as cute as this in an office populated by die-hard dog lovers. By the time they make it halfway down the corridor Napal is so excited by all the attention and so busting to go that he can't hold it in any more. Fortunately, there's a shower in the office block, and Jim keeps a change of clothes at work for incidents such as this one.

It's one of the flip sides of being so popular, Jim decides, but it's something that they're going to have to get used to. It's miraculous the effect this dog has on people. If Jim is rolling to the rest room alone, no one manages much more than a passing greeting: 'Hi, Jim, how's it going?' But factor Napal into the equation and such a simple errand can stretch into a lifetime.

Oddly, there is one person at the office that Napal just doesn't seem to take to. It sounds clichéd, but it's the mailman. For whatever reason – maybe it's the jingling of the keys in the guy's pocket – Napal can hear the mailman a good way off. When he's not out wowing Jim's fellow workers, Napal sleeps under the desk with his head resting on Jim's feet. But whenever he senses the mailman approaching, he raises his head, stares at the door and issues a quiet, throaty 'Grrrrrrrr'.

Jim glances at Napal. 'Hush, little buddy. I know who it is. It's OK.'

It's Napal's aversion to the mailman that gives Jim and his fellow worker Phyllis the big idea. If Napal doesn't like the mailman, then maybe he'll have to take over – or at least that's how Phyllis argues it.

'You think you could get your dog to do that?' Phyllis asks. 'You know, deliver the mail?'

Jim smiles. 'Sure. Yeah. Why not.'

Jim starts Napal's training by taking him around the various key delivery destinations. 'Let's go see the captain, little buddy. Come see the captain's office.'

It makes sense to start there, for the highest-ranking guy is sure to get the most mail. Jim puts Napal on his leash and leads him over. The captain greets the puppy, then gestures at his cubicle, which isn't a great deal bigger than Jim's. 'OK, Napal, so this is my office. The captain's office. So now you know.'

The next time Jim goes to visit the captain, he does so with Napal off-leash, so he can start to find his own way there. He does that a couple more times, on each occasion stressing that they're going to 'the captain's office'. After maybe twenty such trips he figures Napal has the route clear in his head.

Now . . . test time.

Jim has a memo he needs delivering to the captain for his signature. He pops it into an envelope, tucks the envelope into the CCI service dog harness that Napal wears whenever he is working and issues his instructions: 'Go see the captain. Go visit the captain's office.'

With barely a moment's hesitation Napal sets off, tail wagging happily and the memo firmly wedged under the harness. A few minutes later he returns with the memo duly signed by the captain. So begins Napal's informal job of work at the Defense Distribution Depot as the office's Dog Mail.

Two things strike Jim as he trains Napal to navigate his way around the twenty-odd destinations that require Dog Mail deliveries. One: this dog is super-intelligent and smart. Two: he has an amazing drive to serve. He loves being trained. He loves working. And he loves all the praise he receives whenever he gets it right.

After the advent of Dog Mail everyone in the office seems to want a Napal special delivery, and to keep some kind of doggie treat on hand. Napal sure likes getting those treats, but Jim figures he's more interested in earning his human companions' affection and praise. And that in turn promises to make him a fine service dog. When he goes to his eventual life companion, he'll need to be happy to serve without earning any kind of physical reward.

For many people who get a service dog, it's just not possible to keep giving the dog a treat. Their place of work might require hygiene levels that preclude feeding the dog, or the person might be disabled to such a degree that the physical process of giving a dog a treat is simply beyond their capabilities. The ideal CCI dog has to want to work and to serve for no other reward than a few choice words of praise. It's a rare animal that is happy to settle for that.

Of course there is the odd time when Napal gets it wrong. He carries a memo to the captain's office, when Jim tells him, 'Go to Greg's office. Go see Greg.' At which point Jim starts the training over, from scratch. He rolls with Napal to Greg's office, telling him where they are going to remind him how to find his own way there. At no time does Jim ever scold Napal. There is no scolding, and as far as Jim is concerned, there never is going to be any scolding. You only ever use positive reinforcement to train your dog.

Napal's fame spreads. Jim and his dog get a write-up in the Defense Logistics Agency magazine, the official mouthpiece of the logistics chain of the US military. The base's Dog Mail makes for great reading. It's not long before every high-ranking visitor seems to want to pay a visit to 'their' dog – all the way up to generals and admirals.

At the end of their first few weeks together Napal gets to go to his very first party. It's what CCI call a puppy social, and provides some further training, plus it gives the dogs the vital opportunity to be just ... dogs. Which is important. Like humans, dogs need downtime. They need time off from their training to wind down and run free and do whatever dogs do.

It's a Saturday morning, and after a long working week of pre-dawn starts Jim is enjoying a well-earned lie-in. Or at least he was until Napal decides otherwise. Jim wakes to a now familiar sensation – a dog's muzzle snuffling hesitatingly at his face. Napal's nose is just millimetres away, his whiskers brushing Jim's cheek as he sniffs and snorts and tries to establish if his big buddy is ready to greet the day.

Maybe the sheets are a little dusty or something, but Napal gets the sneezes. The first one explodes with perfect aim right up Jim's nostrils. He opens one sleepy eye carefully, only to get a second blast. There is no point trying to sleep any more. He opens both eyes and finds himself gazing into Napal's eager, let's-get-on-with-it, good-morning-Vietnam smile.

Napal may have his own bed but it isn't a patch on where Jim sleeps. Not in Napal's eyes or, rather, not via his nose. A dog's nose is anything up to a million times more sensitive than a human's. We might poke our nose into a mug of coffee to smell if it's been sweetened with a spoonful of sugar, but a dog can detect a teaspoon of sugar diluted in a million gallons of water – in other words, two Olympic-sized swimming pools full.

As far as Napal is concerned, his kennel crate smells of plastic and fake fur, plus the glue that holds it together. By contrast, Jim's bed is replete with the scent of his buddy snoozing comfortably for countless nights on end. It resonates with downtime and idling away the hours – plus there is the odd crumb in there from midnight snacks. That's what Napal's nose tells him, and like all dogs his sense of smell defines his universe. He is a creature of the nose. For him, the world is an incredibly rich tapestry of smells. More often than not, that's how a dog first experiences a new scene – via its scent carried on the breeze.

We humans see the world. A dog smells it.

Right now Jim and his bed sure smell good. But there's a party to get to and things are running late, so Jim insists they get up and get moving. Man and dog load up the Chrysler and head over to a friend's place. Cindy Carlton lives about four miles away on the far side of Santee. Like Jim, she's a seasoned puppy raiser and she's also on her third CCI dog. She's volunteered to host the bi-weekly puppy socials, which from now on will be a big part of Jim and Napal's life.

Cindy is perfect because she's got the energy and the enthusiasm – and with ten puppy raisers and their dogs coming together, she's going to need both. At the rear of her house is a fifty-foot stretch of grass leading up to a steep hill, with a solid brick retaining wall. There are going to be lots of people and lots of dogs, and she's got the space to let them run.

By the time Jim and Napal arrive the puppy party is in full swing. There are eight little dogs tearing up the grass and running wild. These puppies are what the raisers call 'naked': they've been taken out of their harnesses, plus their collars and leads – at which point they know they are being set free. On the 'Release' command each little dog tears off to join the fray.

Jim decides to teach Napal a crucial early lesson. He parks his chair on Cindy's patio, overlooking the dog melee.

Close by the dogs are yapping and barking, grass and dirt flying from their paws as they shoot this way and that. A fully grown Lab approaches from the far end of Cindy's land. At first only his head is visible above the grass as he tears towards the diminutive puppies, all of whom are strangers to this adult male. Then the forelimbs appear, ripping powerfully through the undergrowth, the seventy-pound dog bearing down on the puppies fast. The Lab spies one of the smallest, half-hidden in the long grass. With three massive bounds he's upon the tiny bundle of glistening fur, towering over it. The puppy looks skywards, at the daunting presence rearing above.

The male reaches down and nips the puppy on the ear. The little dog responds by leaping onto the big dog's neck and clinging on with all four paws. Together, these two strangers – one a puppy of ten weeks and the other a mature male – begin to roll around and play as if they're old friends.

Jim meanwhile has given Napal the 'Stay' command. He's still in his harness and he's on-leash, which means he's not allowed to run off and join the fun. Napal settles down beneath Jim's chair, his muzzle pointed firmly in the direction of his four-legged fellows, his nose snuffling up the alluring scents rising from the direction of their high-spirited play. Napal can smell the other dogs. He can hear their squeals of delight as they roll and race and pretend to fight. But he knows he's not allowed to join them. He doesn't know why, and for a moment Jim stopping him may seem cruel, but this is a crucial lesson for Napal to learn. If he's to make it as a CCI dog, he's got to be able to stay focused and not get distracted, no matter what's going on around him.

When Jim figures Napal's learned that vital lesson, he removes his harness and gives the magic command: 'Release.'

Napal bounds across the grass to join in the fun. He doesn't do what a human child might do: he doesn't hang back and eyeball the nearest playmate, or call across to him, or maybe touch him to check if he is responsive. Instead he boldly marches up to his nearest fellow puppy trainee and takes an almighty great sniff. The nose is thrust right up close to the unfamiliar puppy – moist and receptive and vacuuming up the scent. And, no doubt about it, that puppy smells good. She smells Napal back, and clearly she agrees. Moments later, they're bounding around and tumbling over each other as if they've known each other all their short lives.

That's the beauty of dogs. There's no time to waste. No time to be stand-offish or play hard to get. There's a life that has to be lived to the full, and it's got to start right now.

Jim sits on the patio enjoying the scene. It's great to see Napal at play with the others. He pulls a ball out of his pocket and throws it for the dogs. He polices the play a little, making sure that several dogs don't gang up on one, which can happen if they get carried away. He throws a toy into the throng. Napal grabs it and rushes off with all the others in hot pursuit. One catches him. For several seconds they wrestle for the toy, heads tossing from side to side, throats emitting fierce little puppy growls. Then Napal gives up the toy and joins the pack giving chase. This is all good. This is learning how to deal with and relate to other dogs.

After a while Jim notices that Napal seems to have chosen one female as his buddy. He's latched on to her, and she quickly shows signs of trying to be the dominant one. As Jim well knows, a dog that stands over another dog, or tries to mount it, can be showing dominance – behaviour inherited from wolves in the wild.

In a life spent with dogs Jim's studied a little how they've evolved. All modern-day dogs are descendants of the one species, *Canis lupus*, the grey wolf. Wolves are generally pack animals, with two dominant adults – one male, one female – threatening hostility or expulsion from the group to subjugate those under them. But it's important that CCI puppies learn how to socialize properly with other dogs in a 'civilized' manner. Today, Napal reacts to the bitch's attempts to dominate him by trying to dominate her back: he's in danger of picking up bad habits. The dogs gets called in. The female and Napal are separated for a while, so the undesirable – wolfish – behaviour can be nipped in the bud.

The last thing Jim would ever want is to raise Napal to be a wolf in sheep's clothing.

# CHAPTER 9

My name is Jason Mark Morgan . . . and I'm back. Thanks for sticking with my story while I was in the coma: it was one part that I just couldn't tell, for obvious reasons. But from now on I'll be with you all the way.

After I finally had the surgery to stabilize my spine they brought me out of the coma by cutting off the supply of drugs. Slowly, painfully, I crawled back towards the light. After so many weeks mired in the darkness you almost forget that the light is there – or what it's like. My first fully conscious feeling was far from being a good one: it was of unbelievable pain. Pain like you could never imagine possible. It felt as if someone had got a pair of red-hot pokers and had rammed them into my eye sockets. It seemed to drill up from the bottom of my legs hard into my brain, as if my feet were submerged in vats of burning oil.

The pain was so intense that it seemed to me I was almost better off back in the coma. The waves of agony all but blinded me to the here and now. Almost. What pulled me finally into the present was what the surgeon kept telling me – over and over, until it bled through to my pain-racked consciousness.

'Jason, I'm your surgeon. You may or may not realize this, but you've been unconscious for several weeks. You were involved in a road traffic accident while on operations in Ecuador. You're in hospital, and we've been doing everything in our power to keep you alive and to fix you.'

His words could not be ignored. This was the moment when I would fully understand where I was, and that I wasn't in some drug runner's dungeon.

'Jason, I want you to nod if you can hear me.'

I nodded.

'OK. You were injured on operations on the Ecuador–Colombia border. You are now back in the US. You are very lucky to be alive. But I have to tell you – you are paralyzed from above the waist and you will never walk again.'

The bombshell dropped into my pain and my darkness, lighting it up like a nuclear explosion. *You will never walk again. You will never walk again.* Those impossible words reverberated through my brain, cutting through the pain like a laser. I could not believe what I was hearing. This could not be happening.

Deep down inside I knew I had to fight this. Time to break the silence. Time to speak out and be heard.

'Sir, I am going to walk again. Yes, I am.'

My voice rasped and croaked horribly. It was barely above a whisper. I barely recognized myself. It didn't sound like me at all. What in the name of God had happened to me?

The surgeon shook his head. 'No, Jason, you're not. There's no way to sugarcoat this. You broke your back in two places, and you are paralyzed from above the waist. You will never be able to walk.'

I was on massive amounts of pain medication, but I was sharp enough to know this: if I accepted what the surgeon was telling me, that would be it. The battle would be over before it had even started. I would for sure never walk again. I kept telling the surgeon the contrary – that I would walk again. If I believed it strongly enough, I would make it happen. I'd make it a reality. It was hard to keep any kind of a proper focus, but I believed that if I denied it vehemently enough then I'd get there. My only hope lay in resistance.

The surgeon tried to end the debate by asking me to wriggle my toes.

I did as he asked. 'See,' I croaked. 'They're moving.'

He stared at my feet. 'No, Jason, they're not. You just think they are.'

'Sir, yes, they are,' I fired back. 'It's just too small a movement for you to notice.'

'No, Jason. Trust me, they didn't move. You are paralyzed from above the waist. I'm sorry.'

The surgeon was speaking to me gently. He was trying to be as kind and considerate as possible, while telling me what he believed to be the brutal, inescapable truth. Under the circumstances it wasn't exactly easy for the poor guy.

We'd reached an impasse. He wasn't about to give ground, but neither was I, so there wasn't a great deal more to be said. I glanced around at my family. All of my loved ones were gathered. I could read the expressions in their eyes. They'd heard it all before. They'd had plenty of time to prepare themselves. Tears rolled down my mother's cheeks. I didn't know if they were tears of pride at my resistance, or tears of sadness that I was nurturing a false hope. But knowing my mother it had to be the former. She always had been a fighter, and she'd imbued in us the same spirit.

Even if there was no chance that what I said was true, I still preferred to nurture hope. For without hope what is there?

Once the surgeon was done talking, an air force captain in full uniform came to see me in private. He wanted to know everything that I remembered about the 'accident'. I told him the truth: I remembered absolutely nothing. My mind was an utter blank. I'd jumped out of a Hercules and parachuted into the jungle. I'd come back to consciousness here, like this, and in between there was just a ragged black hole full of sheer and utter emptiness.

It was as if someone had lobbed a cruise missile into my brain and blown away a patch of memories. If I tried looking into that hole there was nothing to see – just the torn and shattered edges where the recollections petered out. I knew that something was missing. Something big and significant had been ripped out of my head. But I had no idea what it was that I had lost.

The captain seemed satisfied that I'd told him all that I could. As far as anyone knew I was the perfect survivor of such an operation – I had no memory of what had happened, so there was nothing that I could go and tell.

Because I had been lying down for so long, my blood vessels had dilated to enable the blood to keep flowing, plus my muscles had wasted away due to inactivity. I'd also lost as much as forty pounds in weight. The first time they tried to sit me in a wheelchair I lasted barely fifteen minutes. The combination of dilated veins and weak musculature meant that I couldn't pump enough blood to my head, and I passed out.

Gradually they built me up to being able to sit for thirty minutes in the chair. I had my legs wrapped in bandages, to constrict the flow of blood to my lower limbs and keep it pumping to my head region, but I felt about as capable as a newborn baby, maybe less so. I was going to have to learn how to sit again, and even the slightest movement caused me a tsunami of pain.

My mind felt as if it was being torn into little pieces and pulled in a thousand different directions. I was alive. I could so easily have died. I should be thankful that I was alive. I was in a wheelchair. The surgeon said I'd spend the rest of my life in a chair. I couldn't even manage an hour in it right now. I was racked with pain every waking moment, a pain that made life close to unendurable. So what in God's name did I have to live for? This was a living nightmare. Paralyzed and confined to a wheelchair for life – I'd be useless to everyone, including the military and my wife and three infant boys.

There was a dark truth tugging at the edges of my consciousness: *Jason, let's face it, maybe you'd be better off dead.*

I blocked that out by vowing to fight; by vowing that I would walk again and recover my faculties. *The surgeon was wrong* – that was my only coping mechanism. I chose denial, and I kept telling myself that mind over matter *can* achieve great things. Plus I had my wife and my kids to live for, if only they would accept me for who and what I now seemed to be.

The first time my boys came to visit me after the accident, I was still bedridden, still working my way up to being able to spend an hour sitting in a wheelchair. I managed to prop myself up in bed against a mountain of pillows. I tried my best to act normal, like the daddy they needed me to be, and to screen out the screaming, burning bolts of pain.

Carla and my mom brought them in. Blake, Austin and Grant – what were three boys below the age of four supposed to understand about any of this? Carla had told them only that daddy had been hurt and was recovering in hospital.

She brought a portable playpen and two strollers so the boys could spend some quality time with me. From the get-go Blake and Austin were just overjoyed. To them this was just Daddy lying in bed, like they'd seen me a thousand times before, when they'd burst into the bedroom and bounced about on the bed. *Come on, Daddy. Let's get up. Let's get up. Let's go face the day.*

It was a magical moment having them there beside me. I felt tears pricking my eyes. But Grant, my youngest, seemed inconsolable. The moment he stepped into the room he wouldn't stop crying. He looked in my direction, and it was as if he could see right through to the damage and the hurt and the pain. He just wouldn't stop, no matter what we tried to do, so they really couldn't stay for long.

I could see how hard the adults were finding this too. Carla. My parents. My brother and sister. They'd already been told the harsh truth – your son/brother/husband will be wheelchair-bound for the rest of his life – but hearing is one thing; seeing is quite another. *Seeing is believing.* For the first time they saw me in a wheelchair, and it really hit home. As much as they tried to hide it, I could see the shock and the consternation etched in their eyes.

I felt it too. This could not be me. I had been the sports jock at high school. I'd won a sport scholarship to college. I'd gone into the military instead, for only that seemed to offer me the action and the challenge that I craved. Even there, I'd chosen an elite air force outfit, to push to the max. And, not content with making it into Air Force Special Operations, I'd pushed one step further – getting myself into the SOAR.

So how could that guy end up paralyzed and consigned to a chair?

Before now, my family had been focused purely on keeping me alive. After the surgery on my spine, my life was no longer hanging in the balance. It was hellishly tough and emotional for every one of them. That was when reality hit. *This is how it's going to be.*

I remember the first time they wheeled me outside. It was a couple of days after I'd crawled out of the coma. It was a beautiful summer's day. It was the first time in months that I'd seen the sun. My father took the reins. I think he needed to show that he was not embarrassed or discomfited by what his son had become. He wheeled me along the hospital corridor, into the elevator and out the rear door leading onto the grass. My boys were there with some of their toys, and the idea was that I could sit in my chair with the sun on my face and watch them play. I could hear their squeals of laughter and know that much was good with the world. There were still things to live for.

For the first time in what felt like a lifetime there were no nurses and no surgeons around; no heart monitors and drips; no straps holding me tight to a rotating bed. It was just us, just family. It was August, the hottest time of the year. The grass around the hospital was fed by sprinklers, and it was emerald green. Shimmering with good health.

*What a contrast to me.*

For my dad this moment was about getting his son back in whatever way was still possible. This might be as good as it got, but it was way better than me being in a coma and unreachable. At least they had me out in the sun and seemingly of sound mind.

This was a key moment – one that my folks would relive many times over – when they realized something of vital importance. We define people by the physical, by what we can see. The ability. The physical beauty. The stature of the warrior. But actually what matters is the person inside.

But even that was somehow . . . reduced.

I had lost so many memories. The air force captain had told my family that I remembered nothing about how I had got hurt. But brain damage is a sliding scale: at one end lies minor memory loss, at the other serious mental disability. And scattered in between are countless other points. My mind seemed scrambled. Ill-focused. Unwieldy. But maybe that was all down to the pain that I was feeling – the constant, unbearable pain – and the drugs I was on to fight it.

In truth, any mental fallout I might have suffered wasn't really the key issue right now. The physical was all-important. I was a pain-racked, weak, emaciated shadow of who and what I had been. I was quiet and uncommunicative, and I could do almost nothing for myself. I could barely turn over in bed; one of the medics had to come in and do it for me. My struggles were so very, very basic and immediate right then.

They got me into rehab pretty quickly, and that was when it really hit: *I can do almost nothing for myself.* I was going to have to relearn so many of the basic abilities that able-bodied humans take for granted. Dressing myself. Washing. Going to the rest room. Getting out of bed. Driving. All of those things become a very different exercise when you cannot use your legs.

I felt lost. I was assailed by a thousand uncertainties. What on earth would become of me? How strong would I ever be? What would I be able to do for myself and my family? Would I be able to lift my kids and hold them even?

I was overwhelmed by my lack of capabilities. Just the process of transferring me from my wheelchair to my bed was a massive undertaking. It took an age to achieve it, and there was almost nothing I could do to help.

As a paraplegic – *for that's what I was now* – you have to learn to do all the things your legs used to do by using your arms, back and shoulder muscles. You have to drag the lower half of your body after you, like a useless deadweight. Now, imagine trying to do all of that with a back broken in two places and shored up by a titanium sarcophagus, and with muscles that have wasted away to such an extent that you've lost a third of your body weight, and when every single movement causes you unbearable pain.

Impossible, huh?

It was. Pretty much.

It wasn't so long ago that I'd put myself through air force special forces selection and jump school. I remembered doing the obstacle course, my rucksack loaded down with ten-pound sandbags, getting sprayed with ice-cold blasts from fire hoses the entire way. I had to complete fifty press-ups between each obstacle. I was breathless and soaking wet and my muscles were burning, yet still I had questions fired at me about the technicalities of airborne drops and weather systems.

One wrong answer, one failure to cross an obstacle – the wall, the tunnel, the pond, the ditch – one significant defeat in making the times allowed, and I would not have passed. Yet I did. My body and my mind endured.

At the end of that punishing course I had stood in line with the few and the proud, and I was given my unit coin and my beret. It's a slate-grey one with the 10th Combat Weather Squadron's badge attached – a dagger, point upwards, super-imposed over a parachute and a pair of crossed lightning bolts, with COMBAT WEATHER TEAM AIRBORNE stamped around it. At that moment I had felt so very honoured. And after that I'd made it into army special operations, being assigned to the iconic SOAR.

In 1980 a mission to rescue American hostages in Iran had been aborted due to problems with the helicopter-borne force. After that the US Army began developing a helicopter unit specifically to support special operations. Over the next decade the unit evolved into the 160th Special Operations Aviation Regiment (Airborne) – the SOAR. Long-range low-level penetrations were a speciality of SOAR crews, infiltrating behind enemy lines to insert or extract US or allied forces. SOAR helicopters were also used for close air support or medical evacuation of special operations personnel. From Operation Urgent Fury in 1983 – immortalized in the book and the movie *Black Hawk*

*Down* – through numerous more recent missions, the SOAR was at the forefront wherever elite forces went into harm's way.

For our South American operations we'd been equipped with a pair of MH60 Blackhawks. More often than not our task was to carry out surveillance of known narco-rebel hideouts. Our rules of engagement didn't allow us to fire unless fired upon first. FARC knew this and used it to their advantage. Most of their bases were located on the rivers, which they used for transport. We'd move fast and low, flying just above the water to drown out the engine noise and surprise the bad guys.

On one such mission a man came running out of a hut brandishing a pistol. We had two 30-millimetre Gatling cannons on each side of the helicopter, so he was a little outgunned. He stood outside waving his pistol at us, as if that was going to scare us off. Since we couldn't fire unless he fired first, the pilot decided to hover just above his hut, the rotor wash blowing his roof off.

But the rebels' weaponry and intelligence was actually surprisingly sophisticated. On one mission we recovered a scanner which they used to listen in on the radio chat between our Blackhawks. More worrying still, we received weekly threats that if we didn't leave Ecuador, they would find and kill our wives and kids back home. Chillingly, Carla's name was on one of their kill lists. But despite the threats and the dangers, I'd loved what I did with the SOAR.

And now this. Consigned to life in a wheelchair.

I seemed to have feeling down to the level of my belly button, no further. Any lower and I could pinch myself and feel absolutely nothing. That is the weirdest, most unsettling feeling. Imagine running your hand across your foot or your thigh, and your brain failing to register any feeling, not even the passage of your fingers across your own skin. It's as if a part of your body is no longer yours any more. In my case, we were talking about more than half of it.

And that had to make me wonder: *How can life go on when half my body is lost to me?*

# CHAPTER 10

They've started calling Jim Siegfried the Dog Whisperer.

He can't remember who first came up with the nickname. Or rather, who first used it. Maybe it was Cindy, Jim's Santee neighbour who runs the twice-weekly puppy socials? Either way, Jim doesn't figure he deserves the name. He's no dog whisperer. He's just been blessed with the smartest ever puppy.

Jim first heard the name being used at the puppy classes. Every two weeks a CCI-nominated instructor helps the puppy raisers with the training of their dogs. Mike Fowler runs the Santee classes. A serving police officer with San Diego's K9 unit, he has a handsome and athletic-looking Malinois called Rex. A Malinois looks like a slightly smaller, more compact German shepherd. They're a favourite breed in law enforcement and military circles.

Mike's a down-to-earth kind of a cop. In his mid-forties, he pretty much lets his dog do most of the work. He's approaching retirement age, his hair is thinning on top and he's one mellow, easy-going guy. He's also a total dog lover and a huge fan of CCI. Every two weeks he gathers a dozen-odd puppy raisers together, to teach the thirty-odd commands a dog is supposed to master prior to being handed back to CCI. They include the obvious ones – 'Sit', 'Stay', 'Release' – most of which Napal has already mastered, and some not so obvious ones. Take for example the command 'Speak' – meaning the dog is supposed to bark on demand. Why might an assistance dog need to do that?

Imagine the dog is assisting a person in a wheelchair and that person is home alone and tumbles out of their chair. They may have no way to get back in again unaided. But if the dog gives his signature bark – the woof he only ever does if his charge is in trouble – and the neighbours have been warned about that, then the dog can raise the alarm.

Mike gets each puppy raiser to work a task with his or her dog – perhaps getting it to open a fridge door or to retrieve a dropped item and return it to its human companion. He watches carefully and critiques each raiser-and-dog team, suggesting ways to get them to interact more closely. In the eighteen months that Jim will have Napal, he has to pass Puppy Class Basic and Advanced Puppy Class, all under the mellow – yet all-seeing – gaze of Mike Fowler.

The commands are taught to the dogs purely via positive reinforcement. When Napal gets it right, Jim bends down to him and whispers in his ear, 'Good dog. Good dog.' Napal's tail-wagging is so enthusiastic, the puppy's entire rear end gyrates back and forth. Napal's grown considerably since Jim first got him. When he's sitting, his head is about as high as the side of Jim's wheelchair. It puts man and dog almost on the same level, which Mike figures may help explain the miraculous bond he's forging with this dog.

Of course, there are downsides to raising a CCI puppy from a chair. At all times Jim has to be careful he doesn't run over a soft puppy paw with one of his wheels. He's also got to avoid getting into any situation where Napal might feel cornered, trapped or in any sense threatened by the chair. If he develops any such fear that would be disastrous, for most likely he'll end up assisting someone who is at least partially wheelchair-bound. But the upsides are also very real. Being paired with Jim gets Napal accustomed to being around a human in a chair. And Jim is pretty much eye to eye with his dog. With a dog like Napal, the more on his level you can be, the more receptive he will be to your commands. Maybe that's why Jim's earned the Dog Whisperer nickname.

Or maybe it's all down to the Dick Van Patten's Natural Balance treats Jim's started feeding Napal. They went through a few flavours – Sweet Potato and Fish, Sweet Potato and Bison, Potato and Duck Formula – before discovering Napal's all-time favourite, Natural Balance Duck Formula Jerky. They're like mini-sausages, ones that are soft enough to break into pieces so you can easily feed a snippet to your dog. Suffice to say, with Napal it's one sniff, one gulp and it's gone!

Jim doesn't think the Dog Whisperer nickname is down to any one thing. There is just some incredibly natural ability to communicate developing between him and his dog. Whenever they run through one of Mike Fowler's exercises, Jim talks to Napal the entire time, murmuring little words of guidance and reassurance as they go.

'That's right. Good boy. That's it, little buddy – lift it up in your jaws and pass it my way. You got it.'

But in truth he figures they could complete most exercises in total silence. The communication between them goes much deeper; it goes beyond words. One look between man and dog, and they pretty much know what they're about.

But all work and no play makes for a dull dog. After Mike Fowler's training sessions Jim heads home in the Chrysler, Napal perched on the passenger seat looking forward to some downtime. They roll into the backyard and Jim decides he deserves a Budweiser.

He glances at Napal. 'Go fetch a beer. Go fetch me a beer.'

Napal wags his tail and dashes off inside. He grabs the rope loop that Jim has tied to the door of his mini-refrigerator, pulls it while edging back with his legs, pokes his head around the open door, grabs a can of Bud out of the cooler and returns with it gripped in his jaws. When he hands it to Jim there's not a single indentation in its soft metal skin. That's how gentle Napal's bite can be.

Jim grabs Napal and, gangly legs and paws scrabbling, lifts him up to his position on the Hot Tub Lookout. He reaches into his pocket, pulls out a last length of Duck Formula Jerky and offers it to his dog.

At work Jim has taught Napal to fetch him a Coke from the office refrigerator. Here at home it's more commonly the TV remote, or maybe Jim's slippers. It's so much fun working with Napal and training him, especially as the dog so loves to learn and to serve.

Jim glances at the fast-growing puppy. Every day he seems a little bigger. And every inch the dog grows is an inch nearer to

Jim having to hand him back to CCI. Jim forces that troublesome thought from his head.

'Ain't it a beautiful evening?' he muses. 'So, how about we have the last instalment of my life story?'

Napal's got this expression on his face that Jim knows well.

'Oh. OK, you want your toy? Is that it? You'll listen better if you got something to chew on? Well, OK, go get your toy.'

Napal jumps down and beetles off inside the house. He returns a few moments later with a knitted and stuffed toy chicken gripped in his mouth. It's most likely a cockerel, by the look of the big red comb atop its head and its flash of bright orange tail feathers. Jim lifts the toy chicken and places it feet down on the Hot Tub Lookout. It stands there, looking a bit like one of the penguins from the movie *Madagascar*. He lifts Napal up beside it. Napal stares at the chicken with his laser-eyed look. He's stand-offish and almost discomfited.

His expression says, *Hey! Chicken! What are you doing up here? This is my lookout.*

Napal circles the chicken warily. Then he goes for the kill. He pounces. The chicken doesn't stand a chance. Napal grabs it in his jaws and settles down for a good chew. The look in his eyes says it all: *OK, I'm all ears.*

'So, where was I?' Jim murmurs. 'I know. I was in the hospital, and the doctor guy had just told me I'd never walk again. And I'd just asked him to let my girlfriend know, 'cause I couldn't make it to the dance.'

Jim settles deeper into his chair, enjoying the warmth of the balmy summer's evening.

'So, I was nineteen years old. Nineteen, and I'd just been told that I'd never walk. And you know what the doctors did? They moved me out of the ICU right away, 'cause there were fifty people waiting to visit me. *Fifty*. And they couldn't fit them all in, but they so wanted to raise my spirits.'

Jim drags open the ring pull on his beer and takes a first sip. 'At the time I was coaching football at Los Altos High School in Hacienda Heights, and I was thinking about joining the navy. My dad was a sailor in World War Two and I was tempted to follow in his footsteps. But I hadn't really made up my mind. I guess I was confused about what I'd do with my life. And now this – paralyzed from the waist down and confined to a chair.'

Jim pats the wheel of his chair. 'Don LeGro, one of the senior coaches at Los Altos, had told me to go back to college and try for a football scholarship. He thought I was good enough. But, well, no one plays football in a chair.

'Don said to me, "So, what're you gonna do now?" Meaning, now that I was in a wheelchair. I said, "Well, I can't exactly go to college." He said, "Stick with me and coach football." I said, "Me coach football? How am I going to coach from a wheelchair?" And he said, "Don't worry – we'll figure it out."'

Jim chuckles. 'I was in hospital for four months. I got out in February 1978. I coached at Los Altos the '78–9 school year. I was on the freshman programme. And you know what? We went undefeated that year. How good is that!'

Man and dog exchange glances. Napal's eyes light up and his tail thumps out a staccato rhythm on the cover of the hot tub.

'I coached right through until I got Gigi,' Jim continues. 'She was my first CCI dog. Then I thought, *I can't combine coaching and dog raising*. So I stopped for a year or two. But then I got a call from Mike David, a great coach I know, who'd just taken over coaching at the Bishop's School, which is right nearby. And, listen carefully, little buddy, 'cause you're gonna meet him soon.'

Jim glances at Napal. He's got his head nuzzled comfortably onto his chicken toy, using it like a pillow. He doesn't move, he just flicks his eyebrows Jim's way, as if to say, *You got it. I'm all ears.*

'Mike called up and said, "I want you to come help me coach. You know, work with the offensive line. Get 'em up to speed on the wing T offence. You figure you could do that?" Now I know you don't follow football, Napal, but you're gonna have to learn. The wing T, that's my specialty. And I thought, *You know what, I've missed coaching.* I've missed it. So I told Mike, "Sure, I'll give it a shot."

'I had your father, Terence, right then. I used to take him with me. We have an artificial turf field, so I didn't want him going to toilet there. I'd get him to go in the flower bed, right next to the field. And sometimes we'd be halfway through training and I'd figure Terence needed to go. So I'd tell him, "Go on. Go use the rest room." He'd run off into the flowers, do his stuff, and run back to join us.'

Jim reaches out and grabs Napal's chicken toy, making as if it's trying to escape. Napal growls gently, enjoying the game, and grasps it tighter between his paws. *That bird's going nowhere.*

Jim laughs. 'That's it. Get that chicken. Now ... I'm gonna expect the same kind of good behaviour from you. No goofing about on the football field. The team's easy to recognize: they wear maroon and gold and they're called the Knights. And you'll need to be on your best behaviour at all times 'cause it ain't easy coaching from a chair.

'Pretty much all I've ever done is coach from a chair. But I gotta be a lot more verbal 'cause I can't demonstrate so much physically. So, if it's not coming across to a kid, I have to go home and figure out how I can get into his head what exactly I want him to do. I can use my arms and shoulders and gestures and stuff, but I can't run or show a manoeuvre, obviously.

'In fact, it's a real pain in the shoulders just to roll a chair over grass 'cause the wheels tend to dig in. And you know how you can help? If any of my guys get hurt, just by sitting by them and comforting them, giving them some real good Napal love, you can really make it feel better. So, you figure you can do that? I bet you could!'

Jim caresses his dog's sleek head thoughtfully. 'Season begins early September, so soon now. And you know what? You're gonna love it with the Knights. We're gonna have *fun*.'

Jim is approaching two months into life-after-getting-Napal, which means his dog is pushing four months old. And that means Jim's got sixteen months to go before he has to hand Napal back, which equates to one and a bit football seasons. It's not a lot of time when viewed that way.

He's convinced that Napal will make it as a CCI dog. No way will he ever wash out. He picks up the training in a snap of the fingers, he's so smart. Although they're only eight weeks in, even now there's a part of Jim that's trying to steel himself for what is coming – the parting. Giving up this dog is going to be one of the hardest things that he's ever done. In fact, the closer man and dog become the more impossible the thought seems to be. And it's not just Jim who's daunted by the idea of handing back Napal. The dog has won the hearts of his wider family, in spite of all the warnings.

Jim's father has passed away, and his younger brother Danny – the one with Down's syndrome – is in a rest home. But his mother Virginia lives just nearby. Jim is in the habit of heading over there with Napal to take her out on day trips. From the very first he warns her that some day soon he's going to have to give this dog up.

'Hey, don't get too attached. Don't get too close.'

In a sense, he doesn't know why he bothered with the warnings: Jim's mother has fallen head over heels for Napal.

At first Jim tried telling himself the same thing. There was a voice inside his head saying, *Hey, don't get too attached. This dog isn't your dog, and you won't have him for ever. So don't get too attached.* Intellectually, Jim knew that. He told himself that same thing over and over. But emotionally? Emotionally, Jim just wasn't able to hold back. How could he, when he was putting his entire essence into forging a special bond with this dog and creating the best possible team? How could he put his whole life into the dog, yet combine that with holding back? The two things pulled in opposite directions. In truth, he would only be the best trainer if he gave his whole heart to the dog.

As to their parting, Jim's kicked it into the long grass: he'll just have to find some way to deal with that when the time comes.

# CHAPTER 11

The day arrived when I checked out of Wilford Hall.

They rolled me out of one hospital straight into another, the San Antonio Spinal Cord Rehab Center. For the first time they dressed me in something other than a hospital robe. But the jogging pants were like sacks on me. I'd gone from 185 pounds to 130, and my legs looked like toothpicks. I'd always been a muscular kind of a guy – especially my legs. I used to run like the wind. Now I felt as if a puff of wind could blow me away.

They got me into a body brace, a kind of strap-on sarcophagus that encased me from my hips to my chest. It was to stabilize my spine and give it a better chance to heal. They started to put me through some very basic physical therapy. I was supposed to wear shorts for the sessions. They taught me how to put them on. Without the use of my legs it took me twenty minutes to do so.

Twenty minutes to pull on a pair of shorts.

How could I be so freakin' useless?

I felt like picking up the nearest thing and throwing it at the medical staff, I felt so utterly hopeless. *See! See that? At least my arms still work!*

They told me all about the dangers of pressure sores – one

of the main complications associated with paralysis – and how to avoid getting them. An able-bodied person will be sitting somewhere, and if they feel the circulation start to shut off, they'll simply wriggle around a bit, which enables the blood to flow. But for a person with paralysis, wriggling-around isn't an option; the muscles below the level of the paralysis generally don't work any more. They waste away. If the blood supply gets cut off for a long period of time, a sore develops. It's basically an infection of the flesh, but it can go through to the bone, and that can be fatal.

The only way to avoid getting pressure sores is to push yourself up out of your chair every fifteen minutes or so, and to lower yourself down in a slightly different position – the equivalent of an able-bodied person's wriggle. Plus you're not supposed to do much of any kind of activity that requires you to remain in one position for a long period of time.

In spite of all the rehab, the medics never managed to communicate to me adequately what life was going to be like in a chair. I didn't blame them. They weren't wheelchair-bound, so how could they know? How could they *feel* it? They'd never once experienced the kinds of things that I was going through, so they just couldn't know. But there were other guys who did know – those like me who'd suffered paralysis. A day came when one of them paid me a very special visit, one that changed things for me. He'd been injured years before, and now he played for a wheelchair basketball team that practised in the rehab centre.

Prior to his visit I didn't even know such things existed. *Basketball in wheelchairs. What is that?* But the guy explained the level of disability the guys had and what the team was about.

Then he threw me this look. The expression in his eyes said, *I know exactly what you're going through right now, buddy. I understand.*

He smiled. 'You know what, Jason? Maybe when you're back on your feet, as it were, you can come play for us? Come play some chair basketball?'

Then he did the most amazing thing. He spun his chair round pretty much on the spot, executing this neat kind of handbrake turn, and tilted it back into a wheelie. Right there in my hospital room he lifted his front wheels off the ground and wheelied out, laughing all the way.

I stared after him. For the first time I thought to myself, *Maybe there is life after paralysis? Maybe I can have some fun in a chair, after all?*

The physical therapy was interspersed with occupational therapy – basically relearning all the things an able-bodied person takes for granted, the kind of things you learn to do when you're a toddler. How to wash yourself. How to use the rest room. How to eat. Plus you're also supposed to learn that as a paraplegic there are so many things in life that you will never to do again.

Prior to my injuries we'd done lots of wilderness camping. That had been the Morgan family thing. I'd hook up a trailer to my truck and we'd head off into the wilds. We'd started with a little pop-up camper and worked our way up to a forty-foot RV trailer, with a pickup to pull the thing. For a while we'd lived in Denver, Colorado, which was a perfect place for such trips. Within thirty minutes you could be deep among the Rockies. I was an elite forces operator and my wife was a fitness fanatic;

heading into the wilds had been the most natural thing to do, and it had become a regular weekend pastime for us as a family. I'd slip Grant into a baby-carrier backpack and the two older boys would toddle off on foot as Carla and I hit the trails. In summer it was paradise up there. We'd sit around an open fire in the evening and I'd barbecue some ribs, then throw a football around with the boys. The very best of times.

All of this I was now told would no longer be possible. A guy in a chair can't hook up a trailer to a truck or follow a hiking trail. Wheelchairs are not designed for going off road; they're strictly for hard, level surfaces. Even a moderately thick carpet makes it difficult to roll. As for grass, rock or forest floor, forget it. It's impossible.

I just didn't know how I was going to manage without any of that. I wouldn't be able to wrestle with my kids on the grass, or carry them through a forest's shadows, or lift them over a sunlit stream. I couldn't clown about with them, or throw them into the air and catch them. Rolling along the sidewalk with one of the boys in my lap just wasn't going to cut it. It wouldn't even come close.

Obviously, we were going to have to sell the RV trailer, and probably the truck we used to pull it. We had no need of either any more. It'd be the end of an era – a beautiful, magical time in which I had taken my health and my able-bodied status for granted, as we all tend to. And what was then going to replace it? With Dad in a chair, what would be the new Morgan family normal?

Before checking out of rehab I had to learn to drive again, but this time using only my hands. The Department of Veterans

Affairs (VA) – the government agency charged with looking after disabled military veterans – provided the tools for me to do so. I started in a simulator, a kind of wraparound capsule that projects onto a screen a video image of you driving a car, one that responds to your use of the hand controls as if you are on the road for real.

Driving using only your hands is completely different to how you normally drive. It felt utterly unnatural. It seemed as if I had a car pulling out in front of me every ten seconds, and my brain just couldn't communicate to my body what it had to do. I kept trying to push down on a non-existent brake pedal with legs that didn't respond.

The real-life learner vehicle I graduated to was fitted with a simple set of hand controls. Fastened to the steering wheel was a lever. You pulled this towards you to accelerate, you released it to slow down, and braked by pushing it away from you. Sounds easy enough, right? But then you had to work out how to push forward to brake, steer and put a blinker on all at the same time. That seemed to require three hands.

The driving proved hugely tiring. It required the use of a set of muscles that weren't accustomed to such constant strain. The first time I managed to cover any amount of distance, my fingers and wrists ended up sore and fatigued. But eventually I mastered it. By September, after a month or so of rehab, I was judged ready to be sent back into the wide world.

The day I was injured was the last I had spent in uniform. After that, it had all been hospital gowns or jogging pants and T-shirts. I was discharged from the hospital dressed like that, and I rolled in my wheelchair towards a truck that I'd had fitted out for a disabled driver. In theory I was still on active duty. I had not been discharged from the military, and I still nurtured a dream that somehow, someday I would be able to serve again.

The air force had put me on a five-year 'temporary retirement' package. That meant that after five years I could go back to my unit, to work some variant of my former role. Even if I was still wheelchair-bound, I believed that I could still be useful and serve. With all of my specialist combat weather knowledge and training I believed there had to be a role that I could fulfill.

Because I was only on temporary retirement – as opposed to being permanently medically discharged – I didn't get a VA-supplied vehicle, which all qualifying wounded veterans are entitled to. Instead, I'd paid to get my truck adapted. It had cost $1,200 to fit the hand controls to the vehicle. I'd had a fold-down electric seat installed to lift me from my chair into the pickup, at a cost of another $5,000, plus there was a $4,000 crane-and-winch system that lifted my chair into the back. Over $10,000 in all – and that was just to fit out one vehicle.

We'd also had to find a wheelchair-friendly home to live in, and there were countless other costs associated with my disability. It was growing ever clearer to me that we faced a tsunami of financial needs. But, right now, on the day of my discharge, I was simply looking forward to getting back with my family once more.

I managed to drive the truck all the way to our temporary new home, an apartment that Carla had rented in San Antonio. When I got there, the boys rushed out to greet me. They wanted Daddy down from the truck and throwing a ball around with them, right away. But life wasn't going to be like that any more. Even getting out of a vehicle was a whole new drama in itself.

First, I had to press a button in a console set into the truck's driver door. There was a mechanical whine from behind me and the rear cover – the camper top as we call it – levered open, rising on hydraulics. I pressed a second button and a mini-crane lifted my wheelchair from the rear of the truck, swung it out and round, depositing it on the ground beside the driver's door. I opened the door, unhooked the crane and pressed a third button. The crane retracted into the truck's rear and the cover swung shut once more. I reached down and unfolded the chair. With Carla's help I manoeuvred it in close, got the seat cushion positioned just about right, then levered myself out of the pickup and into the chair.

This was the first time my kids had had me at home for months. I had a photo taken with all three boys perched on my lap. From the waist up there was nothing much to show how my life had changed. I looked young, square-jawed and warrior-like, and I forced a smile. But in the bottom of the photo I was folded into a wheelchair.

My boys were too young to understand much, or to remember much about Dad-before-the-chair. They were preschool age, so it wasn't as if I was suddenly going to turn up at a school football game riding in my chair. In a way they were lucky. The shock of it all was reserved mostly for the adults.

Back home there were the good moments that I'd been longing for, when I got to be a dad again and to play with my boys. Then I knew how lucky I was to be alive. But there were also so many black moments – long chunks of time blanked out by stabbing peaks of pain. I endured hours and hours of sheer agony. My moods proved hugely unpredictable: they could swing from happy to angry to pain-racked to happy again in just a few short hours. I was mixed up and all over the place. Who wouldn't have been?

In rehab the medics had told me that I would have to catheterize myself every time I wanted to use the bathroom. At first I'd refused to accept it. *I cannot do that,* I'd objected. *I cannot live like that for the rest of my life.* But the horrible challenge that presented were actually pretty minimal compared to the relentless, nerve-jangling torture of the pain.

I'd gone from jumping out of airplanes to being stuck in a wheelchair, and the pain was simply horrendous. I was in almost constant pain, the background buzz spiking to unbearable levels many times during one day. Then it would be so bad that I'd be crying out. Yelling. Screaming. I couldn't help screaming. It's like badly stubbing your toe – you just yell out without warning. It was the same, only infinitely worse. The house would echo with my piercing cries.

What kind of father was that for the boys to have come home?

What kind of husband was that for Carla to have around her?

And then there were the in-between moments, those during which I looked at all that had happened – the 'accident' and how miraculous it was that I had survived – and I wondered for what purpose I'd been kept alive. I figured there had to be a purpose, I just didn't have the faintest clue what it might be.

Just prior to leaving the hospital, I'd made a comment to my mom and dad. 'Don't worry about me,' I'd said. 'I'm going to end up helping others.' I had no idea why I had said that or where it had come from. There was no apparent reason. But somehow, deep down inside, I felt that I'd get there. Even at this point there burned a conviction that I'd reach a place in life where I could start giving back. One day.

I got heavily into wheelchair sports. They became my therapy. They gave me a reason and a focus. I got myself a handcycle – a wheelchair bicycle that you pedal using your hands – and I started trying to get myself in shape again. But as much as I tried to lift myself, I kept butting up against the harsh reality: no matter what, I just couldn't get much of my body to work again.

Just the simplest of things were beyond me. Going out for a romantic date with my wife, or taking her dancing – that was an impossibility. I couldn't do it. Or maybe I hadn't learned to. Just giving my kids a proper hug was a huge challenge, because when I tried to lift them up I felt as if I had daggers stabbing into my backbone.

I was recommended to visit a physiotherapist who worked at a civilian facility called Health South. She was young and full of energy, but more importantly, she was the first person from the medical profession who chose to believe in me. I nicknamed her PT – short for physical therapy. She told me there were long leg braces that might enable me to walk again, plus these special Italian boots that could also prove helpful. I was gripped by PT's enthusiasm and her belief. With her there was no *You will never walk again* bullshit. At the very least she was willing to try.

PT wanted me to come to three sessions every week.

I said, 'Three? Let's do five.'

Eventually, she got clearance for me to come to her every

day bar Sunday. Every moment we spent together we worked towards one goal: getting me walking again. I cherished her for the simple fact of her belief in me. She was motivational; I was motivated. It was a fine fit.

One day, maybe six weeks after I had left hospital, she produced a pair of odd-looking high-topped leg braces.

She gestured at them. 'Put 'em on.'

I presumed she just meant try them on for size. With her help I managed to slip my feet into the bottoms and fasten the uppers tight around my legs, to just below my hips. As I could feel nothing below the waist, it wasn't as if I could sense anything different.

'OK, these are the leg braces and this is what we're working towards,' she told me. 'You see those parallel bars. One day some time soon you're gonna strap these boots on and walk the length of those bars. You with me?'

I nodded. 'You betcha!'

It seemed like an impossible dream right then – to walk those bars. But what was wrong with nurturing such a dream? If I believed strongly enough, I figured I would get there. PT helped nourish that conviction, and her belief gave me hope.

By contrast the psychiatrist I was assigned – I had to see one regularly as part of the process of getting my pain medication – seemed angry and frustrated. She kept telling me I needed to get some 'closure'. She told me to 'move on' by accepting my wheelchair-bound status. I told her to go take a hike.

'You're in denial,' she kept saying.

'I am not,' I countered. 'This isn't *denial*. I know I'm paralyzed. I just want to have hope. There's nothing wrong with hope.'

She shook her head. 'You just need to accept that you're in a chair and you're in it for life. You'll never get better until you accept that.'

The conversations went on like that until I was spitting mad.

I really didn't want to see her, but I had to. I almost felt as if she was giving me an ultimatum: accept that you'll never walk again, or there will be no more pain medication. But assessing my pain to see what meds I needed had nothing to do with assessing whether I'd walk again – the two were utterly unconnected.

The contrast between her and PT couldn't have been more marked. One lifted me right up; the other brought me down so low and made me so mad. The conflict between those two opposing perspectives pretty much embodied the conflict that was raging inside of me. One of the challenges with trying to walk again was how to manage my pain. The fewer painkillers I took, the more pain I felt, but the more pain I had, the more I could feel – and the more sensation I seemed to get in my legs. In short, pain equalled movement, or at least the hope of movement.

The psychiatrist wanted to up the painkillers to save me from the pain. But I needed to embrace the pain, for with it might come the ability to do what for me was the dream – to put one foot in front of the other. And, in truth, I really had no option but to get walking again, for I'd made myself a hostage to fortune.

Unbeknown to me, my buddies in the special forces community had pledged their 'jump pay' – the uplift in wages they got for being airborne troops – towards helping me and my family. Colonel Funk, my commander in the 10th Combat

Weather Squadron, had coordinated all of this, setting up the Taking Care of Our Own – Jason Morgan Fund. He'd created a website to give regular updates on my condition. The pay increase for someone jump qualified was around $150 month, and in the four months since my injury the fund had raised some $16,000. Suffice to say a hell of a lot of guys had donated a hell of a lot of jump pay, and most were only making around $25,000 year. It was amazing, especially as a lot of those who had given had never even met me. But the community was so tight knit and the camaraderie so great they were like my brothers, and they'd dug deep.

The fundraising helped pay for all the expenses we now faced as a family. I'd used $10,000 to adapt my vehicle. We had rented the apartment in San Antonio, so I could remain close to the medical facilities treating me. That was costing $1,000 a month. Plus I still had the mortgage to pay on our house in Savanna, Georgia, one thousand-odd miles away.

I hadn't asked for help. Colonel Funk had simply told me what he was doing during a visit to my hospital bedside. I could not believe how generous people had been. I was deeply touched, and especially because the majority of the donors were army guys – helping an air force guy like me!

In a moment of amazement and overwhelming gratitude, I'd promised Colonel Funk the same thing I'd pledged to my surgeon. I had told him, *I will walk again.* More than that, I'd told him that by my fortieth birthday – still a decade or so away – I would run a full marathon.

There was another, deeper reason behind that pledge. Colonel Funk had brought a bunch of my buddies to see me. In Air

Force Special Operations there is a tradition that when you turn thirty you have to run thirty miles. I was twenty-nine years old at the time of my injury. The guys had joked that I'd got myself injured just to get out of running those thirty miles.

I'd shot them a look. 'You know what I'll do? I'll run a full marathon. How does that sound?'

That was the impossible dream of a guy paralyzed from the belly button down.

# CHAPTER 12

Napal loves to fetch a Budweiser. He loves to fetch the TV remote. No reason why he shouldn't love to fetch the Knights' football tee.

The idea comes from one of the boys that Jim coaches. 'Hey, man, you think your cool dog could run out and fetch the tee?'

The football tee is a round cone-shaped piece of plastic, which the kicker uses to balance the ball. Once the kick is taken someone has to run to fetch it off the field. Having Napal get the tee would be far easier.

'Neat idea,' says Jim. 'Let me work on it. Let me see what I can do.'

The first time Jim recognized Napal's drive to fetch was one evening back at home. He and Napal were chilling on the couch. Strictly speaking, Jim shouldn't really have allowed this. CCI dogma says dogs aren't allowed on the furniture. But, hell, you got to break a few rules. Napal wasn't allowed up there all the time. But just occasionally he'd come over, put his head on the couch and give Jim the eyes that said, *Pleeaassse.*

How could Jim resist that? 'OK, up you come. Come up.'

Jim got him snuggled up there and he went to change the TV channel. But he fumbled and dropped the remote. Not a problem for an able-bodied person, but a real pain for a guy in a chair. As he heard the remote hit the floor, Napal perked up: *What was that?*

'You figure you can get that?' Jim asked. 'The remote?'

Napal jumped off the couch and looked at Jim, double-checking what was being asked of him.

'Get,' Jim commanded, using the proper CCI instruction and pointing at the remote.

Napal wandered over, his tail all a-wag, picked the remote up in his jaws and brought it back to Jim – at which point he got oodles of praise and a big treat. From there it had developed into Budweiser from the fridge, and then the early-morning shoe ritual. Jim would get woken by a Napal face snuffle, and he'd issue the command, 'Go get my shoes.' Napal would head into the lounge and fetch Jim's shoes from where he'd kicked them off the evening before by the couch.

Jim figured it wasn't such a stretch from that to fetching a football tee.

Jim talked it through with Mike Fowler, their friendly instructor, and they developed a training programme. Jim started by placing the tee a couple of feet away on the grass. He pointed at it and issued the command, 'Get.' Napal ran and fetched the tee, and Jim fed him a chunk of Dick Van Patten's sausage. Each day Jim moved the tee a little further away. At first Jim got one of the stat girls – those who write down the scores in a match – to take Napal on a leash to collect the tee. It took two weeks for Napal to master fetching the tee from the middle of the field all on his own. It still wasn't a live match with all the fans yelling and screaming, but Jim figured Napal was pretty much ready for his Big Day.

He took a few moments to write an email to Gayle – or, rather, to Terence – with the news. It'd been a good while since father and son had communicated.

Hi Dad,
Jim has been really busy with football. I've learned to get the kicking tee after kick-off, and this Friday night is my big premiere. After I retrieve the tee, the announcer will plug CCI.
Jim thinks I'm going to follow in my dad's pawsteps. I figure I'll be going to Advanced Puppy Classes in May.
Hope my brothers and sisters are doing well.
Best to all,
Napal

Terence replies to the email, and Jim prints it off and reads it out to Napal.

Hey Kid!
I am VERY impressed with all the stuff you are learning. You're giving the old man a run for my doggie biscuits!
I've been holding my own up here with thirteen (!!) puppies, and they were born here at the house. If you run into Kynda or Kelsey (we heard they went to your region), I've got them trained up real good with some fancy moves. Here's a YouTube link showing off one of our practice sessions.
I had to spend a lot of time out on the patio making sure

that no bobcats or coyotes got the little team. Actually, I only saw a skunk – but ya just never know.

Give my two-legged dad a big old nuzzle from his kid. He's the best.

The T-man

That Friday night Napal's tee fetching is scheduled to go live, and it's more than a big deal. The Bishop Knights are playing their old rivals the Christian Patriots, from El Cajon in San Diego. There's a lot riding on the match. Old scores are about to be settled. Knowing this, Jim gets Napal into a good, solid, calm 'Sit' position long before kick-off. He can tell that Napal is 100 per cent focused and itching to do his stuff. The moment the player with the tee walks out onto the field Napal has his number. His eyes track the player, or more specifically the tee in his hand, right to the spot where it's placed on the field.

The guy kicks off, the ball goes dead and the referee blows his whistle, for all of which time Napal has his eyes glued to the tee.

The moment the whistle blast dies Jim issues the command: 'Go fetch the tee.'

Napal bounds away like a streak of black lightning. He dashes half the width of the field in a flash, but that's when the trouble starts. The referee sees a dog hit the field making for the kick-off, and he grabs the tee. Napal skids to a halt at the referee's feet, eyes glued to the tee. The ref stares back at him in consternation.

It's a stand-off.

Napal looks at the spot where the ball was kicked, back at the referee and all around and about, searching for that elusive tee. The referee's not about to give it to him. Jim sees the ref staring at his dog with an expression on his face like *What the hell?* Jim can see that it isn't working. The guy isn't best amused.

He calls Napal back, and the stat girl goes out to fetch the tee. This hasn't gone quite as Jim had planned.

During the break Jim goes to explain things to the referee. He tells him how Napal is a CCI dog in training, and that he's also the informal mascot of the Knights. The ref's a young guy, in his early thirties, and at first he's a little . . . icy and unfriendly. But, as Jim knows well, no able-bodied man can be angry with a guy in a wheelchair for long, especially when that guy is a fellow football coach.

'It's all part of the training,' Jim explains. 'It helps get him used to environments like sports fixtures and stuff. 'Cause you never know . . . He may go to someone who's a big football fan. It's possible.'

At that the referee starts to thaw a little. 'Oh, right. Now I get it. I just kind of saw this dog run out and, hell, I didn't even know we had a dog here. I didn't know what he was about.'

'I'm sorry. I should have told you. I'm sorry about that.'

'Yeah, well, no big deal. Very next kick-off, let's have him fetch the tee!'

Sure enough, when the game restarts Napal dashes out, grabs the tee in his jaws, does a magnificent handbrake turn and dashes back again. It's all over in a matter of seconds, the tee deposited safely in Jim's hand. And the spectators, they're clapping and whooping and cheering the dog like crazy.

The Knights fans chant, 'GO NAPAL! GO NAPAL! GO NAPAL!'

This is more like it. Napal has stolen the show, and Jim is grinning ear to ear.

This tee fetching isn't purely for the fun of it; for the spectacle. A crucial part of CCI puppy raising is to socialize the dogs, to get them used to every kind of environment that their life companion might wish to take them to. A football game could be that kind of place. The dog has got to be cool around fans and players, retain his focus and not get distracted.

Fetching the tee – it's perfect training.

Jim and Napal return home late after the football match. Jim's not feeling particularly hungry, but it is Napal's feeding time. Jim heaps some Eukanuba into his bowl. Napal takes a sniff and throws Jim a look. He knows exactly what his dog is asking for. Just now and again Napal wants a little warm water poured over his dog biscuits, and the whole left to soak for a while.

It's Napal comfort food.

Jim figures he more than deserves it after his performance on the football field. Warm water applied, Jim fixes himself a sandwich and takes it into the lounge. He flicks on the TV and goes to use the rest room. By the time he's back, Napal is lying on the couch right next to the sandwich. He's waiting for his Eukanuba to soak properly. Napal sees Jim roll in, looks his way and sniffs at the sandwich, as if to say *Here it is. Human food. Just where you left it.*

'Good boy,' Jim tells him. 'That's not for you. But, hey, you know that.'

As part of the training you have to test your dog. You have to leave human food in places where the dog could steal a quick bite. If you don't do that, you'll never know if they're up to scratch. A dog like Napal needs to know that if it's not in his bowl, then it's not his food. Everything he eats goes in his bowl.

The amazing thing with this kind of training is that Jim never once scolds Napal. Jim's golden rule is: reinforce and praise the positive. Find the good in the dog, not the bad. Don't overcorrect the bad; seek the good to praise. We don't. Punish. The dog. It isn't right to, and in any case it doesn't work.

After Napal's performance at tee fetching, he is taken right to the heart of Jim's football team. The Knights have a mascot, a guy who dashes around the field dressed like a medieval knight in armour, but now he has to compete with the cool black dog who fetches the tee. The football moms start knitting scarves. The craze begins with the mother of the Chedrick boys, who play running back and defensive back in Jim's team.

The scarf Mrs Chedrick knits is bright yellow, with two black paws across it, below the words NAPAL TEE RETRIEVER. That first scarf is for Napal. He wears it knotted around his neck when on tee retrieving duty. But once Mrs Chedrick has knitted one, all the moms have to. Soon the stands are packed with Knights fans wearing NAPAL TEE RETRIEVER merchandise. Soon, even the fans of opposing teams are calling for Napal by name.

Travel is the other key thing Jim has to get his dog accustomed to. America is a big country, and people tend to fly from A to B. When Jim gets asked to visit some relatives in Canada, he figures both he and Napal should go. They head to San Diego Airport to catch a flight, on the first leg of their journey which is routed via New York.

Normally people with disabilities get to board the flight first. Jim gets ushered to the front of the queue, and he's allocated an entire row of seats adjacent to the bulkhead. By the time he's got himself and Napal comfortable, he realizes he's not had the chance to toilet his dog. They've got a five-hour flight ahead of them and he figures Napal really does need to do this.

He gets the attention of one of the air hostesses. 'Hey, you figure you could toilet my dog for me? Like on the grass beside the runway? He really does like to go on grass.'

'Sure.' The hostess smiles. 'No problem. I know exactly what to do.'

She leads Napal down the aisle, and Jim figures he can afford to relax a little. More and more passengers stream aboard. But by the time the pilot announces that the plane is ready for take-off, there's still no sign of Napal. Jim's feeling a little panicky. This is the nightmare scenario: leaving his dog behind.

He grabs another hostess. 'Hey, can you check where my dog is at? My service dog?'

Finally, he spies Napal being led up the aisle. Phew. The hostess hands him over.

'Sorry about that.' She giggles. 'He's one popular dog. Everybody just wanted to pet him.'

'OK, no problem,' Jim tells her. 'I guess that's what comes with being such a handsome dog.'

Jim chuckles. The hostess laughs. It's all good. He takes Napal's lead, pats the seat and issues the command: 'Up.'

Napal jumps up beside him, and man and dog settle down to enjoy the flight.

The hostess returns to Jim once they're airborne. 'I got something for you. Or rather, for your dog.'

She hands Jim a certificate. It reads across the top, 'Southwest

Airlines welcomes *Napal*. For your first flight on Southwest we proudly salute you on this 26th day of March 2008.' The certificate is ringed by signatures: *Cathy 79358, Jenny 2174, PHX, Buff, David*. Plus little hand-drawn heart motifs and kisses. It even comes complete with a pair of shiny Southwest Airline wings.

Jim is touched. He packs the document safely into his flight bag. He's started putting together a scrapbook of Napal mementoes. He sticks each into the book, and it's as if he's mentally signing that chapter away to whoever will get his dog in the future. The scrapbook isn't for Jim; it's what he'll hand over at Napal's graduation, as a special gift for whoever gets his dog.

After several flights their end destination is Rock Lake in Ontario, Canada. Together with a bunch of friends and colleagues, Jim's uncle purchased 8,000 acres of wilderness surrounding a beautiful lake. Jim and Napal spend ten days camping out at Rock Lake, in the midst of pristine forest and clear, crisp water, plus the occasional wooden pier upon which Jim can roll his chair.

Napal takes to the wilderness like the proverbial fish to water. He gets zipped around the lake in motorized fishing canoes. He retrieves endless floating toys thrown into the lake by the kids. He goes paddling with them in the creeks. A crowd of children escorts him through the woods, to make sure he doesn't eat any poisoned ivy. In short, he goes completely woofing-wild.

Jim breaks out his shorts and his tie-dye T-shirt, and he makes sure to get out on a few boating jaunts himself. The first fish he catches is a smallmouth bass a good eighteen inches long. He holds it up to Napal, his fingers hooked into the gills. Napal reaches out his moist nose and sniffs, vacuuming in the sharp, slimy, lake-water scent of the thing.

He glances at Jim. *Smells like a fish.*

Jim laughs. 'You got it. We'll cook and eat it later.'

This is Napal's first-ever encounter with a big stretch of water. Jim lives close to the beach in Santee, but he's never taken him to the seaside. It could be tough for him to control his dog in a beach environment. He can't afford to take Napal places where him being chair-bound might mean his dog becomes a nuisance to others. But here at Rock Lake, surrounded by his relatives and in the midst of the wilderness, Napal gets to run free. Yet even when he's truly, deeply free, he still seems to have one ear and one eye out for Jim. Their neighbours on the lake are forever stopping by. Whenever they do, the first thing they notice is Napal.

'Oh, what a gorgeous dog. What a well behaved dog. Can we pet him?'

Jim smiles. 'Wait a second. Just one.' He glances at Napal. 'Napal, down.'

Napal lies down beside Jim's chair.

'OK, Napal, Release.'

At that, Napal leaves Jim's side and wanders over coolly to his admirers, offering himself to be petted. He doesn't jump up or cavort or show off. He presents himself royally: *Here I am, ready for some petting.* No wonder the population of Rock Lake is smitten by the dog.

When Jim and Napal fly home to Santee, Jim finds a letter waiting from CCI. He knows what it is even before he's opened it. It's his six-months-warning letter. It's the one CCI send out to the puppy raisers to say, *Don't forget, guys, you got to hand your charge back to us in six months' time. We're six months and counting.*

The letter gives Jim an idea. He senses that he needs something extraordinary to ease the coming parting. Maybe he can ask CCI if he can get another puppy *before he has to give up Napal.* Maybe he can organize some crossover time, so that by the time he's deprived of Napal he's got another CCI puppy to raise? After Napal, it will be tough not having a dog. Emotionally draining. But if he has a CCI puppy to focus on, perhaps that will help to help ease the pain and fill the vacuum? Jim writes an email to CCI, floating the idea.

He'd always intended to raise more dogs, but right now this request is all about . . . survival.

# CHAPTER 13

Hope springs eternal in the Morgan family household.

A few short months after my release from hospital, hope manifested itself in a very special journey. It was my father's sixtieth birthday, and my brother John and Scott, my brother-in-law, were taking him fishing for stripers – a type of bass – on Lake Texoma, where my folks had kept a boat for the last few years. Lake Texoma is a stretch of water that straddles the Texas–Oklahoma border. It was spring and the water was still cold, so the stripers would be down deep, and they'd need to be lured out with some live bait.

But, deeper below the surface, the fishing trip was a cunning ruse. While my dad and the bros were out catching stripers, the ladies of the family were organizing a surprise party on the dockside. Scott had decided it was going to be done real proper. He'd hired a portable margarita-making machine, and driven it to the lake on the flatbed of his truck. Even that was hidden, for every preparation had to be kept absolutely secret from my dad. In all of this I had a very special part to play. I was going to drive my car from San Antonio all the way to Lake Texoma, which is several hundred miles, so as to make a surprise appearance at my father's surprise party. It would be my first social outing since the accident, and my first expedition of any significant distance by vehicle.

At the end of the day's fishing the men headed into shore. The dock was festooned with balloons and birthday banners, and most of our friends and relations were there, plus a good many of the lake's boat owners. The dock was jam-packed. These were people of all different faiths and some with no faith at all, but at one time or another most all of them had prayed for my recovery, especially during my time in the coma. Yet most had never actually met me.

I was six months out of hospital but I was determined to make it all the way – for the symbolism of having driven myself to my father's sixtieth. This was important to me, and Carla understood. As for the boys, they were just excited to be off on a new adventure. I had to stop whenever the pain spiked real bad, so it was mostly one hour on the road and one hour off it. For a normal person the drive to Lake Texoma would take around about six hours. It took me double that, yet eventually we got there. You can drive right up to the dock, but we stopped a little short. Carla had phoned ahead, so John and Scott knew exactly when and where we were going to arrive.

My big brother organized a screen of people to surround me in my chair, as I rolled towards the walkway that led onto my parents' floating dock. Dad had opened all his presents by now, and as I made my way across the wooden planking John went ahead of me and silenced the crowd: 'I've got a special announcement to make. So, Dad, we've got one final present for you. A surprise.'

With that the guys ahead of me drew aside and I rolled into the open. It was the first time my father had seen me out of the hospital and moving independently in my chair. I was very close to home here. We'd spent much of our time as kids by the lake, and I hoped I was looking something more like the boy my father had raised.

He came over and knelt down in front of me. He reached out and enclosed me in a massive bear hug. You could have heard a pin drop as he held me close and his shoulders heaved. He is a big, tough, gruff Texan, and an absolute diamond of a father, but not the kind of guy who wears his heart on his sleeve. I guess none of us Morgan men are. But tonight there was to be no shaking of hands. Instead he hugged me for a good five minutes, and I could feel his chest heaving as he held me tight.

Finally he managed to speak. 'You know, son, this is the best present a dad could ever wish for. The best. I'm so proud of you. So cotton-pickin' proud.'

I found a way to speak though the tears. 'You know, Dad, you can get up now. You can get up off your knees. You can let go, Dad.'

He shook his head. 'I don't want anyone to see me crying.'

I glanced over his shoulder. 'Dad, you're not alone. There's not a dry eye on the dock.'

Like every son, I had always wanted to make my father proud. That was what I'd hungered for. I'd never known that he was proud of me before now. He'd never said it and he'd never shown it. In fact, I'd always thought he'd been saddened by my move into special operations, and worried about the risks that

I was taking. Well, tonight I knew what he really felt of me and my service.

Later that night I had to go to my truck so I could empty my catheter with some degree of privacy. All I had to drain it into was a soda bottle. 'Needs must,' I told Scott and John, who stuck with me for the company. Once I was done, I figured I'd empty it into the bushes beside the parking lot. I was halfway done when some guy wandered by, and it almost went over his shoes.

'Oops, sorry,' I apologized. 'It's just some flat lemonade.'

We returned to the party and inevitably the story did the rounds. It raised a few laughs, and it sure put a smile back on my father's face. That became a Morgan family catchphrase: whenever someone put a foot out of line we'd exclaim, 'Oops. It's just some lemonade.'

A few days later I was out with Mom and Julie in Richardson, a suburb of Dallas. They were taking me to dinner at Pappasito's, a Mexican restaurant. I'd been pushing it hard on my handcycle and working hard in the physio sessions with PT – I was even training to roll a wheelchair obstacle course.

I guess I was starting to feel super-confident – a bit like the wheelchair basketball guy who had wheelied out of my hospital room that day. Plus I was trying to make it so I could laugh in the face of my injuries. Like all good restaurants, Pappasito's has a disabled access ramp, but I decided to go a different way.

'Hey, Mom! Julie! I'm not going to use the ramp. Check this out.'

I headed towards the stairs leading down to the restaurant.

*Proud father.* At home with my two eldest, Blake and Austin, after an exercise with Air Force Special Operations, serving as a Combat Weatherman.

In South America with my Special Operations Aviation Regiment (SOAR) buddies, about to board a C130 Hercules aircraft on an anti-narcotics mission.

In a SOAR Black Hawk, poised to take off from the South American jungle searching for narco-rebels (I'm on the left of the three in the doorway).

The twisted wreck of the Chevvy Blazer after it hurtled down the jungle-clad mountainside. I was thrown free and crushed into a tropical swamp.

*Irresistible.* Napal II at eight weeks, at Jim Siegfried's – his puppy raiser – home.

Jim Siegfried at Napal's Change of Hound ceremony. Dogs from left to right constitute the family: Gigi, Napal, Tatiana (on Jim's lap) and Terence.

Napal at work beside me in my wheelchair. Amongst the countless ways that he helped, Napal used his nose to push an elevator call button or to open a door.

*True love.* I've just rolled the Warrior Games 1500 metre race. I am exhausted, pain-wracked and tearful. As always, Napal knew I was suffering, and his very love and companionship could take away my pain.

*Special Agent Napal.* We got the run of the White House, courtesy of the Secret Service who made Napal one of their own – see the Secret Service lanyard around his neck. We'd travelled to Washington to speak to audiences and Government, campaigning for more service dogs to go to wounded warriors and others in need.

LEFT: *Woah . . . Big pussycat!* Special Agent Napal gets eye-to-eye with a lion at the local zoo – a confrontation that both Blake and I found hilarious.

BELOW: *Freedom.* Scubadiving with my boys – from left to right; Blake, Austin and Grant – courtesy of the Cody Unser First Step Foundation. It was the closest I'd ever felt to being able to 'walk' again; to being 'able-bodied normal'. Sadly, much that he wanted to, Napal couldn't join us!

RIGHT: *Mexico Time*. Napal was easy-going and laid back, and loved his 'chilling-time'. He was just what I needed to de-stress me and mellow me out!

My mom Patti, working with co-author Damien Lewis, around the time that Napal passed away. It was only then that I realized she'd kept everything – every photo, newsclipping or report – about my accident and paralysis.

*The last goodbye.* Saying a final tearful farewell to Napal. There are no words to express what it was like to lose him.

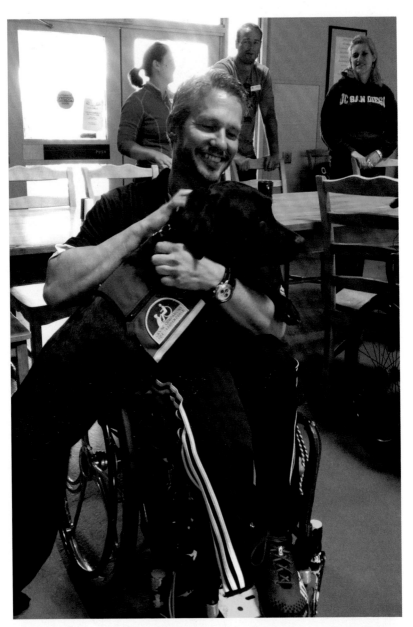

*The whirlwind.* In contrast to Napal, Rue – my replacement service dog who was named after the girl in the *Hunger Games* – was like a canine hurricane! No one could ever replace Napal, but Rue and I had to continue the mission that I'd begun with him, as ambassadors for Canine Companions for Independence.

When Julie saw where I was going she tried to stop me. 'Jason! No! Don't!'

I was laughing by now. 'No, no. I've been working on this. Check this out.'

To wheelie a chair you have to push the drive handles forward while tilting your body backwards, so you balance on the rear wheels. I adopted the position and wheelied myself down the first step.

*Crunch.*

I steadied myself, then dropped down the second.

*Bump.*

Then I overdid it. I tried to wheelie down two in a row and moments later I was out of control. By the time I was at the bottom I had seriously wiped out. My chair had gone over and I had fallen onto my side, blocking the way. At least I'd fallen sideways, which meant I'd been able to use my arms to cushion the fall. If you tumble over backwards you can crack your head real bad.

I glanced back at Julie and Mom. 'Yeah, like I said, I've been working on it.'

Realizing I was OK, the two of them had to sit down on the steps they were laughing so much. To the Morgan family's sense of humour, this was priceless. One moment I was acting so cocky and cool, the next I was lying on my back, utterly helpless like an upended tortoise.

'I guess it needs some more work, huh?' I ventured.

Mom and Julie were crying with laughter.

A guy arrived at the top of the steps and eyed the scene. Below him was a man who had clearly fallen out of his wheelchair and was blocking the stairway. Beside him were two women perched on the top step and crying with laughter. The two parties clearly knew each other, and the scene did not compute.

'Erm . . . hey, d'you need some help there?' he asked.

I shook my head. 'No, I'm good. This is just how I take a rest. It's tiring going down these steps, you know. I'm just resting between steps.'

The guy did a double-take. Guy who has fallen out of wheel-chair. Two women laughing their socks off. All apparently refusing any help. He shook his head and hurried past, stepping over me to get by.

'Hey, I was only joking,' I called after him. 'Hey, I could do with a hand.' I jerked a thumb at my mom and my sis. 'Those two sure aren't any help. They're the worst mom and sister a guy could ever wish for . . .' But he was gone.

The only way to get back into my chair would be to crawl across to the nearby grass, get someone to bring my chair over and get lifted back in. But Julie and Mom were so completely useless right now, disabled by their laughter. Eventually two guys walked by and I persuaded them to help.

A few weeks after Dad's surprise party I was back at our rented apartment in San Antonio when a letter popped into the mail-box, the Department of Defense (DoD) stamp marking it out as official mail. I presumed it was just another of the many they'd sent me concerning the treatment of my injuries.

Wrong.

I ripped it open and had to read it several times over before I could even begin to believe it was for real. It was a typed letter from a DoD clerk declaring that I had been permanently medically discharged from the United States military. Unilaterally, and without the barest word of warning, the DoD had decided that I would never be fit enough to serve. My second family – the military, the one that I loved almost as much as I loved my kids – was done with me.

I could not believe it. I was utterly stunned. Life as I had known it was over. Mine was not just a job. It was so much more. It was a lifestyle. A mission. A reason for being. In an instant all of that was gone. I'd trained relentlessly. I'd scaled the heights and done so well. But now, with the click of a keystroke, the dream had died.

I was so angry I didn't want to talk to a soul. I didn't think there was anyone who would understand. I had wanted to walk again so much, in part so I could get back into the military. In an instant all that motivation was suddenly ripped away from me.

The days following The Letter were dark, but then I became aware of a small chink of light. I presumed that I'd been discharged on standard retirement pay, in which case I didn't have a clue how I could take care of the financial needs of my family. I couldn't rely on Colonel Funk's fund for ever, and I certainly couldn't see who would ever give me a job – not broken, pain-racked and wheelchair-bound as I was. I just kept thinking, *How will I ever take care of my family?* It was then that I took a call from Colonel Funk. He explained with enormous patience the reality of my situation. I'd been retired on full medical disability pay. On disability pay I'd get enough to cover the extra costs that paralysis dumps on you. The not-for-profit Paralyzed Veterans of America (PVA) would be getting in touch and would take care of all the paperwork.

Sure enough, the PVA were fantastic. They sorted everything out and kept Carla and me briefed every step of the way. I felt as if such a burden had been lifted off me. I had been discharged from the service that I loved and for which I had so very nearly given my life, but at least the military were looking after me financially.

That lifted me. And in the Morgan household hope really does spring eternal. Right now, hope would manifest itself in the form of Dr Carl Kao, a groundbreaking neurosurgeon and freethinker who would prove willing to contemplate the unthinkable.

It was my mother who stumbled upon Dr Kao. She read a story in the paper about a sixteen-year-old girl with a spinal injury who'd enjoyed a miraculous recovery after being treated by Dr Kao. Using her considerable medical skills Mom researched all there was to find on him. The more she looked, the more she was convinced. He was a leader in spinal-cord injury research, and a true pioneer.

She called him up and made an appointment to visit him at a clinic in Forth Worth. She and my dad – hell, the entire Morgan clan – were more than willing to defy what the Wilford Hall surgeon had told us: *that I would never walk again*. We had to believe there was a better prognosis. *We chose to believe.* We met with Dr Kao. He explained the procedure that he specialized in. He put patients through an operation to open up the spinal cord, to better enable the flow of spinal fluid – without which there could be no recovery. My spine was so swollen and so beaten about, the flow was badly blocked. But all previous surgery had been performed on the basis that I was never going to walk again. By realigning my spine he could reinvigorate that flow.

Dr Kao offered these surgeries because in his view even a partial recovery was better than no recovery at all. Something was still better than nothing. A chance of being able to walk was better than no chance at all. What he told us was music to our ears. But there were downsides. The surgery would take as much as twelve hours, and because it was unorthodox the VA would not cover the cost. It was $30,000, which was a heart-in-the-mouth kind of amount for us right now. But all of this paled into insignificance compared to the final thing that Dr Kao revealed to us: the location of the clinic where he performed his operations.

Due to his unorthodoxy, he couldn't get insurance to cover his liabilities in the USA. So he carried out his operations overseas. He did them at a clinic in a South American city with good medical facilities and decent nursing staff.

The city was Quito in Ecuador, pretty much the very place where I had received my injuries.

Julie's husband Scott employed contractors at their flooring company. Around this time one of them received an email from an American missionary purely by chance. His name was Steve Sutherland and he was based near the Ecuador–Colombia border. Several months back he'd pulled some America service-men out of a vehicle wreck in the jungle. The email described how the most seriously injured was a guy named Jason Morgan, and he was trying to track him down to see if he'd survived. It was like searching for a needle in a haystack, so he'd cast his net wide.

Julie was shown the email. She called Mom and said, 'This has to be the guy who hauled Jason out of the swamp!'

It was unreal that all of this could have come together at the same moment. My parents made contact to check whether Steve was genuine. After that so did I. I told him that I was thinking of returning to Ecuador for some surgery and Steve encouraged me to come. He was determined to visit me and, needless to say, there was a lot we had to talk about.

If anything would bring back the memories of what had happened, I figured meeting Steve would. A part of me looked forward to the possibility of recovering some of what I had lost. I wanted to remember. I was dying to know the truth, especially when it concerned such a life-changing moment.

I wanted to hear from him the story of the car wreck. It held little fear for me. As far as I was concerned it was just an accident: an SUV driven too fast along a treacherous mountain road. I also wanted to thank Steve. This was the guy who had saved my life, pure and simple. At the very least he deserved my gratitude and my thanks. But my biggest motivation was the prospect of Dr Kao's surgery and what it might do for my mobility.

And so I had to ask myself the hardest question of all: *Do I want to walk again enough to return to the country that almost killed me?*

# CHAPTER 14

Jim's six-months-to-go warning letter also includes some timely prompts regarding Napal's training. It gives a long list of things Jim needs to get sorted so he's ready for Napal's matriculation – the formal term for handing him back to CCI – including the tasks the dog will be expected to have mastered by then. At the next puppy class Jim and his fellow raisers discuss this with Mike Fowler. The dogs have been taught to walk obediently on-leash, to sit and to stay and to shake hands, but those were the early lessons. They're now into the final stages of Advanced Puppy Class.

Napal has to 'Sit-Stay' for two minutes in a room, maintaining his position even though Jim has left. Jim puts Napal into the 'Down-Stay' position – lying on his belly and stationary – rolls around him in his chair a few times and then leaves the room. He returns in two minutes, and Napal is in exactly the same position as he left him. The dog's somehow able to understand exactly what Jim wants, and to do exactly what is asked of him. Jim still hears himself called the Dog Whisperer by those who are having a tougher time with their dogs.

But it's now, just when they're up so high, that Jim and Napal are about to take a big fall.

A year in a dog's life is supposed to equate to around seven human years, in which case Napal is well into his teens. There's been little of the drama or the angst that a human child tends to experience in adolescence, no teenage crushes or rebellions. But when he is on 'Release' time the one thing he loves to do is to run. And Napal has grown into a big, powerful dog. The largest of his litter, he's got a beautiful broad head, wide athletic shoulders and a thick solid tail like a fifth limb. When Jim takes him to the puppy socials, woe betide any who choose to get in his way.

Or at least that's normally the way things are . . . until Napal chooses to pick a fight with Cindy Carlton's garden wall, at the bottom of the hill behind her house. It's a brick retaining wall, so it's thick and solid and built to last. Napal is running wild with the other dogs and he goes to jump it. Somehow he misjudges and hammers into it at full speed. The impact is so serious Napal actually dislodges a brick. He takes a whole brick out.

But in doing so he takes himself out as well.

Jim sees the whole thing happen from his place on the patio. He hears the hollow thud of the collision. And as soon as he hears Napal's long, drawn-out cry, he knows how badly he's hurt.

'HOOWWwwwwEEEEEEEeeeRRRRRRrrrrree.'

Napal has never made a sound like that before. Jim can see him lying on the ground. Mike Bennet, one of the other puppy raisers, rushes down and gets beside Napal. He manages to stop him from moving or trying to get up, as that will exacerbate any injury.

Jim is badly shaken. From the look of things he figures his dog is done for. He must have broken his shoulder, and that means Napal will never graduate as a CCI dog. If a dog is badly hurt, the injury tends to return to haunt them. And an animal dogged by injury just won't be able to take the kind of strain a service dog needs to be able to handle, day after day after day.

Having checked him over, Mike Bennet lifts Napal up and carries him to Jim's vehicle. He's laid across the back seat of the Chrysler. Jim prepares to fire up the van and motor over to the nearest veterinary surgery. He knows of one that is only fifteen minutes up the road, but right now with Napal being in such bad shape, that feels like a whole world away.

Napal lies on the back seat covered in a towel, and he is quiet as a mouse. He doesn't make any effort to move. He knows he's hurt, and he's relying on Jim – his big buddy – to get it sorted. Jim sets off at a breakneck speed. As he drives he feels waves of nausea wash over him: he is sick with fear for his dog. If the shoulder is broken it'll need to be put into a cast, and Napal will wash out of the CCI programme – in which case, Jim pledges to himself that he will adopt Napal as his own. But every effort of the last year has been focused on making Napal the dog of dogs, a top CCI graduate capable of changing a life. An image flashes through Jim's mind – of the boy with cerebral palsy and autism and how the dog lit up his very existence. There is a person out there waiting to get Napal. Jim knows it. But after today he might never make it.

Jim reaches the vet's in record time. It's a Saturday, but luckily this is an emergency clinic open all hours. Jim has to roll into reception and ask someone to come out to the van to help with his dog. Napal is rushed into the examination room while Jim remains hunched in his chair, worried sick and making calls.

He phones Napal's regular vet at home. 'You won't believe it, but Napal's been hurt real bad. Yeah, he ran into a wall . . .'

The vet does his best to reassure him: 'Jim, you're where you need to be right now. Just let us know the prognosis.'

Jim manages to raise one of the head trainers at CCI. The guy confirms his worst fears. CCI can't graduate a service dog that they know has a health issue, not even if he does appear to be fully recovered. They need a dog that can give eight to ten years' good service. In short, an injury like the one Napal seems to have suffered means that he's out of the programme.

It's two long hours before the vet finally comes to speak to Jim. That amount of time can't spell good news.

'So, there's an upside and a downside,' he begins. 'The upside is the shoulder's not broken. The downside is he'd dislocated it. Fortunately, it seems to have popped back in of its own accord. So it's badly bruised, but there's nothing that's broken.'

Jim breathes a partial sigh of relief. 'Not even a minor fracture?'

'Not even a minor fracture.'

'So what does that mean? I mean, he's supposed to graduate as a service dog in a few months' time.'

'Just keep him calm, quiet and rested. Try to keep him off the limb. Soon as you can, go see your regular vet and get a longer-term prognosis. Meantime, if he loses his appetite or loses his desire to drink, bring him back in immediately, OK?'

'Sure. If there's anything I'll be in.'

The vet hands Jim a packet of drugs. 'Steroids. For the dog, not for you. They'll help with the pain and they'll speed up the recovery of the muscles around the dislocation. Instructions for their use are on the packet. Just try and keep him as calm as possible, and keep him rested and warm.'

'How long do I rest him for? Like keeping him immobile?'

The vet spreads his hands. 'After the first twenty-four hours let him do what he wants to do. A dog is not going to push himself to the point where he's going to do any harm. But don't let him run around or jump up and down too soon. Go see your regular vet and get him to do some oversight. OK?'

Jim heads home. Napal is lying on the Chrysler seat looking very sorry for himself and not a little uncomfortable. Fortunately, Jim's regular vet lives less than a mile away from his place, so getting him to oversee Napal's recovery shouldn't be too much of a challenge. They reach home, and Jim manages to coax Napal down from the van to hobble the short distance inside.

Once there, man and dog climb onto the couch. Time for both to kick back and take it easy. Jim feeds Napal a few chunks of Dick Van Patten's sausage as a bumper treat. Napal eats them, but in a half-hearted I'm-feeling-sorry-for-myself kind of way.

'It's not your fault,' Jim tells him, putting an arm around his dog and ruffling his floppy, velvet-soft ears. 'It's not your fault at all. Don't beat yourself up about it.'

Napal tries wagging his tail, but it's a very muted few thumps that it delivers to the couch. *Then whose fault is it?* his look seems to say.

Jim shrugs. 'I guess the wall moved. The wall moved is all. Gotta be.'

There's nothing much on TV, and Jim figures he'll finish off telling Napal his life story. Not only is his dog a fine listener, but whenever Jim talks it seems to lull his dog into a deep sense of contentment. He's more than happy to lie still and do nothing but open his ears, which is exactly what the doctor ordered right now.

'So, it was twelve years after the accident that a friend called. He said they were looking for a speaker for the Disability Awareness Foundation. "Hey, you figure you might want to share your thoughts and experiences?" I told him I might. A guy from the foundation called me. He explained they had a speaking programme in schools across southern California, and they were looking for a new speaker.

'The schools programme was called Tools For Success. The aim was to teach kids *without* disabilities that with a positive attitude and perseverance you could overcome just about any obstacle in your life. You don't focus on the disability; you focus on the positive. If a paralyzed guy sitting in a chair delivers that kind of message, it's pretty powerful, obviously.

'I started doing those talks. You gotta give something back. At the end of one a teenage kid stood up, looked at me very directly and asked, 'Do you think you'll ever be able to walk again?' I hesitated for a second. I didn't want to break his spirit. Then I said, 'Well, if by me coming here and talking to you that puts something in your mind that you can maybe cure my paralysis, maybe you'll be the doctor that's going to fix it. Maybe not for me, but for others in future.'

Jim glances at Napal. 'And you know what? His face lit up with the biggest ever smile. That was just so great. I've given over a hundred talks and, just like I'm doing with you, all I do is tell them my story: how my paralysis happened, how I bounced back, how I overcame – that kind of thing.

'I was at one talk called Spend a Day in Our Shoes at an Orange County school. There was a guy there called Al Ryes, speaking for CCI. After we'd done our stuff he came over and introduced his dog – a big beautiful yellow Lab called Manny. I asked him how I could get into doing stuff for CCI. I was struck by the idea of working with dogs and helping kids, kind of combining two of my passions in life.

'I thought, *I love kids; I love dogs. If I could do stuff for CCI I could kill two birds with one stone. Plus I could speak to schools about the dogs, and all kids love dog stories. How neat would that be?* So I phoned CCI. I spoke about being a puppy raiser. Right at the end I said, "So, by the way, is it going to be a problem that I'm in a wheelchair?" And the guy kind of laughed. "Well, I don't know. I mean, it's sure gonna be interesting 'cause I don't think we've ever had anyone in a wheelchair *raise* a dog before."

'I didn't get my first dog until 2000, twenty-three years after my accident. And that was Gigi. Then came Terence and then came you. And the rest, as they say, is history. And, you know, it was always for the kids. Which is why you gotta lie still, take it easy and recover.'

Jim scratches Napal under the chin, where he loves it. 'That is why you just gotta get well again. 'Cause somewhere out there we got a little life that we're gonna change.'

# CHAPTER 15

I decided I did want to walk again badly enough to risk that trip to Ecuador. But first we needed to raise the $30,000. My folks dived right in, setting up the Help Jason Morgan Walk Again Fund. Within two weeks they'd held a silent auction, and from donated gifts and services – including a football signed by Roger Staubach, the veteran Dallas Cowboys quarterback, plus some fine pieces of art and jewellery – they managed to raise the money.

The next question was: who would go with me? My dad wanted to, but with Jim Lake Senior recovering from his heart surgery he couldn't spare the time from the office. My wife wanted to go, but who could she leave three young kids with? She decided that Blake, Austin and Grant had been through enough, and she couldn't risk being away from them for so long.

By contrast, my mom wasn't constrained in these ways. She'd raised her kids already and she'd given up her business. As a bonus she spoke passable Spanish. But the idea of returning to the place that had all but killed her youngest son had Mom all knotted up with tension and nerves, especially as the only way to pay for the surgery was in cash. Mom did her research. It was illegal to carry more than $10,000 across an international border. She bought herself a money belt, put the $30,000 in that and stood before a full-length mirror, checking for bulges. She figured she'd pass muster.

It was six months after my accident when we prepared to set off for Ecuador, flying from Dallas Fort Worth to Quito. Carla drove me to the airport. We were halfway there when I happened to glance in the back of the truck. There was no sign of my wheelchair.

'Uh, Carla, where's my chair?' I asked.

I was panicking. I was thinking, *Without a chair how do I get on the aircraft? How will I go anywhere?*

Carla was certain that she'd loaded it. Somehow, it must have tumbled off. We did a U-turn and retraced out steps. We came across my chair lying on a railway crossing. When we drove over the rails, the truck must have kangarooed a bit, the tailgate fallen open and the chair tumbled off the rear. Amazingly it had landed on its wheels and was undamaged. Carla loaded it back in; we made sure it was fastened properly and continued on our way. We met up with my mom and dad at the airport, and steeled ourselves for the goodbyes. I felt daunted. I was used to flying into such places as an elite forces soldier, with my brother warriors at my side. Now I could not even protect myself, let alone my mom.

As for her, she looked absolutely petrified. She held on to my dad until the very last moment, when final boarding was called for our Continental Airlines flight. She knew that the moment she let go of my father she would be on her own with her wheelchair-bound son, returning to the country that had all but killed him. She didn't know if she could do it.

Finally we had no choice but to head for the security gate, or miss our flight.

Mom forced herself to turn away from my dad, knowing that the $30,000 cash was strapped around her belly. Her heart was in her mouth. Surely it would get picked up by the scanners before boarding or, worse still, when we hit customs in Quito? *What would they do to an American grandmother smuggling $30,000 into their country?* she wondered. *What would they accuse her of?* Anything was possible. She could even be accused of coming to Ecuador to buy drugs.

By the time we reached the aircraft Mom was sobbing, she was so scared and so burdened down with her responsibilities. For most of her life she'd grown used to going places with her big tough husband or her big tough sons by her side. This was a total reversal. She had me and my wheelchair to manage. She had the $30,000. She had my fold-up mattress pad, which I used to lie on in an effort to avoid getting pressure sores. She had luggage for the both of us for a three-week stay in Ecuador. And all she had by way of comfort was an email from one of Dr Kao's staff saying that she would be waiting for us at Quito Airport.

One stranger among an alien city of over two and half million souls.

The city where six months back I had almost died.

But, as my mom and dad had repeatedly said, their hopes were greater than the sum of their fears, and that's what drove them on. My mom had researched Dr Kao and his career exhaustively. He worked with the renowned University of Miami Spine Institute as one of their key experts. He'd achieved such amazing results in getting the level of paralysis to drop that demand for his services was snowballing.

We were an hour into the flight when we heard the fateful announcement: 'This is your pilot speaking. I just want you to know that there is thick ground fog in Quito and we cannot land. We will have to divert to the next available airport, which is Guayaquil, on the Ecuadorian Pacific coast.'

*This could not be happening.*

My mom turned to me, her face ashen, her lower lip quivering. 'Guayaqu-what? Where the hell is that? Jason, get me a parachute and let me down.'

'Guayaquil is a long way from Quito, that's for sure. Mom, we're screwed.'

She looked wide-eyed and desperate. 'We can't even call them to tell them we won't be there. And we'll have no one there to meet us when we land. Jason, what are we gonna do?'

'Mom, they just have to land this plane in Quito. They cannot reroute it. I got surgery scheduled for tomorrow!'

'I know.'

I managed to grab a flight attendant. 'Ma'am, I have to get to Quito. I have spinal surgery scheduled. I have to get to Quito.'

'I'm sorry, sir, there are a lot of people desperate to get into Quito, but the fog just won't allow it.'

'But I got surgery—'

'I'm sorry, sir, but we cannot land.'

'But—'

The hostess was already making her way down the aisle. Mom

turned to the window in horrified silence. Below us was just a whiteout of cloud.

The plane came in to land at this unknown city – Guayaquil – at dusk. We popped out of the cloud cover, and below us were ribbons of street lights snaking off towards the horizon. It looked like a big, sprawling, scary kind of a place. Guayaquil is actually Ecuador's second city after Quito. While Quito sits high in the Andes, Guayaquil lies on the coastal plain. But my mom and I, we knew nothing right then.

We touched down and taxied to a standstill. I was carried down the steps of the aircraft in my wheelchair and deposited on the runway.

To one side of the airport lay the city, to the other was a ragged fringe of palm trees. The smells and the atmosphere hit me immediately: the heat and the humidity, the scents of wet and rot and riotous vegetation, the *preeep-preeep-preeep* of a zillion night-time insects. Instantly, my mind was back on my last mission, the one where we'd parachuted in to lay an ambush for the drug-boats.

*What in God's name had possessed me to return here?*

The crowd of passengers headed for the terminal. We followed as if on autopilot, for what else was there to do? Mom was in such shock that she didn't even seem to register the customs officials, or to worry about the money strapped around her waist. She'd withdrawn to a place where the shock just didn't seem to reach her any more. She stumbled through Arrivals in a daze, after which she had to grab all our bags and kit off the carousel and pile it onto a trolley. As she pushed it away from the conveyor, we were accosted by a Continental Airlines ground official.

He gestured at the exit. 'Make your way to the cab stand outside. The cab driver will know where to take you guys, OK?'

*OK? No, this was freakin' well most definitely not OK.* But neither of us had the energy to argue right now.

We headed for the cab stand, Mom pushing the mountain of luggage and me rolling in my chair. While operating in Ecuador our unit had been based in a run-down town called Coco, a place that had seemed awash with cocaine. The streets outside Guayaquil Airport struck me as being pretty much the same: riotous, noisy, chaotic and lawless.

We rolled over to the lead cab in the line, a small, yellow Japanese Toyota-type vehicle. The cabbie lunged across to us and grabbed the trolley. I couldn't even begin to imagine how he was going to squeeze me and my mom, plus all of our luggage, my wheelchair and mattress into his cab.

I managed to manoeuvre my chair close enough to the passenger door to lift myself out of it and into the seat. But my mom had not yet learned how to dismantle and fold my chair. The cabbie got the wheels off, which was easy enough, and then he eyed the roof of his vehicle. There was no roof rack. Regardless, he laid my mattress on the roof, lifted my chair onto that and roped the whole lot down.

He grinned at Mom and me. '*Ningún problema. Todo va bien!*'

The cabbie spoke no English, but Mom understood enough Spanish to grasp what he told us next: *I know where I'm going. I'm taking you to your hotel.*

As for us, we knew nothing. He could have been taking us anywhere.

He set off like a bat out of hell. My chair was already dented and scarred from where it had fallen off the truck onto the railway line earlier that morning. Now I figured it was utterly finished. I turned to Mom as we careered around a tight bend.

'That's it. The chair's finished. The surgery better work. I got no option but to walk out of here!'

Beneath the forced humour I was a total bag of nerves.

Finally, we made the hotel. Mom got out and, miracle of miracles, the chair was still there. She and the cabbie reassembled it on the street, then held it steady while I lowered myself in. We thanked the cabbie as best we could and headed towards the hotel. There was no disabled access. No ramp in.

'*Ningún problema!*' the hotel porters told us. '*Esta bien! Bueno!*'

They lifted me up and carried me into the hotel.

We checked in and I turned to Mom. 'You know what, after that I need a freakin' drink.'

Mom sought out the way to the bar. Needless to say, it lay up a long flight of stairs. 'But, how you gonna get up there? There are all those steps, Jason.'

'Mom, I need a drink, and I don't care how many steps there are.'

I gestured to the waiters in the bar. I mimed them carrying me up the stairs. Just as soon as they understood what I wanted, they were all smiles.

'*Ningún problema! Esta bien! Bueno!*'

They lifted me up and carried me into the bar. I ordered myself and my mom each a Bandido Alta. That was the key thing right now: getting my paws on a beer. After the last twenty-four hours we'd more than earned it.

We drank some beer, nibbled on some bar snacks and tried to calm our frayed nerves. Once our heart rates were something like back to normal, we got the bar guys to carry me to our hotel room. Mom and I crashed out fully clothed and utterly exhausted. We had been told to be ready for a 6 a.m. start, when we'd head back to the airport.

It was still dark when we left the following morning. We never even got to learn the name of the hotel. We reached the airport, but no one seemed to know what was happening. We were on standby, and mid-morning we were instructed to board a plane. We did as we were told, although no one told us where it was flying to. We took off, wondering if we were Quito-bound and whether anyone would be there to meet us.

Imagine our relief when the flight did indeed touch down in Quito. The scenery – soaring jungle-clad mountains cloaked in wisps of snowy white cloud – told us as much. Once again I was carried down from the aircraft.

No sooner had my chair hit the runway than a cry rang out: 'Jason! Jason Morgan! Jason! We await you!'

I glanced across to the crowd thronging Arrivals. A woman was waving at us frantically. I guess it wasn't hard for her to work out who was Jason Morgan. There weren't any other gringos wheeling themselves along the runway in a chair.

Mom and I made a beeline for her. 'You must be Jason and you must be Patti? I am Patti too! That is also my name!'

Mom couldn't hold herself back any more. She grabbed her namesake across the Arrivals railing and burst into tears. Ever since leaving the US Mom had been pretty much on her own. For some reason our cell phones wouldn't work, and we doubted we'd have Internet where we were heading. She was bawling her eyes out with unadulterated relief that we'd made it and that someone was here to receive us.

We were loaded into a minivan and driven out of Quito. I was heartened to discover that the van was properly fitted out for the disabled, with an access ramp and the ability to strap down my wheelchair. Things were looking up.

An hour's drive east of Quito was Cumbayá, the neat-looking town where Dr Kao had chosen to build his surgery. The clinic looked smart, clean and functional. It had its own accommodation, and Mom and I were taken to the one-bedroom apartment that we would share. All things considered, Mom seemed to have weathered the storm pretty well. She made herself up a bed on the sofa so I could have the bedroom. The next thing she did was unburden herself of the cash. She put the $30,000 in the clinic's safe, breathing a sigh of relief like no other.

While the staff readied me for surgery, Mom went out with Patti to the market to purchase some roses. Growing flowers is big business in Ecuador, and she could buy an armful for less than a dollar. She told me she'd head out with Patti every morning to buy fresh flowers, just to brighten up our day.

My surgery was already twenty-four hours overdue, so I was put under a general anaesthetic just as soon as I was ready. Nine hours later Dr Kao was done. I came to lying on my back on a recovery bed, with Dr Kao tidying up his equipment beside me. He stopped and asked me how I felt. I guess it was just a standard question to ensure I was back in the land of the living again.

I told him I was fine, although I had the world's most crushing headache. He told me that was only to be expected; it was a side effect of the operation. They'd give me something for the pain and, with time, it would subside.

Then he said, 'Jason, I want you to try to move your legs.'

I did as he asked, sending the signal from my brain to where I figured the right nerve endings were situated, although for the last six months nothing had worked below the level of my navel.

Dr Kao smiled. 'That's good. Excellent. Take a look. They're moving.'

I looked. I sent the same message again: *Move*. My hip flexor muscles twitched up and down and up and down again. I tried even harder and found I could lift my knees a fraction towards my chest. Wow. At that moment I could have cried.

Mom was there with me. She did cry. In fact, I think she blubbed almost as much as she had when dragging herself away from my dad at the airport in Dallas.

Imagine it. Imagine the very idea of being able to move your legs just a fraction representing such a miracle.

That's exactly what it was for me.

# CHAPTER 16

Shannon and Jeff Reh are a husband-and-wife team, and their Rancho San Carlos Pet Clinic lies just around the block from Jim Siegfried's place. They looked after Gigi and Terence before Napal, so they are more than accustomed to the kind of dogs that Jim rears for CCI. In fact, so impressed are they that they've asked Jim to train their own dogs.

A week or so after Napal's fight with the brick wall, Jeff gives him a full check-over. He tells Jim that his dog is doing just fine. 'He's looking good. Let him go. Let him be who he wants to be.'

'Really? That fast? Jeez, that's . . . amazing. But what about the steroids and the painkillers?'

Jeff eyes Napal for a moment. 'He doesn't seem to be in any pain. If he does start to suffer, give him something, but not the steroids. He's young, he's strong and he's in the very best of hands. Let him heal naturally and in his own time.'

Jim heads home in the Chrysler feeling on top of the world. He figures it's time to celebrate Napal's speedy recovery. He opens the freezer and grabs a rare and special treat – a Frosty Paw. Manufactured by Purina, the peanut- or vanilla-flavour ice cream is made especially for dogs. He rips off the covering and hands the plastic cup to Napal.

'There you go. Your favourite. A Frosty Paw.'

Napal stares at it for a second. *A Frosty Paw. You serious? What have I done to deserve this?*

'You gave me a scare, little buddy. But you're over it. So take it into the yard and lick your heart out.'

Napal lifts his head, grips the ice-cream cup in his jaws and heads out to the backyard. While he enjoys his Frosty Paw, Jim drafts a short email update for CCI. He forwards Jeff Reh's report as an attachment with a summary of Napal's recovery so far. Each month he's sent a similar message, briefing CCI on how the training is going and whether he's experienced any issues with raising Napal.

Email written and Frosty Paw licked out of existence, Jim takes Napal for a gentle stroll, rolling along beside him in his wheelchair. They walk some, then Jim lets Napal have a little run off-leash. Over the week that follows he allows Napal to run and run some more, and he's soon coming back like a champ.

Pretty quickly life returns to their regular routine, the one that Napal seems to love. Early morning, man and dog roll out to the Chrysler and drive into work. Napal does the rounds greeting all the office staff and delivering the Dog Mail. After lunch they head home and stop off at the football field for an afternoon's training. Napal gets to grab a few kick-off tees, and he's not showing any signs of pain any more.

Jim phones CCI and delivers the good news. Napal is back on track for the handover. Physically, he's almost as strong as he ever was. There's just a niggling doubt in Jim's mind as to whether his dog will be mentally up to the coming separation. Or maybe that's more himself that he's worried about.

On that front Jim receives some good news. Gayle Keane emails him. She reports that Terence has mated with a CCI bitch, and the litter is due in several weeks' time. If Gayle's done her sums properly, Jim should be able to get one of the pups just a couple of weeks prior to giving up Napal, to help ease the coming parting.

Of course, Napal has come to feel as if Jim's home is his home. One of the biggest fears when handing a dog back to CCI is separation anxiety – the stress a young dog can feel when removed from its home and human family. But CCI has strategies to deal with most scenarios. When Napal has recovered enough from his injuries Jim will start sending him for sleepovers at another puppy raiser's house, so he gets accustomed to separation.

It will start with the odd weekend and build eventually to four- or five-day stretches. It'll show Napal that it's OK to be fed and petted and to sleep at somebody else's place, and that there are other humans who know what they're doing. If he only ever stays with Jim he'll get real bad separation anxiety for sure.

At worst, a dog with separation anxiety will stop eating completely. It'll develop a bad attitude around other dogs. Small things may cause the dog to snap because it is so badly stressed. Eventually, separation anxiety can make a dog ill. And humans can suffer from separation anxiety just as much as dogs can, as Jim well knows. Jim's trying to steel himself. He's trying to find some distance. But it's impossible. At times he looks at

Napal when he's about to go to another puppy raiser's house for a sleepover and thinks, *You know, this dog knows. He knows we're gonna be parted for good some time soon. He knows we're getting ready. And he's just so sad.*

But then Jim tells himself this is him anthropomorphizing Napal. He reminds himself that dogs don't know what's coming tomorrow and they don't care about yesterday; they live in the moment. So maybe the fear and the anxiety is all Jim's, because Napal simply doesn't know what's around the corner.

As Jim knows full well, there is no way to insulate himself from the pain of the parting. You can't. He knows how tough it's going to be. He's been down this road before with Terence and Gigi. He's made that drive north to CCI's facility, knowing what he has to do and understanding the reasons, but that still didn't ease the hurt.

Jim guesses this is what sending a kid off to college must be like. It's a bittersweet moment. You're happy for the kid, but you're sad for yourself because you know he's not going to be around any more. You raised him, but soon he'll be gone. There will be a hole in your life. You'll have to either close that hole or fill it with something else.

Just the idea of the coming separation gets Jim teary-eyed. And he's worried about Napal. As much as he tells himself that Napal lives in the moment, he still worries. He worries about separation anxiety because Napal is just too in tune with him right now. Too close. It's reached the stage where Jim can think of something, and he swears that his dog can read his mind. All Jim has to do is throw Napal a look, and Napal *knows*. He doesn't need verbal commands. Jim looks at Napal when he wants him to lie down and Napal does it. He doesn't know if it's in his eye movements: a glance at Napal and a glance at the floor. Can the dog read such signs?

Jim's even started to think of it as telepathy. Napal seems able to read his every emotion. On the rare occasions when Jim is feeling down, Napal wanders over and places his head in his lap, his eyes saying it all: *Hey, don't stress. I'm here for you. Let's do stuff. Outside it's a beautiful day.*

Jim begins a long series of 'lasts' with his dog. It's not deliberate. It's not as if Jim and his dog are making their final tour. But each time they do something together for the last time Jim is acutely aware of it. And each time someone has to say a final goodbye to Napal, it kills him. For Jim this really hits home when Mrs Chedrick – the football mom who knitted Napal his first TEE RETRIEVER scarf – has to say farewell. A lot of the football moms gather that day, Napal has pulled so many people in close. The separation is more than the football moms seem able to bear. They have an idea. They volunteer to prepare the breakfast that will be served when Napal graduates from CCI. That way they are sure to get one more hit of this wonder dog before he disappears from their lives completely.

Because of course, no one has a clue where Napal will go. America is a big country, and CCI provides service dogs all across the nation. Napal could go to a needy recipient 3,000 miles away; it's highly unlikely he will be allocated to someone local. It's a very real possibility that after the graduation breakfast Jim and the wider Napal community may see him no more.

People like Jim aren't technically trainers; that's why they're called raisers. Sure, they teach those thirty-odd commands, but the real professionals are the in-house trainers at CCI – and they're experts at matching a dog to a recipient.

CCI actually offer four types of dog, each with a specific skill set. They provide 'hearing dogs' to assist the hard of hearing. They train 'facility dogs', which are provided on a temporary basis to families experiencing problems – for example in a difficult divorce situation. A facility dog may help a kid handle a courtroom experience, standing with the child in the dock to ease the stress of testifying. Facility dogs are also called comfort dogs, for that's the basic role they fulfil. Then there are 'skilled companions' – dogs that go to children with disabilities as friends for life. The little boy with cerebral palsy and autism that so inspired Jim, he was given a skilled companion. And finally there are 'service dogs', which become life companions for wounded warriors and the disabled in general.

Whichever role Napal ends up fulfilling, Jim knows for sure that soon he'll be gone. So it's doubly fortunate that his plan to ease the coming separation comes to fruition. A few weeks before he's scheduled to give Napal up, he takes a call from CCI. Terence's new litter of puppies is ripe for going to their raisers. There is one bitch, called Tatiana II, and she's Jim's if he'd like her.

'Yes, please! I'll take anything,' Jim tells the caller. 'When do I come to fetch her?'

From the get-go Tatiana is . . . a puppy. Like puppies always seem to, she makes Jim chuckle. Napal too. Napal is in the Chrysler when Jim goes to collect her. He takes one look at the tiny ball of glistening black fluff, sniffs her underside, nudges her with his nose and sneezes, before breaking into a goofy, lopsided smile. *Oh wow. A living, breathing, walking, talking chew toy!*

Jim cracks up laughing.

For the next ten days Napal and Tatiana are inseparable. She follows him everywhere. Napal gets up on the Hot Tub Lookout and peers down at his little baby sister, eyes sparkling. *See. Up here, this is the best. Up here you get to watch all the birds. Up here big buddy will tell you lots of stories.*

Napal whispers words of advice in Tatiana's tiny ear, nosing it so he can really drive the message home. Jim's certain these are tips and hints on how to train their human charge. Tatiana responds with a few words in Napal's ear, though he's got to bend real low so she can reach. Napal is showing her the ropes. Jim is glued to every moment, every interaction. It's beautiful; priceless.

Normally the person in the wheelchair holds one end of his or her service dog's leash, but recently Jim and Napal have got into the habit of Napal carrying his own leash. Napal and Tatiana develop a variation on the theme. Napal takes the free end of Tatiana's tiny puppy lead in his mouth and takes her around the house and for walks in the yard. It's a classic big brother–little sister combo.

The first time Jim brings both dogs into work, Napal is in his element. He takes Tatiana's leash and runs her down the corridor of the 32nd Street Naval Station Defense Distribution Center, leading her direct to Phyllis's office, so both dogs can get their early morning greet and treat. By day's end, there isn't an office that they haven't been enticed into. They're the stars of the show.

That evening Tatiana curls up with Napal, exhausted. Being part of an all-star double act sure can be tiring. In his bedroom

Jim's got a big kennel crate for Napal and a small one for his new charge. They're positioned face to face, so brother and sister can sleep with their breaths touching. Jim looks at the two of them, nose to nose, blissful and snoozing deep. He realizes that he's got the happiest family a guy could ever wish for – but at the very moment when it's all about to end.

The worst is the final puppy social at Cindy Carlton's place. One of the raisers has baked special goodbye cookies for all the raisers and their dogs. While Jim knows well what is coming he doesn't much want to talk about it. He doesn't want to dwell or wallow. He doesn't see how that will help. The talk becomes very emotional. The women start to cry. They are really, truly wailing their hearts out, and all Jim can think of doing is getting away. He calls for Napal. His dog comes running from the doggie fray, then notices all the grief that's in the air. He eyes Jim with a puzzled but stoical look on his face. *Man, what's with all the emotion? What's going on here?*

Jim thanks everyone and rolls towards the door. 'He's coming back!' he calls over his shoulder. 'Napal's coming back. He's not going to make it. I got nothing to worry about!'

But, in truth, Jim is struggling to keep his composure. He reaches the Chrysler and sets off home, fighting back the tears. He glances at Napal, riding shotgun in the van.

'You OK, buddy? All that crying and wailing . . . Jeez.' He shakes his head. 'You don't know what's going on, do you, boy? You're a dog. You're not gonna look back, are you, boy? A dog never looks back.'

Except, this one will.

This one will look back like no dog has ever done before.

# CHAPTER 17

In the days after Dr Kao's surgery I could feel more and more sensation returning to my lower limbs. Movement came back in little, miraculous, spine-tingling bursts and starts. Somehow my brain was communicating through my hips and down towards my knees. I could have someone lift my leg into a bent-at-the-knee position, and I could *hold it like that.*

A week after the operation I was able to sit up in bed and watch the Super Bowl on TV. Mom had discovered a local Domino's Pizza. She ordered for everyone: every patient, the medical staff, the drivers, the cleaners, plus the two of us. We got my bed rolled into the common room and together we watched the Tennessee Titans play the St Louis Rams on a local TV network. It was all in Spanish, but it was still fun. I didn't need the commentary to get what was happening with the match.

As the days went by I felt strong enough to face the truth: it was time to meet Steve Sutherland and learn what had happened out there in the jungle. Steve brought his wife and family to visit. They'd cooked Mom and me a special American lunch. It was a home-baked lasagne and it was delicious. Yet my mind wasn't on the food.

I had been so nervous prior to meeting Steve. I was wondering how on earth I would thank a man who had saved my life. What would I tell him? There were so many different emotions running through my head. I was desperate to know the truth about what had happened to me in Ecuador, as the military had told me next to nothing. I wondered what Steve might know that had made the military so reluctant to give me his contact details.

After the meal Steve's folks departed, leaving him, Mom and me alone. Steve turned to the window of my room, which looked out over mountains cloaked in jungle. He pointed at a near peak. 'Do you know, that was the site where you were injured? That cleft in the mountains, that's where it all happened. That's where we found you.'

Mom stared at him in disbelief. I did likewise. We had had no idea that we were this close.

Cumbayá perches on the side of a mountain. Below it lies the wide expanse of the Tumbaco Valley, and on the far side rises the towering volcanic mass of Ilaló. Through the valley runs the San Pedro River, and it was in a pass leading into the river valley that Steve had found me. Steve worked for Voice of the Andes, a missionary radio station which broadcasts across much of Latin America. On the mountain peak they had a radio mast, and they'd been up there making some repairs. They were driving back to Quito when they came to a stretch of notoriously dangerous road. At the tightest of the corners there were skid marks and crushed vegetation, as if something had gone off the road.

Steve didn't know if it was a recent accident, but he decided to stop anyway. It was just him and his local driver. They peered over the edge of the ravine. Below they could see a white SUV lying on its side. Nearby, one figure was wandering about in a total daze. Steve and his colleague clambered down the slope, following the path of crushed vegetation made by the vehicle. The guy stumbling about in shock turned out to be the vehicle's driver. There was a second guy wedged into the front passenger seat, who was also badly injured. Apparently there was a third guy, but he was missing. Steve and his colleague began a search. They only found me because they stepped on my back when checking out a patch of swampy ground.

I was mostly submerged and covered in muck and vegetation, which made me hard to see. Steve could tell immediately what had happened. The soft ground had saved my life, giving way as the vehicle rolled over me, but it had also practically drowned me. He could tell that I had a back injury, but he knew that if he didn't move me I would drown.

He and his colleague dragged me out of the swamp. They got me onto my back, face up. I was breathing, but only just. Steve figured one lung had collapsed and the other was partially full of swamp water. They were at around 14,000 feet, so the air was seriously thin, which made it all the more difficult for me to get enough oxygen. At 15,000 feet pilots who are not in pressurized aircraft have to wear oxygen masks.

Steve knew I wouldn't live long enough for an ambulance to reach me, especially as it would most likely have to come from Quito. Somehow they managed to carry me up the hill. They removed the seats from their minivan so they could lay me down flat, and lifted me inside. They returned to the crash site, pulled the other injured guy out of the wreck, carried him up and loaded him in beside me.

Steve decided to call for an ambulance. Trouble was, we were deep in a ravine and there was no cell-phone signal. Then he had a brainwave. He used his shortwave radio to contact the radio station and got them to call for the ambulance. He was told it would take three hours for it to get there.

'This guy doesn't have three hours,' Steve replied. 'Get them to meet me halfway. I'm bringing him in.'

Steve knew that his injured passengers were Americans. He also knew that, officially, there weren't any US servicemen in the country. He guessed we had to be on a classified military operation, and so he got a radio call patched through to the US embassy. He explained what he had found, asked if there was somewhere safe where the ambulance could take us and was given the name of a medical facility.

Steve set off down the mountain. He knew I was on the edge. My breathing was short and rasping, and it sounded horribly watery as I tried to drag enough oxygen into my partially flooded lungs. All the way he kept telling me, 'Come on, buddy, keep breathing, keep breathing.'

They made the RV with the ambulance and somehow I was still alive. But the moment they tried to move me from one vehicle to the other, I stopped breathing altogether. It was almost as if I'd thought I was safe now and had given up, the effort of breathing proving too much. There and then the ambulance crew broke my ribs, shoved in a tube and pumped in air, reinflating my lungs and starting me breathing again.

Just minutes later and I would have been dead.

Before Steve left we talked about him taking me back to the scene of the crash. There was a part of me – a big part of me – that couldn't resist the urge to go, yet once Steve was gone and I was on my own I began to feel worried. Scared almost. At first I didn't understand why. But that night I had my first nightmare. It was as if the darkest of the lost memories were starting to bleed back through. It was so real that I woke screaming. I had hallucinations of running from capture. I had horrible sensations of being tied down and held. I didn't know what, if anything, was real.

In due course Steve did take me out to the scene of the accident. I gazed along the road and sensed our approach to the dead man's curve. I knew this was the spot without anyone having to tell me. Peering into the ravine, I felt a massive chill run down my spine, and I found myself fighting back the urge to vomit.

Seeing it all triggered an avalanche of memories. Once again they came to me at night, in my dreams. I had no idea if what I saw was real or not, but I presumed it had to be, it was so visceral and so vivid. I'd been told that I was asleep in the back of the SUV at the time of the accident, but in my dreams I was very much awake. We were driving along a mountain road that cut through thick jungle. I was with two other SOAR operators, and we were heading to Quito to collect some parts for a damaged Black Hawk helicopter. The road was prone to ambushes by FARC, so they had asked someone to ride security. I had volunteered.

I was in the back, M4 carbine cradled in my lap. We neared a bend in the road. A vehicle came up fast from behind and

I heard gunfire. We were under attack. I leaned out of the window. I was hanging half out as I loosed off bursts of fire at our pursuers. The driver stepped on the gas, but he didn't make the bend. Instead, we left the road and for a second we were airborne.

Our unmarked white Chevrolet Blazer rolled eight times as it plummeted down the mountainside. I was thrown free, but the vehicle landed on top of me, breaking my back and crushing me into the swamp. I was still conscious. I couldn't move and I was breathing in the stinking black water. I was trapped, and I was convinced that I would die.

What a shitty way to go.

I'd been drowning for a long while before my world went totally black. After that there truly were no more memories.

The nightmare was terrifying. It was so real it *had* to be real. But I didn't tell anyone, not even my mom. I was too scared – scared that it would terrify her, and Lord knows she'd been through enough.

It certainly scared the hell out of me.

That nightmare was the first detailed recollection of the accident that I'd ever had. I felt I knew in my heart what had happened now. I understood why the military were reluctant to give me and my folks any details, but I'd got to the truth anyhow. It had been inside my head all along – it just needed a trigger to fire up the worst of the memories. From now on I'd have that dream many times over, and as the months went by more and more details would become clear to me.

While I was at Dr Kao's clinic I'd been seriously worried that somehow FARC might learn of my presence in Cumbayá. There was zero security and the rebels clearly carried out operations in the vicinity, for the site of my injuries was no more than fifteen miles distant. Fortunately, word didn't leak out, or at least not to our knowledge.

Of course, Mom had accompanied me on the trip to the site of the accident. At numerous points during our Ecuador journey I had realized that there was more bravery in my 59-year-old mom than there was in many an elite forces soldier.

At the end of our three weeks in Ecuador, Mom cried again. She was sad to be leaving all the dear friends that we had made – Dr Kao and his staff, plus Steve Sutherland and his family.

Having said our fond goodbyes we flew out of Quito, bound for Dallas Fort Worth. My dad was there to meet us. He handed my mom a bunch of red roses to welcome her home. She glanced at them, teary-eyed, then burst out laughing. She pointed out the label: GROWN IN ECUADOR.

Mom and I had left for Ecuador in a state close to meltdown. We'd returned having pulled off the seemingly impossible. And it all had been so worthwhile. I'd recovered the memories, and for that I felt so much better; so much more complete. But more importantly, I was so much better physically, as events were about to prove.

I headed home to San Antonio for a sweet reunion with Carla and the kids, and I told them all my stories. The next day I went for a session with PT. I arrived at the gym and she laid out some raised mats, with the leg braces waiting for me in the middle.

'OK. We're gonna try these things out. Let's give 'em a whirl.'

By the end of that morning's session I had managed to walk along a pair of parallel bars, using my arms to support myself.

I'd taken maybe a dozen steps, using my upper body to roll one leg round after the other. The effort of doing so had totally finished me. After twelve tiny steps I was sweating and shaking as if I had just run two marathons back to back.

Twelve small steps, but to me this was like a miracle.

I called my parents. I was close to tears. 'Mom, you have to come down. I'm starting to walk a little.'

I worked on the walking relentlessly, day after day. The Italian boots braced my legs solid from the ankles up. With them I could use my hip muscles to lift each leg and swing it around. Doing that, I worked up to being able to take 250 steps in one go.

I was so determined to show my mom and dad what I could do that I walked all the way down one of the corridors at the gym, turned the corner and completed another. But by then I was utterly exhausted – it was worse than anything I'd ever done in the military. I was soaked in sweat, shaking like a leaf and on the verge of passing out. My dad had to run to fetch my chair. But you know something – I had even been able to stand up and hug my mom properly. Imagine how good that felt.

Those were the upsides. Those were the benefits I had reaped from the return to Ecuador. But there were downsides. I had more sensation, which meant more pain, and I had more memories, which meant more nightmares and flashbacks. But more than anything, I was overjoyed to walk again. Just as I'd vowed that I would. Yet it's only when you're up so high that you can be pulled down so low again. As I pushed and pushed with the leg braces, plus all my other get-me-fit-again training regimes, disaster struck. I developed my first pressure sore.

It was just below my right hip. I had to check with mirrors

and feel around my lower limbs every day, and that was how I discovered it. At first I tried to ignore it. *I'm doing great. It'll soon go away.* But then the sore opened up. I went to the hospital and I was admitted immediately. The sore required surgery, which meant an automatic six-week stay. I had to lie on a bed with a sand-filled mattress. The sand shifted around minutely, so as to stop any part of my body developing sores. But I had nothing to do, and the only way the staff could get me to keep still was to drug me to the eyeballs. To be honest, I was in masses of pain, so I needed those painkillers.

The operations failed again and again. The sore kept opening up. I ended up spending eleven months in hospital. Imagine it. *Eleven months.* Three hundred and thirty-odd days, all exactly the same: totally immobile, with nothing whatsoever to do. Some 3,600 waking hours – and most of that time spent racked with pain. Twisting and crying out in agony.

I was given a big dose of morphine every four hours. I killed time watching the clock until my next shot. The longer it went on the worse it became. My state of mind became so dark. A few months back I had walked again. I had done it. And now this . . . waiting for my next morphine shot. It was the worst of all.

As time wore on I noticed Carla and the kids were coming to see me less and less. I couldn't exactly blame them. There was nothing to talk about, and I could do nothing with my kids because I wasn't allowed to move. I couldn't even hold them.

And, in truth, it broke my heart.

In truth, it was maybe better they didn't come.

In truth, I did not want my three boys to see me like this.

That 4th of July I woke to the sound of fireworks, but I felt as if I was back on that mountain under fire. I gazed out the window of my hospital bedroom and, once I could see the fireworks, I felt a little better. Yet when they just suddenly exploded out of the dark night, it freaked me completely.

Just prior to getting released from hospital I had brain surgery. The aim was to lessen my pain, which had spiked to unbearable levels. The doctors explained to me that pain travels like a telephone signal. If you have a good line, the pain will come through loud and clear. If you have static and interference on the line, the pain will be disrupted and muted. In essence, the aim of the surgery was to insert a scrambler into my brain to disrupt the pain signal. In my more lucid moments I argued that I didn't want the surgery if it would also disrupt my ability to feel and to try to walk. I was assured it would not. Pain signals and those associated with movement travelled along different phone lines.

The day of the surgery they put me into a head brace, to keep my skull absolutely still. I had to be sitting for the operation, and they kept tightening and tightening the screws until it felt as if my head was about to explode. The pain was worse in my right leg, which is controlled by the left side of the brain, so that was the side they intended to drill into. I also had to be conscious, to tell them where in my body I had sensation. They switched the drill on and started the insertion. They flicked a switch, and my right arm flew up as if I was possessed. *What the hell!* I thought. *It's supposed to be my right leg!*

'OK, that's good,' the surgeon reassured me. 'That's what's supposed to happen.'

I could hear and feel the drill rotating and I could smell burning flesh. Finally it reached a place where I could feel a tingling in my right leg. This apparently meant that they'd hit the exact spot. A device was implanted that I was supposed to be able to activate by remote control, to block the pain. But it never did a thing for me; it never seemed to lessen the pain at all.

As a result of the operation I had half my head shaven and a semicircle of staples holding my scalp together. Before being released from hospital I was allowed to visit a hairdressing salon, to have the other half shaved so it matched. I went there with a hat on. When I took it off the girls in the salon almost had a heart attack on the spot.

I guess I was more than a little like Frankenstein's monster – and that was the last way in which I ever wanted to return to my wife and kids. But, as matters transpired, I would not have a wife to return to. At some stage during those eleven months of hopeless, screaming, pain-racked despair, my wife had decided enough was enough.

She'd decided to leave me.

Now, I do not want your sympathy. Not ever. No one should ever pity me because I am paralyzed and in a chair. But I guess you need to know how my wife left me and how my life crashed and burned. And to understand quite how low my paralysis took me, you've got to know where I came from. How I was before.

Growing up I was one of the fastest runners at school. I was an ace at football, soccer and track sports. My dad coached my football team and he gave me some sage advice early on in life: 'Son, you can be good at many sports; you can only be truly great at one.' He advised me to choose my sport and go for it, and golf became my thing. By the time college approached I was in the high school team that won the state golf championship. I won a golf scholarship, but college just didn't give me the buzz that I craved. Dad had been in the air force in an air-refueling wing, and I decided to follow him, signing up for Air Force Weather School and then special operations. We combat weathermen were known as the Gray Berets.

My dad never could figure out how I'd got into the air force only to end up jumping out of planes, as opposed to flying them. But I loved it. Prior to Ecuador, I'd been deployed on numerous active missions, including one to unseat a notorious African dictator. I believed we could be righteous warriors and a force for good in the world. Every time I jumped out of an aircraft on a mission, that's what I hoped to achieve – including in Ecuador. I wasn't out there fighting a war against drugs; I was out there battling the criminals and the murderers who feed off and profit from the addicts. I was out there trying to do my bit to free a country and a people from that evil.

Almost overnight I'd gone from that to a guy paralyzed from the waist down and confined to a chair. My refusal to zone out on pain medication made me hell to live with. It put enormous strain on my marriage, but I would not give up the dream of walking again. And then there were the eleven months of drugged despair and darkness, confined to my hospital bed.

In a sense I'd faced a choice between keeping the dream of walking alive and saving my marriage, though I hadn't known that at the time. I believed I needed to feel the pain to keep trying to walk, but the pain made me very bad company. Eventually my wife had had enough. I came out of those eleven months in hospital and she was pretty much gone.

At first she told me she was leaving for a two-week holiday, spending some time with her uncle in the sun. She said that she was desperate for a break. But once she went she didn't come back. The 'holiday' thing was really just a way for her to try to shield me from the truth – that she was leaving.

There was no way that I could try save my marriage; I didn't know if I could even save myself. I didn't blame her either. Imagine the man you'd married going from being the golden jump boy to the guy who lies in bed for days on end, screaming and cursing with the pain. At times it felt as if I had daggers stabbing into my thighs; as if my muscles were being sliced off the bone.

In our marriage ceremony we had vowed to stay with each other 'in sickness and in health', but after my injury I was not the person that Carla had married. I was another person entirely. During those eleven months she had come to see me less and less, but if the shoe had been on the other foot, would I have wanted to keep visiting someone drugged up to the eyeballs, and dragging my kids in there too?

So when I came home from those eleven months and found out that my wife was leaving me, I tried to understand. It had all got too much for her. The life I had right then I would not have wished on my worst enemies. But the last thing I ever expected was to have to look after my three small boys, on top of everything else.

My youngest was three years old, the oldest, six. Their life had gone from being part of a beautiful, sunny, happy family, to having only their wheelchair-bound dad for company. But you know something? It was also the responsibility of having my boys to care for that gave me the will to go on.

I knew that I had to get myself healthy, and be a good dad to my kids. I needed to be the dad they needed me to be. Now I had them full time I had to step up to the challenge. It would turn out to be a blessing in disguise, but right at that moment I felt as if I had the weight of the world on my shoulders, and some.

I figured maybe Carla had left the boys with me because she knew it would break me to lose them. I hoped and presumed that was the case. She knew I loved them dearly and would take good care of them – at least to the best of my, now limited, abilities.

But in losing Carla I lost yet another part of my identity. My work and my family had defined me. My military service had shaped who I was. I loved the missions, my brother warriors, my country. Now I was reduced to being a disabled veteran confined to a chair with three young boys to raise. A lone, stay-at-home, wheelchair-bound dad.

Of course, Mom stepped in to help, and the boys sure grew to love her home cooking. But she couldn't be around 24/7. When she wasn't, Blake, Austin, Grant and I learned to live off frozen meals, sandwiches and nachos. We became a regular feature at the local takeouts – Taco Bell, IHOP and Wendy's – wheelchair dad with his three hungry boys.

But there were so many times when I kind of just stopped and thought, *How in the name of God did it come to this?* It was no way to live. It was bad enough that my life had been turned upside down and back to front, but I couldn't even go onto the grass to throw around a ball with my kids. If the boys wanted to go on vacation, they'd ask, *Hey, can we go camp in the mountains?*

*I can't. My chair won't roll off-road.*

Hey, can we go to the beach?

*I can't. My chair won't roll on sand.*

Time passed. The months became years. People got into the habit of saying to me, *Things always get worse before they start to get better.* I'd tell them, *Yeah, I used to think that way. I used to think that it can't get any worse. But it just keeps seeming to . . .*

There just seemed to be no light at the end of the tunnel. Or, as I got to saying, the only light was the headlamp of an oncoming freight train.

# CHAPTER 18

In the final days before Jim has to hand back Napal to CCI, he organizes a change of hound ceremony at the naval base. They always have a change of *command* ceremony whenever a new captain replaces the outgoing one, so they figure they'll have a change of hound ceremony to mark Tatiana replacing Napal. The ceremonials normally come complete with formal dress, plus a red carpet weighed down by bullet stanchions on either side and with swinging ropes stretched between them. In lieu of that Jim has organized a 'carpet' made of newspapers and lined by red fire hydrants with dog leads stretched between them, and he's invited his two previous CCI dogs to attend.

The arriving animals get piped in, just like military dignitaries would be. Jim sits on a stage out front, officiating. Gigi appears, complete with her owner, and takes to the newsprint carpet.

Jim rings a ship's bell. *Ding-ding! Ding-ding!* 'Change-of-career dog Gigi – arriving.'

A CCI dog that's failed to graduate gets called a change-of-career dog. No one wants to taint a dog with any stigma, especially when the dog hasn't really failed. Beautiful Gigi just loved to run and run and she wasn't destined to be a service dog, that's all.

Jim rings the ship's bell a second time. *Ding-ding! Ding-ding!* 'Breeder-dog Terence – arriving!'

Gayle Keane leads Terence down the carpet to join Gigi.

Jim rings the ship's bell again. *Ding-ding! Ding-ding!* 'Dog-in-training Napal – arriving!'

Napal is led forward to join the others.

Jim rings the ship's bell for a fourth time. *Ding-ding! Ding-ding!* 'Puppy-in-training Tatiana – arriving!'

Down either side of the newspaper carpet are ranged the 'side boys' – an honour guard at a traditional change of command ceremony – comprising Napal's buddies from his puppy classes. The corridors and offices have emptied, as all the staff crowd around.

Jim Piburn, the captain of the base, delivers a speech saying how much Napal has meant to the facility, and welcoming Tatiana, as she takes over his duties. It's then time for Jim to speak. He's decided to give a personal kind of talk about what a difference Napal has made in people's lives. But as he gazes out over all these people who so love his dog, he suddenly realizes what this signifies: he is seven days and counting from handing Napal back to CCI.

The reality strikes home, and Jim finds himself lost for words . . . and in tears. He sits on the stage, crying into the microphone, and for a few long seconds the words just won't seem to come. Thankfully, Jim isn't alone. Most of his DoD colleagues are also choking back their sobs.

The grand finale of the ceremony is when a symbolic bone gets passed from the old dog to the new, whereupon all is declared complete: change of hound ceremony done and dusted.

Afterwards, Jim leads Napal over to Terence. As male dogs tend to at a 'first' meeting, they come up to each other limbs stiff and wary, nose thrust to nose. Napal is eighteen months old and Terence is three years, and it is hard to tell the two dogs apart. All of a sudden Napal backs away and his head goes down to touch his forepaws in front of the older dog. He bows. Deep and long, he bows. Jim reads that move as a son paying his respects to a father. *Hey, you're my dad. You're the man.*

The day of parting finally arrives.

It's a crisp November morning in 2009, and Jim has got to be at CCI's Oceanside facility for 10 a.m. sharp. It's an hour and fifteen minutes' drive, and he has to drop Tatiana off with a friend. He's had no trouble sleeping, but that's only because he took a sleeping pill. In truth, he's a total bag of nerves.

He takes the drive slowly. There's hardly a bright and breezy atmosphere in the Chrysler as they pull onto Route 76. Jim tries to focus on Tatiana. How she'll help get him through this. How it'll make it so much easier for him just having her around. He tries to focus on her training and what kind of things they'll be doing over the next few weeks together. But in the back of his mind a voice is screaming, *After today you might never see Napal again. This could be the last moment ever.*

They park, and man and dog roll towards the coming separation. Today there will be a joint matriculation and graduation ceremony. Eight CCI dogs are graduating and forty-odd are being handed in. Napal is one of those. The graduation comes first. Jim is barely aware of what is happening. He's sat there in his chair, trying not to lose it, his arm looped around Napal's neck and his eyes front. He's got one hell of a fight on his hands.

Finally, his name is called. He rolls up to the stage, Napal trotting quietly at his side. Jim rolls across the stage and takes up a position facing the audience, though he's blind to the faces before him. And inside he's screaming, *NOOOOOOOOO*.

'OK, so this is Jim Siegfried with Napal,' the CCI announcer declares. 'Jim's a veteran puppy raiser. He's raised three dogs for Canine Companions for Independence, and Napal is his third. Let's have a round of applause for Jim and Napal.'

The audience claps. Jim doesn't hear them; he's lost to the world.

He rolls out of the hall. There is a sign outside that reads, CANADA THIS WAY. MEXICO THIS WAY. Below the words is a pair of arrows pointing in opposite directions. It's kind of a joke. The sign means, you're here to hand in your dogs, and the only way out of it is to run, either to Canada or Mexico. In other words, there is no escape.

Jim and Napal follow the others towards the handover room. It's basically a training facility adapted for today's purpose. People have volunteered to be here, to help ease the matriculating dogs away from their raisers. Jim hovers outside the entrance along with a number of others who are reluctant to go inside.

The tears are flowing freely, though somehow Jim's still managing to hold his emotions in check. Puppy raisers are bawling their eyes out, their separation anxiety kicking in, but the dogs are mostly just checking out all the other interesting canines around and about.

A volunteer approaches Jim. 'What is the name of your dog, and are you ready? Whenever you're ready you can go right in.'

Jim can't find the words to reply. He can't even look at Napal. Instead he puts his gloved hands to the drive wheels of his chair and begins to roll towards the door . . . and the parting.

Jim rolls inside and a faceless volunteer comes up to process him. She's faceless only in the sense that Jim is blind to everything right now, apart from the swirling void that is threatening to swallow him: *separation*.

'So, good to see you,' the volunteer declares. 'Are you ready? Ready for the handover?'

'Yeah, yeah,' Jim mutters. He can't believe he's doing this, but he reaches out and hands the leash towards her. 'Here.'

She takes it. 'OK, so what's your dog's name?'

'Napal.'

'OK, so come on, boy. Come on. '

She tugs the leash and moves off towards the kennels. Napal knows better than not to obey, especially as he's seen Jim hand the leash to her. But as he steps away from Jim's chair, the volunteer hesitates for a moment and turns back.

'Sorry, what did you say his name was again?'

'Napal. He's called Napal.'

The moment Jim says his name, Napal turns right around and looks back at him. He fixes Jim with his laser-eyed stare. *Hey, did you call? You need me right now? If so, I'm always there for you. Just say the word, I'll be right by your side.*

It kills Jim.

That look – those unspoken words – they kill him. He is the most polite and easy-going guy you could ever hope to meet, but he loses it with that hapless volunteer.

'You stupid . . . Why did you have to ask me to . . .'

With that he spins his chair around, and with Napal's puzzled gaze burning into his shoulders he sets himself going and rolls out the door. Someone outside recognizes him, and he realizes that Jim is most definitely not feeling himself right now.

'Jim! Hey, Jim, are you OK? Hold up a second.'

Jim shakes his head and keeps rolling. 'I can't talk. I can't talk.'

He waves everyone away and wheels himself towards his Chrysler. He brings down the ramp, rolls himself inside and shuts the door firmly behind him. Finally the dam bursts. He sits in his van, hunched over in his chair, alone and bereft of his dog, and he sobs his heart out.

The tears keep falling. He doesn't seem able to stop.

One thought keeps whirling around in his tortured mind: *What am I going to do now?*

Jim cries all the way down Rancho Del Oro Drive. He cries his way along Route 76 and right out onto the Ocean Road. In fact, he cries all the way home to Santee. As the tears roll down his cheeks his head is full of the memories of the dog he's left behind: Napal waking him up in the morning with a sneeze and a dog kiss; their chats on the Hot Tub Lookout; Napal grabbing him a cold beer; Napal delivering the Dog Mail; NAPAL TEE RETRIEVER fetching the kicking tee.

By the time he collects Tatiana from his friend's house, Jim has just about managed to stem the flood. But it's only temporary. The moment they set foot inside his door, there are Napal's food and water bowl. Jim glances at them and the tears stream down anew. He glances at Napal's bed in the lounge and they keep flowing.

He tries to tell himself that life goes on. After all, he's got Tatiana to worry about now. He's got an eight-week-old puppy to raise, to train and to love. He's got to take her out every two hours to use the bathroom. He's got to teach her to 'Sit' and to 'Stay' and to 'Go potty' on command. He tells himself that at least he's got Tatiana to help ease him through.

He tells himself all this, then he rolls into his bedroom, and there is Tatiana's kennel crate, with an empty space beside it where Napal's ought to be. Jim knows there's not a day will go by when he isn't reminded of this dog. There isn't another like him.

Jim knows he will never get over losing Napal.

# CHAPTER 19

Due to their experiences dealing with my disability, my mom and dad were inspired to get involved with a not-for-profit organization called Challenge Air. Challenge Air takes kids with mental and physical disabilities and gives them the experience of actually flying an aircraft. The philosophy behind it is: if you can fly one of these, you can do anything. The sky's the limit.

After a while I started going to Challenge Air events too. I got to meet a lady called Jackie, a volunteer with an organization I'd never heard of before. It was called Canine Companions for Independence, CCI for short. Jackie was there with her yellow Labrador–retriever cross, a puppy she was raising in the hope that he would qualify as an assistance dog. She was the first person to suggest to me that I might try to get one.

'But I thought you had to be a quadriplegic,' I told her. 'Or you gotta have a higher level of paralysis. Like be more disabled. I mean, I'd love to have one, but I'm far too independent.'

'No, no, no. I can't guarantee it, but I really think you'd qualify.' She handed me a brochure. 'Go on, apply. See if you qualify. What have you got to lose?'

I was amazed and excited. *Could I get a dog? Could I have a dog again?* Dogs had always been in my life. I'd just presumed that now I was confined to a wheelchair there was no chance of ever having another one. And it had never crossed my mind that a dog could actually help me.

I always have loved dogs. My all-time favourite was an Australian shepherd called Blue. Despite the name, they're an American breed. Blue was actually Scott's dog before he married my twin sister, Julie. But I loved that dog so much it reached the stage where everyone figured she was better off with me.

Blue followed me everywhere. I used to mow the lawn using a ride-on tractor and she'd sit up on top. When she got bored she'd jump down and run behind, and no matter how tired she got she'd never leave. Sometimes she even came after me if I drove somewhere, only giving up when she ran out of puff. It was like we were joined at the hip, and when I got married and was posted to Keesler Air Force Base, it was only natural that Blue came with me.

But Blue couldn't share me with anyone. She just wasn't willing or able to. And she sure didn't like the idea of having to go halves on me with Carla. Whenever I left for work she'd go wild, giving Carla hell. If Carla left the door open, Blue would run off after me. It reached the stage where I had to call Mom and Dad and ask them to take Blue. She lived with my folks until the day she died, and I saw her whenever I was home. It wasn't perfect, but there was just no other way.

Blue was the last dog I'd had in a life in which dogs were always around. The idea of getting a CCI service dog was like an impossible promise of hope, one that I sure needed right now. I allowed myself to dream. If I could get a dog it could walk me and the boys to school. Wow. Imagine that.

*They're no longer the kids with the dad in the chair.*

*They're the kids with the world's coolest ever dog.*

It's very hard for special forces types to ask for help. It's not in our make-up – not even when you're former special forces and confined to a chair. It took me several years to do so, but what drove me to contact CCI was when I reached my lowest ebb. The dream of walking again that had sustained me had started to fade.

The brain surgery I'd had did nothing to stop the pain, and a few months previously the pain had finally triumphed. It had got the better of me. I was having ten to fifteen attacks every twenty-four hours. It spiked in three different ways. In the first, my right leg felt as if it was on fire, like it had been thrust into a furnace. In the second, it was as if someone had sunk an ice axe into my thigh. It was visual: whenever the pain hit, I would see the ice axe. The third was as if someone was burning me on my calf with a red-hot branding iron.

The doctors suggested further surgery. They proposed severing the nerves to my right leg, to reduce the pain. Reluctantly I agreed. When Carla had left I'd moved nearer to my folks, which had been a great help in raising the boys. We'd settled in McKinney, a suburb of Dallas. I was no longer in the military of course, so any surgery had to be at a civilian facility. This one would take place at the Centennial Medical Center, in nearby Frisco.

In part I agreed to have the surgery for my boys. I didn't want them to have to suffer pain-racked, tortured Dad. But although post-surgery I did have less pain, the paralysis rose higher up my body. On my right side it was now just below my waist. On my left side it was just below the level of my chest. And I could barely get any sense of movement in my legs at all. After the miracle of Dr Kao's surgery, this was a major reversal. I actually fell out of my chair a few times due to the resultant loss of muscle use and feeling.

But at least I could live. The pain had dropped to manageable levels, and that was heavenly.

If I could have kept the feeling in my legs there was always the chance of walking again. Now that was gone. The hope that Dr Kao had given me had pretty much died. That was devastating. At times it overwhelmed me. Sure, the pain no longer drove me to the very edge of madness, but the depression at my loss of mobility at times overwhelmed me.

One day I was flying somewhere and the airliner hit some really bad turbulence. All around me people were ashen-faced and some were panicking. I stared out the window with an icy calm. I said to myself, *I really do not give a shit if this flight goes down. Maybe it would be better that way.* That was how bad my state of mind had become.

Right then, getting a service dog was all the more vital for us as a family. It was the one thing that gave me hope. Potentially, it could be a lifesaver.

I sat my boys down so we could talk it through. 'Listen, guys, I've been thinking about getting a dog. A service dog. A dog that's trained to help guys like me – guys in a chair. The dog can help me around the house, open cupboards and stuff, and maybe even pull me in my chair when I'm tired. Plus it'll be someone to play with, just like we used to with Blue. So, what do you say?'

The smiles that lit up their faces said it all. They were overjoyed. *A dog? Could we really have a dog?* They'd figured with me in a chair a dog was impossible.

I explained some more about what it might be able to do for us as a family.

They were unanimous.

'Oh yeah, let's get a dog.'

'That'd be so cool.'

'Yeah, Daddy, let's get one.'

As I've said, it's in my nature not to reach out for help. I'd recently scalded my lap real bad, and all because I wouldn't ask someone to carry a takeout coffee for me. I was coming out of a fast-food joint with a litre cup perched in my lap, balancing it as I rolled along in my chair. But the person ahead of me let the door slam, and it smashed into the front of my chair. The impact knocked the coffee over. I had it jammed between my legs, and of course both hands were rolling my chair, so I had nothing to catch the cup with. The scalding hot coffee drained into my lap; I suffered third-degree burns and had to spend a week in hospital.

Ever since being in a chair, people would tell me, 'Oh yeah, I spent a week in a chair once when I broke my ankle. I know what it feels like. I can relate.'

I knew they were trying to be sympathetic, to empathize, but a voice would reply in my head, *No, you do not. You have absolutely no idea. One, because you knew it was only temporary, not for life. Two, because you have no idea of the pain.*

At times I'd endured three days in a row not sleeping, the pain was so bad. I had spent well over a year in hospital, which left me thinking, *When will it ever end?* Deprived of my dream of walking, I'd started to feel as if I had no worth. The paralysis was increasing – not decreasing – and it was stopping me from doing all the things I wanted in my life. *In our lives.*

I was left doing circles in a wheelchair.

While I didn't know exactly what a CCI dog could do for me, I was pretty desperate. Hell, I'd give anything a try. As Jackie had said, *What did I have to lose?*

There was a real gulf between what I wanted to do for myself, what I aspired to do, and what I was actually capable of. And it was killing me. But maybe, just maybe, that gulf could be filled in part by a service dog. Maybe with a dog at my side I wouldn't be confronted so much by my shortcomings. Maybe a dog could step in to help so I wouldn't have to ask.

Eventually I made myself pick up the phone and ask for help. I dialled CCI. From what I told them, they figured I would certainly satisfy their criteria. I was a wounded warrior, I was wheelchair-bound, and I was trying my best to raise a young family. After a little to-ing and fro-ing, I was told that a CCI trainer would be in the Dallas region shortly, and that I should see her for an interview.

I knew it was vital that I gave the right impression. I needed to be on time, pain-free and focused. Otherwise, how would I seem responsible enough to handle a CCI dog?

I drove out to the meeting, which was being held at one of the airport hotels at Dallas Fort Worth, but en route my truck went over a loose manhole cover. *Clang-bang!* The noise and the sensation threw a bolt of lightning up my spine. But worse, the sudden metallic thump from beneath the wheels brought it all flooding back to me . . .

Instantly I was in a white Chevvy SUV rolling down a jungle-clad mountainside. It was horrific. In my head I could see it all happening. It threw me completely. I had to pull over onto the roadside. I was hyperventilating and my mind was full of dark images. It wasn't the first time this had happened. Loose manholes could trigger some really bad shit. It seemed to take for ever to get my head back to something like normal, but I knew I just had to make that meeting.

I forced myself to drive and I reached the hotel just in time. The CCI trainer met me at reception. Her name was Becky Miller, and she looked to be in her mid-twenties. She had shoulder-length brown hair and a pleasant but efficient manner. No doubt about it, she was here in part to test me. She took me into a conference room and outlined the steps a candidate goes through to get a CCI dog.

Step 1: you had to show your level of disability qualified you for a dog. *Check.* Step 2: you had to establish that the kind of tasks a CCI dog can do would be useful in your day-to-day life. *Check.* Step 3: you had to ensure you had the financial means to keep a CCI dog. *Check.* Step 4: you had to meet a trainer and be able to handle a 'carpet dog'. *That's where we were right now.* Step 5: you would go to a CCI facility and get matched with a dog. *That's if I did OK today.*

CCI are rightfully very protective of their dogs. After all, it's a lifetime commitment for both human and animal. At any step – even number five – a candidate could fail.

In the conference room they had my carpet dog, a spool of heavy wire roughly in a dog shape, covered in brown carpet and with a lead attached. The goal of today was to see if I was able to handle a CCI dog. Some people are simply too disabled for that to be possible. Today I needed to prove I had the strength and the ability, not to mention the temperament.

Under Becky's instruction I had to issue the basic commands – 'Sit', 'Stay', 'Down' – and interact with my carpet dog so as to demonstrate my suitability and needs. Once I was done with the carpet dog, Becky asked me what I thought a CCI dog could most do for me. I pondered on that for a second. It was a question I'd not been anticipating.

'I mean, where should I start? There's just so much.' I glanced at Becky a little nervously. 'I guess one big need would be for my dog to retrieve my wheelchair. With three young boys they're forever messing with my chair. To them it's kind of a plaything. And I don't want to discourage that 'cause I want them to feel comfortable around my chair. But then I need to go somewhere and my chair's nowhere to be seen. Wow. If my dog could fetch that . . .'

Becky smiled. 'Sure, the dogs can be trained to go retrieve a chair.'

I felt encouraged. 'Or I just park it on an uneven surface. You know, like a wooden floor that's not been laid too well. Next moment I look and it's gone. Or I heard the dogs can help pull a chair. So, maybe I need to get over a kerb. Maybe the dog can help pull me onto the kerb. Help get my rear wheels up there. Front wheels, you just flip 'em up. But rear wheels, you got to lift your entire body weight.'

Becky nodded. 'There are some dogs, the more powerful ones, we do train with the 'Pull' command. We'd need to match you with that kind of dog.'

I smiled. 'Sure. That'd be great. That'd be just awesome. You know, we always had dogs as a family. My favourite, she was an Australian shepherd called Blue . . .'

I left the interview feeling pretty positive. Becky had kept her cards close to her chest, but I understood why. This wasn't her decision, and it would depend on whether they had a dog to match my needs. But there was one big positive. There were clearly lots of things I could do with a CCI dog that were near-impossible without one.

I thought Becky had seen that too. Or at least I hoped so.

There is always a long line of hopefuls waiting for a CCI dog, but wounded warriors – especially those who are single moms or fathers – do get priority. I got a call a few days later.

'We've got an opening in two months' time, in our November class,' the CCI caller told me. 'And we may just have a dog to suit your needs. Would you like me to book you into that training class graduation?'

I told her I would like that very much, and the date was set. I felt already as if I was walking on clouds.

A few weeks later I caught a flight from DFW to San Diego Airport, the nearest one to CCI's Oceanside facility. After all the trauma, pain and disappointment, I had taught myself not to hope too much. No great hopes, no massive let-downs. But as we jetted towards San Diego, I allowed myself to dare to dream a four-legged dream.

*A dog. A service dog. A battle buddy. Was there really one out there for me?*

I knew that even now it wasn't 100 per cent guaranteed that I would get one. I was still to be matched with a live animal. They would be testing me to see if I could handle the relationship, master the commands and make the right fit with the dogs they had available.

But, for the first time since flying into Ecuador for Dr Kao's surgery, I felt buoyed by a surge of hope. This was so different from my last flight anywhere. Then, I had been in a really dark place. But now the barest promise of hope had changed everything. Just the idea of a dog – the tantalizing possibility – so lifted me.

That may not seem like much to you, but trust me, to someone in a chair it is the promise of a miracle.

# CHAPTER 20

I hire a car with hand controls and drive to CCI's Oceanside facility. For the entire thirty minutes I am burning up with excitement. I hope they'll have my dog just waiting for me in a kennel and raring to go. But no, it's we humans who are about to be put to the test here.

My first impression of the CCI campus is what a beautiful location and set-up it is. There are lush semi-tropical gardens at every turn. I check in and get introduced to my class. There are eight of us, and rumour has it there are sixteen dogs from which we all have to find the perfect match. *The one.*

I get talking to one of my classmates. His name is Matthew Keillor, a former marine and a quadriplegic, so he's lost the use of both his legs and his arms. Being former military, he and I bond right away. He tells me his story. He was shot in the head by a sniper in Iraq. He's there with his wife, Tracy, who's had to do so much for him since his injury. It's clear from the get-go how much more Matthew needs a dog than me. He's as excited as I am. He's also nurturing similar hopes . . . and he's plagued by similar fears.

There is a part of me that still wonders if I'm worthy, but

then we get to see the dogs. The trainers demonstrate them in action, and I'm so excited I feel like I'm hyperventilating. I worry I won't be able to sleep a wink the entire time that I'm here. The dogs are incredible. I can only imagine how one of these will change my life. I can't wait to make one my own and take him home to meet the boys.

Matthew is immediately drawn to Guss, a yellow Labrador. The two of them fall in love. It's clearly the perfect match. They make eye contact straight away. Guss is pretty laid-back – like Matthew, in a way. But he clearly loves to work, and he gets very excited when he's running through his commands with Matthew in his chair. Because Matthew has such limited hand movement he needs a dog that can get right up into his lap to give him anything that he may have dropped. Guss is especially good at that.

I can't work out which dog I'm drawn to most. But there is one – Jackson – that I can't help thinking is right. He's a black Labrador–retriever cross, and he's a big, powerful, potent-looking beast. He strikes me as being outgoing and warrior-like, which curiously enough is still how I see myself. He's a dog with real posture and a tough-guy attitude. I can see us making a fine team.

We're a couple of days into the matching process and we head for dinner at a local restaurant. By chance, the CCI instructors are at an adjacent table. It's pretty funny really, because we know all their talk is about which of us will get matched with which dog.

'I'm pretty set on Guss,' Matt tells me. 'He's the one for me.'

I tell him what's obvious: 'Buddy, you and Guss, you're perfect.'

'So what about you?'

'Jackson. Jackson, it's gotta be. There's Napal too . . . I mean, if I had to. But no, Jackson. He's the one.'

'Yeah. You and Jackson seem good.' Matt glances in the direction of the CCI trainers. 'So, you figure we could bribe them with food and drink and stuff? Just to make sure we get the dog we want?'

I laugh. 'Sure. Screw the cost, whatever they want!'

The morning after the dinner we head to the main hall for our pre-match. This is where we get our initial pairing. Matthew's name gets called out, and sure enough he gets Guss. I tease him that must have cost him a fortune in bar bills. I wait. I am on edge. Before now none of us has had any alone time with the dogs; it's all been spent working with them under the scrutiny of the trainers.

After the pre-match the dog we're given will pretty much be our dog, that's unless the match goes off-track somehow. It will be the first time we get to relate to and love our dogs, rather than working with them. I hear my name called. I roll into the centre of the room. I'm looking towards Jackson, but little do I know my heart is to be claimed by another.

The instructor announces my match.

Suffice to say, I'm not getting Jackson. Jackson gets paired with a lady in a chair suffering from multiple sclerosis.

After the pre-match you get thirty minutes alone with your dog. It's a chance just to be. Prior to this all our time has been spent with the dogs on-leash, working through the fifty-odd commands they've mastered. We've had zero time just to be with them as a dog.

During our thirty minutes together I get a sense of the dog within the dog. I've been paired with a deeper, gentler soul – the lover not the fighter – the one who's ready to promise me his life, if I'll have him.

His name is Napal.

One thing had really struck me about Napal over the past two days. With some dogs, Jackson included, I had no idea who their CCI trainer was – the person responsible for their months of intensive in-house training. With Napal I knew instantly. It was Becky Miller, the lady who had interviewed me. I knew because every time she walked past he would stare at her intently. I had liked that in him. I liked that loyalty. But that's the first thought that strikes me now that I am matched with Napal. Will I be able to attract the same loyalty and devotion as Becky did?

Napal and I work together, running through all the commands and exercises that he knows so well. He even has this extraordinary special bark that he's been trained to produce if ever his companion is in trouble. It's a monstrous, ferocious 'AAAAROOUUUGGGH!' It's like an explosion in his lungs.

I imagine what this would mean for me. I can warn the neighbours: 'Hey, if you ever hear my dog bark like this you need to come to my aid, 'cause it means I'm in trouble.'

Amazing.

That evening is the first in which we get to keep the dog we're paired with overnight. We each have a room to ourselves, with a shared kitchen and common area. I go to fetch a Coke and wish my fellows goodnight, and it's the first time that day I'm not with Napal. I've left him lying on the dog duvet in my room. The CCI trainers are really particular that the dogs aren't left to wander around, so I've made sure the door is shut tight.

As I left Napal threw me a look that could melt anyone's heart. It spoke to me so powerfully. *There's so much love, devotion and companionship in here, if you'll only have me. Stand by me, and I'll be your battle buddy until the day I die.*

I'm in the kitchen chatting away with Matthew and some of the others, when all of a sudden they start to smile and to laugh. Something behind me has got their attention. I turn to discover that it's Napal. He has his head poked round the common-room door and his doleful eyes are upon me. *Just checking that you're still here. We're friends for life, right?*

Somehow he's managed to open the door to my bedroom and find me. It's so incredibly touching I can't find it in myself to reprimand him. Instead, I join the others in laughter. I figure I can see the hint of a smile on Napaly-wag's face. Napaly-wag is what the trainers have nicknamed him, because whenever he is especially happy he wags so much his entire back end gyrates to and fro.

We return to our room. There are two beds: a single, hospital-style bed that I can lower, making it easier to get into from my chair, plus a normal double. I take the hospital bed, with Napal on his mattress on the floor. I'm just drifting off to sleep when Napal stands at the bedside, his eyes on mine, pleading.

I know what he's asking: he wants up on the bed.

'Come on, boy. Jump! Jump!'

With one leap he's got his bulk beside me on the narrow mattress. This sure feels cramped. I guess he wants a quick snuggle and then he'll jump down. But I don't know Napal. He inches closer and closer, until finally he's got his full weight laid right across my chest. That's seventy pounds of black Labrador we're talking about here.

It's clear he has no intention of moving, so I get us to shift across to the double bed. That way there'll be plenty of room for him to lie beside me. But, oh no, not this dog. Napal gets right back on my chest again. I can feel his heart beating skin-close to my own. I figure he can feel mine. It's as if they're one.

And somehow we sleep like that all night long.

I wake in the morning cramped and stiff and sore, but very much smitten. We've spent just twenty-four hours together, yet already I know I am exactly where I need to be. I've bonded with my dog, and I know already this is a bond that can never be broken.

I am so glad the trainers picked the dog and not me. It's one hell of a skill to be able to do that. I owe it to them that I have got Napal.

It feels as if we were meant to be. Like it's predestined; like we have known each other all our lives. All our lives we'd been building up to this one special moment – the meeting.

That morning we have a round-table discussion. The trainers go round us all asking the same questions: 'What was your experience like?' 'Any concerns?' 'Any good things or bad things?' 'What did you do?'

When it comes to me I only have four words: 'I love this dog.'

The room dissolves into laughter.

'OK, hey, that's good. But can you expand upon that a little?'

I tell them the story of Napal lying on top of me all night long. 'I ache all over, but I wouldn't have it any other way.'

That becomes my catchphrase for my entire time at CCI: *I ache all over, but I wouldn't have it any other way.*

Napal and I enter a period of intensive training, learning to address any special needs that I have. One is getting to my wheelchair. If ever I am parted from my chair, crawling and dragging my legs behind me to get to it really isn't an option. We also try to work out a procedure for Napal to help me get my chair over a roadside kerb. Neither of these is within the standard CCI repertoire; they're not among the fifty commands the dogs get taught. I work with the lead trainer, a guy called Todd, who is a true magician with dogs. We adapt the 'Fetch' command: 'Fetch my chair! Fetch my chair!' In no time Napal has learned to go to where my chair is, grab it with his teeth and drag it back to me.

For the kerb manoeuvre we need to find something that Napal can grab and pull, to help get my wheels over. Todd works out that the best thing is a tough pouch clipped to the bottom of my chair seat. We practise me rolling up to a kerb, wheelie-ing up the front wheels until they're resting on it – at which point Napal grabs the pouch in his teeth, helping pull my rear wheels over.

We run through the fifty other commands, just to ensure we've got them sorted. Some are positional, indicating where exactly you want your dog. 'Front' – positioned right in front, facing you. 'Rear' – similar but behind you. 'Heel' – the left side of the chair, snug and close. 'Side' – the same but on the right. 'Under' – under a chair or table, to get him right out of the way (particularly useful in a crowded bar).

Others are action commands. 'Get' – grab an object off the

ground. 'Give' – place that object in your hand. 'Drop' – drop it on the floor. 'Up' – put two front paws on whatever surface is indicated (so, for example, to give a cashier your wallet). 'Tug' – grab a rope handle and open something (say a fridge). 'Switch' – flip on a light switch with the nose. 'Push' – close a drawer or a door until it latches shut.

I learn to use all the commands with Napal. It is amazing. Magical. I feel as if I can talk to this dog and he understands my every word. More than that, I feel almost as if I'm getting some of my lost mobility back. My partnership with Napal is going to give me the kind of freedom I could only dream of.

The final few days at CCI are a flurry of tests. I have to take Napal to a shopping mall, load up a basket, pay at the checkout and pack it into the car, all with him assisting. At times the CCI trainers are pushing him to the very limit. They drop a juicy steak at Napal's feet and expect him to carry on with his duties regardless. They scatter doggie treats all around him. They pet him and make a fuss of him and try to get him to abandon his task. But for every moment that we are together Napal is faultless – he sticks rigidly by my side.

The written exams follow, in which I have to prove I understand the use of the verbal commands and show I can read and interpret a dog's body language. Some of it is obvious: with Napaly-wag, tail wagging means that he's happy, and he's always wagging his tail whenever he's working. But I need to know when my dog is in pain or if he's unwell – telltale signs being drooping ears or a dryness of the muzzle.

We move on to more complex problem-solving. A laundry basket is placed in front of a light switch. Task: get your dog to turn the light on and off. I get Napal to grab the rope attached to the laundry basket and give the 'Tug' command, at which point he pulls it out of the way. I point at the light and issue the 'Switch' command. He turns it on. I give the 'Push' command and he flicks it off again.

Task complete.

The two weeks seem to have flown by. The day of our passing-out comes around. The entire CCI campus fills with visitors. I wonder who all these people are. I had no idea this was going to be such a big deal. I was down so low before I flew up here I haven't invited anyone. Not a soul. I didn't have a clue what a life-transforming experience this was going to be.

But back then I hadn't met Napal.

Just prior to the graduation ceremony Becky, Napal's trainer, lets me in on a secret. 'So, I shouldn't really say this, but we knew you and Napal were the perfect match. We just knew it long before you met. With most handlers we don't know until they've got a feel for the dog. But with you, there was only ever the one.'

I shake my head in wonder. 'Yeah, I'm so thankful. I hate to say it, but at first I was kinda looking towards Jackson. I'm so glad you guys called it, and not me!'

Becky smiles. 'Napal. It was only ever going to be Napal.'

# CHAPTER 21

This year's graduation takes place off campus, in the nearby Mission San Luis Rey church hall. It's the only place that's big enough to house everyone: graduates, families, friends, supporters, dogs.

There are forty-odd dogs being brought in by their puppy raisers to matriculate, plus our entire class is graduating. The hall is packed. It's standing room only. Luckily, it comes equipped with two giant video screens on which the events will be shown, so even those at the very back can see.

Everything is carefully orchestrated. First, the forty puppy raisers gather on stage and formally accept this is the moment to hand back their dogs. Then it's time for the eight graduations. I'm scheduled to go on last, because I've been chosen to give the graduation speech. I figure I'll tell the audience a little about my accident, my disability, and how Napal will turn my life around.

I guess that should do it.

Right now Napal isn't with me. He's somewhere in the audience with his puppy raiser, Jim Siegfried. Jim drove over this morning and he's been enjoying a little time alone with Napal, while we graduates prepare for the coming ceremony. I've yet to meet Jim, and I know next to nothing about him.

The announcer reads out a short biography of each graduating dog, as a video showing images of the dog's life plays on the screen. The puppy raisers have sent in photos and video from which CCI have compiled the clips. Napal's bio and his video come last. Once that's done, Jim Siegfried makes his way through the audience towards the stage, leading Napal by his leash.

'So, our last graduate today is Jason Morgan, one of our wounded warriors . . . with Napal,' says the announcer. 'Napal was raised by puppy raiser Jim Siegfried, a veteran supporter of CCI.' Jim meets me mid-stage and hands across the lead, as the announcer continues: 'And guess what? It's Jason Morgan's birthday today, and what better way to celebrate than getting his service dog.'

He turns to me. 'So, Jason, I'll hand over to you to say a few words.'

He's right, of course. It is my birthday. With all the excitement and the emotion of the past few days I'd almost forgotten. But it isn't that which leaves me all but speechless. Dumbfounded.

It's that Napal's puppy raiser is also in a wheelchair.

As I take the microphone and turn to face the audience, I've got a zillion questions pinging through my head. I figure Jim Siegfried must be a fellow paraplegic, yet somehow he can find it in himself to be a CCI puppy raiser. I find myself thinking, *Here's a guy who could use a dog himself, but he dedicates his time to raising them for others. He's paralyzed from the waist down, and yet he's raised a dog for me.*

It is truly amazing. I am blown away.

'So, you know, I guess most people spend their birthdays

having a party with family and friends,' I begin. 'But, on balance, I'd far rather be where I am now –' I glance at Napal and at Jim Siegfried '– with a new family and friends . . .'

As I talk, I can't get my mind off this stunning revelation: *Napal's puppy raiser is himself in a chair.* I don't know how my speech has gone down because my mind's only half there. I figure I should conjure up a bit of theatre to round things off. Over the past few days I've taught Napal to wave. He's even got into the habit of doing it with the other dogs, which is hilarious.

I give the 'Wave' command. Napal lifts one paw and . . . he waves to the crowd. The audience breaks into a wild round of applause. There is no doubt that Napal – and, well, maybe me too – has proved something of a hit today.

After we're finished, a figure from the crowd seeks me out. She shakes me by the hand and asks if I remember her. I have to confess that I don't, but I explain that my pain medication can make my memory somewhat hazy.

'I'm Jackie,' she tells me, 'the lady at the Challenge Air show, the one who persuaded you to reach out to CCI . . . and now you're here getting your dog!'

I'm touched that she's there, and touched by all those who share their happiness that I've finally found my battle buddy, Napal. But mostly, I'm fascinated to get some quality time with Jim Siegfried, and to learn something of his story – chair to chair, as it were.

This is an intensely personal moment, one that I guess we feel should be shared by just the two of us, somewhere alone. Jim says he knows of a nearby bar, on El Camino Real, the historic 'Royal Road'. It's called The Back Stop, and it's a bit of a spit-and-sawdust kind of place, but it should be real quiet this time of day.

I tell him it sounds perfect. We head over there. The Back Stop is a big sports bar – maybe a 250-seater – the kind of place that's just right for two guys in chairs to lose themselves with their dog. For I guess that's what Napal is now: right now, at this moment, he belongs to the both of us.

It's late in the afternoon and there's a football match playing on several widescreen TVs. It provides a background buzz to cover our talk. We order a couple of dark beers and clink glasses.

'To Napal.'

'To Napal.'

'So, quite a day, huh?' Jim ventures. 'All I knew about you was you were an injured air force vet. I had no idea you were in a chair.'

'Hell, me neither. I mean, you raised Napal in a chair?'

'Uh-huh. He's my third dog. My third CCI puppy.'

'You raised three dogs in a chair? Jeez. How did you do that?'

Jim tells me his story. He explains the life path that put him in a chair and what took him to CCI. I am amazed that he has raised three dogs, yet never had a service dog of his own. I tell him a little about my own life. He is amazed in turn that I am raising three small boys from a chair, and pretty much on my own. I guess I've never looked at it that way. I guess it is amazing.

I explain to Jim that I've started doing a little football coaching with my boys. He tells me he's been coaching pretty much all his adult life. It's another bond that we share.

'Well, you know, I was thinking about teaching Napal to go

fetch the kick-off tee. You figure he could do that?'

Jim spreads his hands. Smiles. 'Already done.'

'You already taught him that?'

'Yeah! I mean done.'

'I figure I can teach him to fetch stuff for me around the house, like my shoes from the lounge . . .'

'Uh-huh. Already done.'

'Shoes?'

'Shoes. From where I leave 'em by the couch.'

'Jeez. Well, this is perfect. He's the dog of my dreams.'

'Uh-huh.'

Jim reaches into his bag and pulls out a big, heavy leather-bound book. It's fastened with a blue ribbon, and doubly secured with a small clip-together luggage strap. Threaded onto the strap is a key ring, and on the key ring is a bunch of metal dog tags. I can see right away they are Napal's tags.

Jim slides it across the table to me. 'So, this is for you. It's kind of like a handover album.' He smiles. 'I've never done one before, 'cause the first dog didn't graduate and the second became a breeder dog.' He opens it at the first page. 'So, this is Napal with his brothers and sisters – Nelson, Naya, Nella – and that's their family tree. See Terence there, that's his father. I raised him too.'

He turns the page. Staring out at me is a photo of Napal as a puppy, his head nestled on the edge of a blue puppy carrier. Below runs a typed caption: 'Napal. 3 months old. Sitting in his carrier while visiting Jim's sister.'

'Yeah, you know, that's Napal not long after I first got him. Well, the captions kind of tie it all together.'

I flick through the pages, the album chronicling the life man and puppy led long before I got to meet either of them. I can sense the closeness between Jim and Napal. It speaks powerfully from these pages. I can feel the special connection. I can sense how difficult it must have been for Jim handing over this dog, this very special dog.

The album is a precious record of their lives together and all the love that has been poured into making this moment possible – the final handover. It chronicles their adventures together as far away as New York and Ontario. Jim and Napal's exploits have clearly been legion, and I know that I will always be indebted to the incredibly humble and generous-hearted guy sitting in the chair before me.

It's a sign of the greatness of the man that he can tell me he's so pleased that Napal has made the grade and graduated. He's deeply honoured that Napal is going to a wounded veteran and that he's accounted for himself so well. These are difficult words for Jim to say. In essence he's saying, *I'm glad Napal can forget me enough to bond with you.*

But a dog never forgets entirely. It never forgets a person or their smell. Napal will never forget Jim no matter how long he may live. But I appreciate his words enormously. He's an easy-going guy and a truly warm-spirited individual. He and Napal must have made the perfect match.

'For every glory there comes a little suffering,' Jim tells me almost as if he can read my mind. 'For every glory there comes a little suffering.'

I respect and cherish him for it.

We say our farewells in the parking lot, me promising to come back and visit. There is a CCI fundraiser planned in a few weeks' time, and Jim figures maybe I could speak at it. We make some promises to meet, and I thank him from the bottom of my heart. Jim rolls towards his Chrysler, me towards my hire car.

He half turns back to me. 'You got a great dog there. You've got a great dog.'

I smile my heartfelt gratitude. 'Yeah, I know. And Jim . . . thanks.'

As Jim turns away and rolls across to his vehicle, he's struggling to hold back his tears. He pauses for a moment at the wheel of his Chrysler. He'd raised Napal for a special person, that disabled kid who had such pressing needs; to help a kid like his own Down's syndrome brother. Instead, Napal has come to me, a wounded warrior with three young boys to raise. Jim's ended up rearing a four-legged angel who will help *four lives* – three of whom are children.

It's perfect.

On the drive home to Santee Jim's smiling and crying. He's smiling through his tears all the way home.

# CHAPTER 22

The very next day Napal and I have to fly back to Texas. It will be my first experience of taking a dog on an aircraft. One of the final lessons at CCI was about preparing for the onward journey with our dogs. There is no charge for taking a service dog on a flight, and no carrier can refuse passage. At the very least the dog must be permitted to lie beneath your feet. That's the law.

But once you're home, there are no laws governing how your family should treat your dog. So you need to impose some. The golden rule is no petting when the dog is in his or her CCI harness. The harness means the dog is working and cannot be treated like a pet or distracted. In fact, Napal's harness has printed on it in big letters I'M WORKING. PLEASE DON'T PET ME.

We board the flight to DFW airport and a friendly flight assistant finds a place for me with a spare seat beside it for Napal. A gaggle of air hostesses takes the row behind us. I can hear them chatting away about my dog. Right now a group of pretty ladies are paying me – or, rather, Napal – some serious attention, and this is an entirely new experience – or at least it is ever since I've been in a wheelchair.

I eye Napal and give him the 'Up' command, nodding in their direction. He gets onto his hindquarters, turns his head round and breaks into a wide, goofy smile. He really can dazzle when he wants. I've cleaned his teeth this morning with a special doggie brush and toothpaste and the results speak for themselves.

There is a chorus of gushing 'Ooohs' and 'Aaahs' from the ladies. One of them turns to me, her face radiant. 'Hey, you know something, that is such a gorgeous dog. Where did you get him?'

The flight is seriously delayed, but I'm in seventh heaven chatting with the girls all about CCI. I'm starting to think that there may be unexpected spin-offs from getting a dog like Napal.

I can't wait to get home and show him to my boys. Blake, Austin and Grant have been staying over at their mother's while I was away at CCI. She's moved into a house in McKinney to be near them. I want the boys to see her as much as they can, though it does feel odd dropping them over at her place.

Recently I bought myself a silver Mercedes SUV. It's second hand, which was all I could afford, but it's smart and a joy to drive. It doesn't have a winch or a crane or even a disabled ramp. The only concession to my handicapped status is the hand controls.

We touch down at DFW, and Napal and I roll across to the airport parking lot. I park my chair beside the driver's door and use my shoulder and arm muscles to lift myself from there into the driver's seat. The Mercedes sits high off the ground and it's a real lift to get up there, but at least it keeps my upper body in shape.

Yet, as I swing myself into the driver's seat, I hear something fall. I know instantly what it is. I've dropped my car keys. Normally this would be a real drama. I'd have to lower myself back into my chair, bend to retrieve them, then repeat the entire process of getting back into the vehicle. But barely have I had the thought before Napal whips up my keys in his mouth and holds them up to me.

I didn't even have to issue a single command.

I take the keys, then lean down to give him a pet. 'Good boy. Good dog. Hey, you're one good boy, Napal.'

He snuffles and sneezes and gives that Napaly-wag – entire butt gyrating back and forth – just to show how happy he is right now.

I collapse my chair, removing the wheels, flip it up into the passenger seat and shove the wheels into the rear. Last, I give Napal the 'Up' command and pat the seat beside me. He jumps in, riding shotgun.

I drive us home. The boys and I live in Stonebridge, a large subdivision of McKinney. The houses are built of this warm, golden-brown stone – hence the name – and all the power cables and phone lines have been routed underground. There are parks and golf courses interspersed with blocks of housing, and this gives the area an open, almost country feel.

We've got a four-bed house with a yard out the back, which is fine for the four of us. Well, five now with Napal. There is only one drawback. The house has a short driveway, which is kind of steep. If I try to get into my chair on the drive it has a habit of rolling away from me and scooting down the road. If that happens, I'm trapped until someone – usually one of the boys – can retrieve it. So, just having Napal beside me and knowing he can fetch my runaway chair gives me this wonderful feeling. It's one of confidence; of mobility. I can arrive home, park and not have to worry about being stranded in my vehicle, or face the embarrassment of having to ask some passing neighbour to fetch my chair.

We head inside and I show Napal around his new home. I take him to the games room, which is full of my boys' football trophies, plus memorabilia from my time in the military. I show him each of the boys' rooms and explain who sleeps in which. I show him our room, as Napal will sleep in there with me. As a service dog he's always on call.

The bedroom overlooks the rear yard, which is ringed by solid wooden fencing. There's a ceramic garden warmer – a chiminea – on the patio, so the boys and I can sit out long into the evening gathered around our 'camp fire' as we like to call it. It isn't exactly going hiking in the Rockies, like we used to with their mom, but it's something. There's even a dog door set into the rear door of the house, which means Napal can go out and use the bathroom whenever he feels the need.

I kill time until the boys are due home by grooming Napal. In the lounge we have a wraparound, L-shaped sofa. It's got electronic push-buttons, so you can recline the seats and extend the footrests. When fully reclined it's about the most comfortable place I can be, for most normal, upright chairs cause me back pain.

I take up a position on the couch and pat the seat beside me. 'Come on, up! Up! Come join me!'

Napal leaps up, giving a comfortable kind of growl-yawn. *Wow. This looks great. Couch time.*

CCI taught us how important it is to groom our dogs, because grooming time is special time. It's real one-on-one bonding with your dog. I use a normal toothbrush to clean Napal's teeth. You can buy special dog toothbrushes, but they don't seem much different to me. Careful with the toothpaste though: if you've ever put dog toothpaste on your brush by mistake, you'll quickly realize your mistake! *Yuk.*

I lift up Napal's top right lip, exposing a row of teeth, including his big white canines. As I start to scrub he keeps trying to lick up the toothpaste. I get him to hold still long enough to scrub them all clean, but then he shakes loose and laps up all the foam. We have that fight three times: right side, left side and dead front.

I give his teeth a final inspection. They're gleaming. 'Good boy. Oh, your breath smells good! Good boy. You don't have that puppy breath any more.'

I give the command 'Roll left,' and Napal rolls onto his left side. I grab a tube of Nutri-Vet Ear Cleanse Liquid for Dogs. It comes in a soft plastic tube, with a photo of a Golden Lab on one side. Emblazoned across the other is the promise '100% guaranteed removes dirt and dissolves wax.' I lift one of his ears, take a cotton-wool ball and work it deep inside.

We spent an entire day at CCI learning how to clean, groom and care for our dogs. Labs have floppy ears, which tend to hold in the moisture, leaving the inside prone to infections. So a good, regular ear clean is key. Dogs don't have eardrums, so you can push the cotton wool right in as deep as it can go.

Oddly enough, Napal likes having his ears cleaned. I can see his eyes flickering around, as he tries to get a look at me. There's an expression on his face that he only ever has at ear-cleaning time: *Man, that feels weird. But you know what . . . Keep doin' it! It's good!*

Napal is less keen on what comes next: nail trimming. I grab my Dremel 7700 electric drill. It's fitted with a nail-file attachment – a small, abrasive metal cylinder, like a tiny electric sander. I tell him 'Paw' and – slowly, reluctantly – he stretches out a forepaw. I flick the 'On' switch and the drill emits a horrible high-pitched whine. I hold the whirring disc to a nail and start to grind some of the excess away. I can imagine how unpleasant this must feel. But I have to be firm. I have to get those claws short enough so that he won't scrabble and flail about on the stone tile flooring, or gouge the walls when turning light switches on and off.

Napal relaxes into it, or at least he tries to. I keep talking to him and reassuring him: 'Good boy. Good boy.'

I issue a firm 'Don't' when he tries to pull his paw away. 'Napal, don't. 'Doh-on't. Come on, boy. You're OK.'

One after the other I grind his nails down. I know how much he hates this, but we both know there is some really good stuff still to come. Nail grinding done, I grab a Kong Zoom Groom rubber dog comb, and using long strokes from his shoulders down to his tail I shake loose any fur. Napal stretches out on the couch and shivers and groans with delight.

'You just hate this, don't you, Napal. This is horrible. *Horrible*.'

Then I move on to the Furminator. At the end of each Furminator stroke I hit the 'Release' button and drop a comb full of dog hair into the carrier bag that lies open on the couch.

I get him to sit up facing me, so I can do his head. 'Sta-ay. Stay. OK, good boy. There you go, Napal, there you go.'

I finish with his tail. The tail is the worst for shedding hair, especially with Napaly-wag. It'll spread fur all over the house if I don't regularly 'furminate' it.

'You know what?' I tell him. 'One of these days we'll get you down to PetSmart. Bet you'd love that, eh? They do a massive discount for service dogs. I hear it's twenty dollars for a full shampoo and trim. A bargain.'

I issue the final grooming command: 'Napal – stand.' The last area I have to do is his tummy. 'Good boy. Stay. Stay. There you go.'

Once I figure I'm done I give him a proper look over. 'OK, I got everything but your back paws. Pretty good.'

The carrier bag is half full of dog hair. The last thing you'd ever want is to take your dog into a restaurant, and for him to leave the floor covered in hair. It may be the law that your service dog is allowed everywhere you go, but we've been taught to treat it as a privilege as well. Our dogs can go where no other dogs are allowed. We have to respect that.

Grooming done, I figure we're ready for Napal to meet the boys.

When I was a kid there was a cat that used to sit on top of the dividing fence between our backyard and the neighbours'. It would taunt our dogs and send them barking wild. So one day my dad went into the garage, came up the side access where the cat couldn't see him and popped it with a BB gun. All we could hear was the cat going 'WOOOOOOUUGHHHH' as it tore off out of there. Dad had used a soft pellet, so the cat suffered no lasting harm, but it sure never sat on our fence again!

We have a cat that sits on our McKinney fence line. As I wait for the boys, I try to get Napal to see it through the glass. 'Napal! Napal! Cat! Cat! See it off! See it off!'

Napal jumps and barks at the glass, but he can't seem to see past his own reflection. I roll into the yard and call him out there. 'Cat! Cat! See it off!'

He jumps and prances about, knowing there's something exciting going on, but no matter how much I point him in the direction of the cat he just doesn't see her. She sits there with her fur fluffed out against the cold, eyes staring big and unblinking at my dog. Finally, she leaps down lazily on her side of the fence.

Her claws scratch the wood as she jumps, and Napal hears. His head snaps round to where the cat's just been; he hustles over to the fence, snuffling about busily . . . but he's five minutes too late. The cat's long gone. This dog is no natural-born hunter but, hell, you just got to love him.

As I hoped they would be, Blake, Austin and Grant are instantly smitten with Napal. I'd phoned them from CCI, so they knew what kind of dog we were getting, but still they've been dying to get home and meet him in person. When I do a show and tell of what he can do – including a selection of the fifty-odd verbal commands – they're speechless.

They gaze at Napal with big, round awestruck eyes.

'Wow. You can talk to him.'

'But how does he understand?'

'Awesome.'

It's one thing getting a new pet; it's quite another getting a $50,000 service dog who will revolutionize our lives. Plus the boys can see immediately the change that Napal has wrought in me: *I'm smiling*. To them, that's close to a miracle. If that's all my dog ever does for us, it's enough. With Napal at my side I am happier than I've been in an age.

'Hey, you know, can I be the one that gets to feed him?' Blake, my eldest, asks.

It's tough for me to feed and water a dog from a wheelchair, and I sense how much Blake wants this. He has this natural way with animals, a certain special kind of magic. I'd figured this was how it would pan out, and Blake is overjoyed when I appoint him as Napal's official feeder and waterer. From now on that will be his duty exclusively. Like many kids, Blake can find it hard to relate to adults unless he knows them. Sometimes he has a problem making eye contact or working out if someone is joking or not. It is completely different with animals, and especially with my new dog.

I give Napal the 'Release' command, which lets him know that he's no longer working, and my boys and their new friend dash out into the yard. They spend a good thirty minutes out there, playing ball and rough-housing. Once they're done Blake asks if it's time to give Napal his chow. I tell him to go right ahead. He's overjoyed.

But mostly my boys are happy just to see their dad so full of life and laughter. Somehow, just having Napal around seems to have made their pain-wrecked father happy. It's almost as if the dog has managed to de-stress me and take the edge off my pain, and it's the pain that brings on the worse of my moods. This is the impossible joy of a dog who has brought us . . . hope.

Blake feeds and waters Napal. I watch, quietly, as a beautiful scene unfolds between the two of them. Austin and Grant have headed for the games room to watch some TV. But not Blake. He gets Napal to roll onto his back on the cool, tiled floor of the lounge, so he can scratch his tummy. Napal goes all gooey-eyed and floppy, and his paws curl over with delight.

Then Blake takes one of Napal's paws gently in his hand and touches his fingers to each of my dog's velvety-soft pads. Palm to palm, boy to dog. Blake does the same with each of Napal's four paws, one finger to every pad – as if this is their special ritual, as if now he's really got to meet and to know my dog.

Wow. This is just so incredible. What a gift this dog is. I really did need the lover, not the fighter.

I had thought I needed Jackson. In fact, I needed Napal.

# CHAPTER 23

Late that afternoon I head out with Napal for our first real experience flying solo, just the two of us getting some groceries. My boys consume milk like it's going out of fashion, plus I use it to wash down my painkillers, so as a family we drink it by the bucketful. I need to buy two one-gallon cartons plus a few other supplies.

As we roll out the door I issue a little apology to my dog. 'Hey, I hope you don't mind, buddy, but I used your toothbrush to clean your grooming comb. To get the hair out. Hope you don't mind that.'

Napal doesn't seem bothered. He's just excited to be heading out on a mission, and what a mission it will prove to be.

I'm used to rolling around the grocery store real quick. Folks tend to give me a wide berth, and I can understand why. It's hard to tell just by looking why I'm in a chair. I might have mental disabilities. I might not be able to hear or talk very well. People are afraid of what they don't know, so it's easiest to pretend the guy in the chair isn't there. To walk on by.

So, I'm used to rolling through superfast. But today proves a little different. Everywhere we go people keep stopping me, and it's all because they want to talk to my dog. Kids in particular are drawn to him. There is something about Napal that speaks to children. Kids adore him.

There is a dilemma here. People love to pet my dog, but they shouldn't pet my dog when he's working, because it stops him from working. It takes Napal and me an hour to do what would normally take five minutes. At one point I get real frustrated at all the interruptions; I just want to grab the milk and get out of there.

I'm cornered at the dairy counter and I just can't seem to break away. The pain is peaking, and all I want to do is get home and wash down some of my painkillers with a long slug of milk. But Napal has a way of making everyone light up, and finally he gets me smiling too. I de-stress, and magically the pain seems to melt away. Eventually, I'm laughing along with the rest of them. It's impossible to be bad-tempered around this dog.

'Hey, Napal, grab the bread. Go grab the bread.'

Napal grabs a loaf by the sealed end, so as not to damage it, and drops it in the basket perched on my lap. The crowd watches and they're fascinated. Captivated. If you've never seen a service dog at work, the first time is utterly amazing. You'll never believe a man and dog can be so close; so intuitive. The kids follow us around the store. Even the over-large lady at the checkout seems smitten. Before today she's never much noticed me. Now she gives me the broadest of smiles.

'Y'all real showstoppers, huh? You and your dawg.' She packs my groceries and helps lift them into my lap. 'Y'all come back now, y'hear.'

On the way to the car I roll my chair with a hand on either

wheel, the right also gripping Napal's leash. By law and for his own safety he has to be on-leash at all times when we're out in public, although I know he'd never dream of wandering an inch from my side.

Halfway to the vehicle something falls from my bag. It's a packet of frankfurters, another Morgan family staple. I go to pick it up, then catch myself. Imagine trying to bend to ground level when you're paralyzed from the waist down, and when stretching your back causes a mass of pain. Plus I've got the basket perched in my lap.

But today I remind myself that I have Napal.

He eyes me excitedly. *Oh can I? Can I? Can I?*

This is his big moment. I give the command 'Get.' He whips the frankfurters up in his jaws and places the packet daintily in the bag nestled in my lap. The car is still a distance away. I think, *To hell with it.* I'm tired. I'm in pain. That hour in the store was so unexpectedly uplifting, but also wearing. I tell myself, *Let the dog take the strain.*

I grab the pull handle attached to his service harness, give the command 'Pull,' and Napal runs me to my vehicle. If I turn my hand left it twists the harness left, and Napal steers that way, vice versa if I twist right. By the time we reach the Mercedes a crowd has gathered. My car has plates that ID me as a disabled veteran, so I guess most can figure how I ended up in a chair. They ask if they can help load the car. I thank them but let them know my dog and I have got it.

*My dog and I have got it all.*

The last time I ever felt this much the centre of attention – let's be honest about it – I was tall, dark and handsome. I was the guy who dived out of planes and could run like the wind. I don't blame people for looking askance at me in my chair. It's hard to approach someone when you don't know the boundaries. It's easier to ignore them. I get that. I really do. But today, with Napal at my side, all of that seems to have changed. Maybe this is a one-off. Maybe with time the wonder-dog effect will wear thin. But right now I'm walking – or, rather, I'm rolling – on clouds.

On the drive home I reflect upon the miracle of our first day flying solo. With Napal it's not so much what he does for me physically – the assisting, the service – so much as what he does for me socially and psychologically. Today, in that grocery store, with those everyday people, he was my bridge to the outside world; to the able-bodied normal. I wasn't expecting that. No one at CCI briefed me about that. And, right now, it is the most amazing revelation of all.

We reach home. I take my meds and figure I need a shower. We're planning on having a barbecue later, so I'll need to get busy. I get in the cubicle, turn on the water hot and strong, and the steam fuzzes up the glass. It's then that I spy something on the outside of the misted shower cubicle. It's a nose. It's a moist, wet, jet-black nose with a curious eager pair of eyes behind it. I know exactly what my dog is thinking. I can read it in his eyes. *Hey! That's water. You're in there in the water! I love water. I wanna be in there with you!*

That evening my boys and I spark up the barbecue. It's winter and there's a chill in the air, but it's a dry night and there's not a breath of wind. I get a blaze going in the chiminea and we stop out late, the boys sipping colas and me a beer. The heavens above us are crystal clear and star bright. For a suburban kind of neighborhood McKinney still has real wide-open spaces that let the sky and the earth breathe. It's one of the main reasons we chose to live here.

When the chill gets too much, the four of us retire to the massive L-shaped couch in the lounge. Sorry, that's *five* of us. Napal refuses to countenance not having his place on the sofa. He ends up stretched out across the laps of my three boys.

They're in heaven. So am I. So is my dog.

'You good boy,' I tell him. 'You big baby. You comfortable? You crazy dog. You crazy dog.'

It's a weekday night, and the boys have school tomorrow, but I allow them to stay up late. Finally they retire to their rooms and it's just me and Napal. He does a repeat of our first night together at CCI: he climbs on top of me, until he's lying right across my chest. He's blocking any view of the TV but I don't mind.

'Attaboy! There's room for us both up here. Good boy.'

But Napal is a seventy-pound dog and he's lying right on top of my worst injury. The pain in my back starts to spike.

I pat the seat beside me. 'Come on, buddy, you're going to have to get off. Come on, over here.' Napal doesn't want to budge. 'You don't want to get off? Come on! Look at this!'

By refusing to get down Napal makes me laugh. I laugh at myself. I laugh at the two of us, and the laughter relaxes me. Miraculously the pain starts to fade away.

We retire late. I place Napal's doggie duvet on the floor beside my bed, lift myself from my chair onto the mattress and wish Napal the warmest-ever goodnight. We're two weeks and one day into our partnership and already this dog has changed everything. I thank him from the bottom of my heart.

But it's not long before I sense Napal beside me. He's restless. I can feel his eyes upon my face. I'm tired, the pain in my back and legs seems to have dropped to near zero, and I have to take advantage of the pain-free hours to snatch some sleep.

I open one eye. I take a peek.

Napal's got his head on the side of the bed, his fire-bright eyes on mine. I know he wants something. I guess it's time for a goodnight pet. I reach out to stroke his head, but he pulls away. Odd. Weird. Why is he doing that? Is he upset with me somehow? He puts his head back, I try to pet him again, but again he pulls away. I figure I must have done something wrong, but what?

He turns away, heads to the bottom of the bed and puts his chin on it, where he's too far away for me to reach him. He's trying to tell me something, I just don't know what. Eventually I get it: it's his way of asking to come onto the bed. It has to be. We've had hours cuddled up on the sofa, but for Napal that just isn't enough.

I let him up, and as I drift off to sleep I can feel him creeping ever closer. I figure he'll soon be on my chest, crushing me, but what a fine way to be suffocated.

I wake some time later in a cold sweat. I've been having the dream. Over time I've been reaching further and further into my memories. Tonight I was on a jungle mission with the local special forces, the PATRIA boys. To a man they hated the drugs cartels – the billionaire narco-barons and the criminal gangs they armed and funded. Few among them hadn't lost a sister or a brother or a mother or father to the drugs war, and they believed utterly in what they were doing. They didn't particularly care about stopping the flow of narcotics to the USA. Why should they? They wanted to bring a modicum of law and order to their country, and to put an end to the death squads.

In my dream I had four deep scratches on my face caused by an ocelot – a jungle cat about the size of a small dog. The dream had me in a prison cell somewhere deep in the jungle, and the narco-rebels were using the ocelot to torture me. They were forcing it to claw me to pieces, before ripping out my guts.

In part the dream was based on reality. Capture was by far the greatest fear for all of us. And the ocelot part was also partly true. We'd found a baby ocelot abandoned in the jungle and reared it as a pet. I used to walk around our camp with it draped across my shoulders. With its dappled golden coat and its huge dark eyes, it was beautiful.

One day I was playing with it and something snapped. I'd forgotten it was basically still a wild animal. It raked me across the face with its claws, and boy did it draw blood. I even had to get an injection, in case I contracted cat flu! But still I loved that ocelot. I still carried it with me wherever I went in the camp. That was just me and animals.

As with other dreams I keep having, I figure this constitutes the gradual bleeding back of my memories. Like sand falling through a timer, gradually, grain by grain, each dream recovers a little more of what was lost.

Mostly when the nightmares wake me I can't get back to sleep. I'm too wired. But tonight Napal has woken with me, and just the knowledge that he's there helps. I know he's fully conscious because he's got those dog tags that Jim gave me attached to his collar, and they clank together whenever he moves or shakes his head. I can hear them doing that now.

I catch his eye, and he gives me a look. *You OK, buddy? I'm here for you, you know that? The demons can't get you, not any more. Nothing's gonna get you with me by your side.*

And you know the most amazing thing? With Napal there lying half on top of me, I believe him. Absolutely. I drift off into a deep sleep, and it lasts right through to morning, when it's time to get my three boys up to face a new and beautiful Napal-filled day.

Over the years since my injuries I'd got into the habit of making like a vampire and sleeping during the day. I'd get the boys to school, then return to the house and curl up to rest. For some reason – and this is common with those with such injuries – the pain is most bearable just after sunrise. That's when I was most likely to snatch a few hours' good sleep.

I'd come home from school and crash out, praying that the pain would dissipate. Pain management. It had become like an art form. It had consumed me. But with a bright-eyed and eager Napal pulling at the bed sheets on our first morning home together – *Come on, Dad, up! It's a fine and beautiful day!* – I guess my vampire days are over.

I buy myself a little time. 'Napal, go wake the boys! Go wake the boys!'

He dashes out and first he noses his head round Blake's door. It'll always be Blake to start with. He spends a second scenting the air and listening hard – just to make sure his prey is really in there. I can sense all of this from my bed.

I shout, 'Go get him, Napal! Go get him!'

Napal tears inside, jumps on top of Blake and rips off the covers. There's no sleeping now. Moments later the three boys come bouncing into my room.

A big part of my stress has been that I can't be the dad they need me to be. Chair-bound dad they can just about handle. In fact, they're too young to remember me before the chair. To them I've always been chair-bound dad. But a dad so zonked out on painkillers that he can't function? That I am determined not to be. So I fight the pain and I fight the meds. They're morphine-based, which means for most people a dose would send them to Happy Valley for hours on end.

I ration myself, to stop getting mushed out. I fight the pain so I can be the dad my boys need me to be. And, with Napal, I've got an ever-faithful buddy to stand with me on that battle line. The pain is still there. A dog can't cure the pain. In my right leg – the one the doctors say I can't have any feeling in – it jabs into me, like a bayonet is being thrust into my flesh.

At times I lie in bed fighting not to cry out. The difference is, before Napal the pain would conquer me. It would keep me in bed the entire day. Many in my family – my mom first and foremost – argued that the pain was stress-related. My mom argued it was a vicious circle. Pain creates stress, which in turn creates more pain. And that's the beauty of Napal: he takes my stress away. With him around that first morning, my stress dissolves, and with it the pain. Not all of it. The pain in my back – the site of the injury – is still there. It never quite gives up. It's like a dull, throbbing, ever-present ache. But with

Napal beside me I know I can handle it, which frees me up to face the day.

We fix breakfast, and then my dog and I roll and stroll with the boys to school. We head down our drive, turn left and make for the Stonebridge Trail, a bike and walking circuit. One of the coolest things about this neighbourhood is the way it's designed with walkways and underpasses, so kids can avoid the busy roads by crossing underneath them.

It's a five-minute walk to Bennett Elementary, and it's so safe around here I've taken to letting the boys come home alone. But this morning there is something extra going on. We're twelve legs now – including the four canine ones – and somehow we feel complete. Our family feels complete.

I send the boys over the crossing that leads into school, telling them that our wonder-dog will be waiting for them when they get home. They're smiling and laughing and waving Napal good-bye, and no one seems to notice any more that I am in a chair.

I'm aware of a newfound burst of energy. I plan the way I'm going to run this family from here on. I sketch out the Morgan household chores. Since I'm in a chair there are certain things I cannot do: I can't mow the grass and I can't put out the trash. Those things are a given. So I set the boys a rota.

Grant, my youngest and the quiet one, gets trash duty. Austin, my middle boy, the more confident, noisy one, becomes chief sandwich maker. And boy, will he be serving up a lot of baloney sandwiches - a Morgan family staple - over the next few years. My oldest, Blake, is already appointed Napal's chow and water guy.

I stack the fridge high with pre-wrapped grated cheese, hot dogs, mustard and Miracle Whip dressing, and, of course, baloney. That'll be our base diet, plus nachos, which I can just about stretch to. I hate cooking, but nachos I can manage. We'll still get the takeouts: Blake loves his Tex-Mex food; Austin is a double-cheeseburger addict; Grant is an IHOP pancake guy. But in the spring and summer months I figure we can break out the barbecue most evenings, and I'm good to throw burgers or steaks on the flames. I figure I'll get a low circular barbecue pit built by the rear patio, where I can cook from my chair. Barbecues – they'll become a Morgan family staple.

There's Mom too. I'll get Mom cooking her homemade meals – the ones we love the most – and we'll fill up the freezer, stacking them high. That way, all we'll need to do is haul one out, put it in the microwave and press the right buttons.

That afternoon Napal senses somehow that the boys are coming home. He starts pacing back and forth by the door. Finally, he lies down right in front it. Blake charges through first, knowing that my big, ultra-loving dog will be waiting. Napal ambushes him, and moments later they're out in the yard tumbling around like a couple of crazies.

Finally, a breathless Napal tears into the kitchen, grabs his bowl and drops it at Blake's feet. *Come on, buddy. You're forgetting something, aren't you? It's chow time!*

With Napal among us we feel like a family again, one blessed with a dad who smiles.

That may not sound like so much to you, but to the Morgan household this is like a miracle.

# CHAPTER 24

A few days into life-after-getting-Napal I have to head down to the local YMCA. I'm on the board and coach flag football for their team. Each month we have a regular early-morning meeting, prior to most of the dads heading off to work. Today I roll in with Napal at my side. Over an hour later and all anyone has talked about is my dog! The agenda went completely out of the window.

I figure I need a note that I can pin to Napal's harness: 'Napal is a two-year-old black Labrador from Canine Companions for Independence. He is a service dog and he knows fifty-odd commands . . .'

It would have been nice to spend five seconds talking about the football, but not a hope. I realize I'm going to have to learn to settle into this; to embrace it. I still find myself fighting it – the Napal effect. *Let's get on with what we're here for.* But wherever we go I guess Napal's going to attract this kind of attention, and I've just got to keep seeing the upside – the magic he brings into so many lives.

If I compare today's YMCA meeting with some of the bad stuff that went before, you'll understand completely what I mean by the 'magic'. A while back I volunteered to coach football. Most of the dads were just too busy. It was the real youngsters I coached, so they were playing flag football – no tackling allowed. I figured I could handle that.

Funnily enough my chair put me on a level with even the youngest kids, and I soon had us winning just about every game. Only one coach was allowed on the field during matches, and as head coach that was me. Then there came a day when this young twenty-something administrator came up to me in the middle of a game and told me that I had to leave.

'Sorry, buddy, what d'you mean, *leave*?'

'Uh, leave the field. Like, we're having complaints from the parents. They say you're a danger to the kids. You've got to leave the field.'

This guy was the athletics administrator at the YMCA. Sure, he was young, probably fresh out of college, but that was no excuse for such ignorance. He should have known better. I told him how wrong he was. I told him this was so against the ADA it wasn't funny. Under the Americans with Disabilities Act (ADA) of 1990 it is illegal to deny a wheelchair-bound person access to any public space, whether a restaurant, shopping mall or sports centre. Anyone working in sports should doubly know that. I wondered where this guy had been hiding. Maybe he'd been living under a rock?

I could have punched him I was so angry.

But because it was kids and football I agreed to leave the field. I did not want to make a scene in front of the kids, or ruin their game. But imagine how I felt – the team coach being forced to roll his way off the field, mid-play. And you know what made it infinitely worse? Austin played running back and quarterback, and he was the star of the team. No question. And he'd just seen his dad, the coach, get ordered off the field.

When the parents heard what was happening, they were outraged. They knew what I had done for their kids, turning the team around. People were visibly fuming. They wanted to know who exactly had complained, so they could have it out with them. Then a woman approached me, to have words. She was a near-neighbour of ours, and her boy played for the opposing side.

'It was me who asked for you to leave the field,' she told me. 'I thought my kids were in danger of running into you and getting hurt by your chair. I'm just scared my son's gonna run into your chair and get hurt.'

She didn't attempt to apologize, and I was so surprised I was all but speechless. I mean, what do you say in the face of such blind ignorance from your neighbour?

I tried to force a smile. 'You know something – those kids are so small I could stop any one of them and scoop them right up. And you know something else – that's why they need their coach on the field: because they are so young. They need me there to direct them and to call the play. I got all our plays mapped out on these laminated cards, so if I call a play a kid knows exactly what route to run, and where I want him to catch the ball. And that's exactly why I need to be out there on the field.'

She turned her back on me, with a throwaway comment: 'I'm just scared my son's gonna get hurt, that's all.'

I had no option but to send the assistant coach out to oversee the game. Having their head coach sent off destroyed my team's play. I was furious. Burning up with anger. But I was not about to blow up in front of my team. There is a time and a place for everything, and this was not it.

After the match I called the director of the YMCA. I told her what had happened, and said I needed a meeting with her and the young athletics administrator. Sure, it was my neighbour who'd made the complaint, but the guy should've known that by law I had every right to be on that field.

The first thing the director did when we met was to get the athletics administrator to apologize. 'I am truly sorry for what I did. I didn't know the law.'

'We really appreciate the utter professionalism with which you handled the situation,' the director added. 'You were so upset – and rightly so – and we know your passion for the kids and the sport. We've heard how good a coach you are from the parents. In fact, we'd like to invite you to be on the board.'

That's how I'd come to be a part of their monthly meetings – the ones at which Napal will henceforth play a seminal role, becoming famous for bringing proceedings to a close. I've realized already that whenever Napal gets bored, he emits a drawn-out groan-yawn of a yowl. It's a massive long 'YOOUUU-WWLLL-ARROULL-ARROUUL' complete with obligatory shake of the head.

Pretty quickly everyone at the meetings gets in tune with this. It becomes our inside joke. As soon as Napal let out his signature yowl, everyone declares, 'I guess we're done. Napal's had enough. Time to go!'

This is the Napal effect.

But I guess in life there are always the exceptions that prove the rule. After Napal's first YMCA visit we head down to Walmart. I always have loved to drive and especially since I got a second car. It's a beautiful orange Mustang with black racing stripes, and it's a real driver's car. A total head-turner.

I crack open the window – just enough to grab a dog-sized breath of fresh air. Napal gets his paws up on the armrest and thrusts his nose towards the window, enjoying a blast of cold winter breeze. I ease the Mustang along the McKinney freeway, and his eyes are squinted tight, his muzzle vacuuming up the fast, rushing air.

I imagine the plethora of scents being carried to him on the Mustang's slipstream. Hot engine oil. Rubber hitting the road. A McDonald's in full-on fry mode. The scent of a freshly mown golf course.

*Ah, smells good out there. I dunno where we're going, Dad, but it sure smells good.*

I park in the disabled bay outside Walmart and start the procedure to get chair-mobile. With Napal watching me closely from the rear I pull my chair off the passenger seat, drop it down beside me, fit the wheels, anchor the chair, then lower myself in. The entire procedure takes about five minutes.

That done I wheel myself round to the rear door where Napal is eager to get out. The moment he's got his paws on the tarmac he's right there beside me. I look up to check the way ahead – *Where's the disabled access ramp?* – and I realize that we've drawn a small crowd.

A seriously big lady dressed in Walmart uniform elbows through. She takes one look at my car and bridles. 'Y'all know this is a disabled bay? It's for the disabled. Y'all know you shouldn't be parked here?'

I can't believe what I'm hearing. 'Yes, I know, and this here is my wheelchair and this here is my service dog.'

She's got her eyes glued to my car. It seems to blind her to everything else. 'Yeah, but it's a disabled bay. It's for the disabled.'

I tell her to check my disabled-veteran plates. I see her move round to the Mustang's rear. She stares at the plates for a long second, then does a slow circle back to us.

'Well, you know, I didn't know disabled could have a car as nice as this.' It's a throwaway remark made over the shoulder as she heads back towards the store. 'A car as nice as this . . . I didn't know that was for disabled . . .'

I am left speechless. Steaming. *Because I'm in a chair I can't ride in a Mustang? I have to drive what? A disabled minibus?*

I can feel the pain rising as my stress levels peak. I'm about to roll into the store and demand to see the manager, so I can unload with both barrels. But then I take a momentary look at my dog. His eyes say it all: *Hey, let's not sweat the small stuff, OK?*

Napal's dying to get into the store and grab a shopping cart, knowing that the kids and the moms and the Walmart staff – all except the ignorant one we just met – will be all over him.

*This is gonna be fun*, his eyes tell me. *Don't worry about her. You've got a damn fine dog and damn fine car, and she's just jealous is all.*

It takes a lot to accept wisdom from your dog, but gradually I'm learning to listen, and Napal's got so much to teach me. Before Napal I would have stormed right in there spoiling for a fight. I guess that's maybe why CCI teamed me up with the peacemaker. Conflict brings stress, stress brings pain, and we'd be into that vicious circle once more. All things flow from there.

Napal and I roll around that Walmart and I experience only fun, laughter and kindness. It is drawn to me via my dog. By the time I leave, the confrontation over the Mustang – *I didn't know disabled could have a car as nice as this* – is forgotten. And it's so much better that way.

A day or so later my pain is spiking real bad. It's often like this come a change in the weather. With a wet snap blowing in I've stayed in bed, pain stabbing through my legs and fire burning up my spine. Before Napal this was where I would remain – in my den, curtains closed, riding out the agony. But not now.

Every half-hour or so I hear Napal pad in, collar jingling hopefully. Up to now it's always been: *With pain like this what is there to get up for?*

But today Napal places his head on my bed and lets out a long deep sigh: 'HARRUUUMP.' His eyebrows twitch, and he flicks his gaze up to meet mine, hopefully. *Come on, Dad, let's go. Things to do, places to see. Let's get out there!*

He's right of course. I do have stuff to do. Blake's playing in a football match and I've promised I'll be there. But there's no point going as pain-racked Dad. That would just be horrible – me twisting and crying out on the sidelines. Yet with Napal beside me I know I can pull through.

We make it to the match. When Blake sacks - tackles - the other team's quarterback Napal does something quite extraordinary, something that he's never done before, at least with us. He let's out a massive, explosive, celebratory bark: 'ARR-ROOOUUUFFF!'

My dog has the deepest, gruffest, loudest and most awesome bark that I have ever heard. But that isn't what is so amazing. *Somehow, my dog knows that my son has made a great play.* I figure we can expand the repertoire. The next time our side wins a big play, I whisper into Napal's ear, 'Speak.' That's the I-need-you-to-bark command.

'ARRROOOUUUFFF!'

I get Napal to bark every time our team has something to celebrate during the game. The kids love it.

I see one turn to his mother and point at my dog. 'Mommy, that dog is so cool! He's so smart! Every time our team makes a good play, he barks! Wow! How does he do that?'

The kid is convinced that Napal is following the game and understands the rules. Maybe he does. Maybe he doesn't need my 'Speak' command. I wouldn't put anything past this dog.

I can feel Napal straining at his leash every time a kicker goes onto the field with the tee. I remember Jim Siegfried telling me about how he trained Napal to be a tee retriever. I get the badge of my kids' team sewn onto his harness. The very next match I have a word with the coach, and I'm cleared to have Napal do his stuff. I figure I don't have to teach him a thing.

The instant the kick is taken I give him the word: 'Go get the tee! Go fetch the tee!'

Napal dashes onto the field, snatches up the tee in his jaws and runs back triumphantly, ears flapping behind him in the wind. Everyone on our side – moms, dads, kids – is going wild. In a few precious moments I've gone from wheelchair dad to the coolest father a son could ever wish for. That is the magic of this dog, and it's a magic that so many will want to have a part of – understandably.

I take a call from Corey Hudson, the director of CCI, who saw me speak at the Oceanside graduation. Partly he's calling to check how Napal and I are doing, but also it's to ask a favour. He believes I have one of the most inspiring stories of any CCI graduate, and he wants me to speak at an event. It's a CCI fund-raiser called Paws in the Park and, as chance would have it, it's exactly the same one as Jim Siegfried has invited me to already.

I tell Corey that after getting Napal I'd climb any mountain for CCI. In the military I'd got accustomed to speaking before crowds; I was trained to brief rooms full of special forces types on the weather for a particular mission. But this is an entirely different ball game. Corey wants me to speak before a bunch of 'normal' people and tell them my and Napal's story: how the two of us came together, and what it means for me.

To do that I'll need to describe how I got injured and what life was like before the chair. It's a daunting proposition, especially because I make a point of not talking about life prior to my paralysis. I didn't go into it much in my graduation speech, and in truth I've blanked out that existence. It's as if it wasn't me – as if there was no Jason Morgan before the chair. It's a coping mechanism, but one that I'll have to abandon publicly if I'm to give the speech that Corey's asked for. Yet I never consider not going. I wouldn't dream of refusing any such request or letting CCI down.

It's hard to explain why I've blanked my life prior to the chair. Even I don't fully understand it. After coming out of the coma

I felt almost as if I had been reincarnated. My injuries changed everything about me and how I was with everyone around me. It was as if I had lived two different lives. Life before the chair felt like an impossible dream. Like an ancient existence, one only dimly remembered. So, it's daunting going to speak before an audience of strangers about life before the chair.

I'm nervous even before the flight, and then I'm involved in an unfortunate incident with a guy who should know better. Before Napal I'd have taken this guy on in full verbal combat, but now I make him my friend. Ironically enough, it's because of Napal that the trouble happens.

The flight is crammed. I ask for a seat by the bulkhead, so there's extra room for Napal to curl up at my feet, but there are none free. Instead, we get one by a window. The guy who sits next to me complains to the air hostess about something. I don't know if he's bitching about my dog, but I have my suspicions. I guess he doesn't have a clue that I'm wheelchair-bound – you wouldn't necessarily know when I'm sitting down.

The hostess asks me to move to the aisle seat, as the guy's complained that he has no space to stretch out with my dog curled up on the floor. I do as asked. I have to lever myself up with my arms, swing myself into the other seat and get Napal to follow. Whichever way he tries to curl up, Napal's now got his nose stuck halfway into the aisle. I have to keep moving him, or he'll get hit on the head by a trolley or trodden on by those using the bathroom.

The guy realizes what he's done now. He tries apologizing. I tell him he should just have spoken to me direct and we could have worked something out. He tells me that he's never seen a dog on a plane before; that he didn't understand. We get talking and I tell him a bit of my story. The more he learns about what Napal means to me, the more he's mortified. He ends up wanting to do a fundraiser for CCI and inviting me to speak at it.

That's the magic here; that's the way that Napal and I can turn a situation around.

# CHAPTER 25

We fly into San Diego and meet up with the amazing Jim Siegfried. It is fantastic to see him again – both for me and Napal. He drives us over to the event, which has been nicknamed Balboa Barks, a pun on the venue, Balboa Park, in downtown San Diego.

It's spring and the weather is beautiful. Balboa Park is magnificent at this time of year – a sweep of grand old trees running through the heart of the city. We're to complete a two-and-a-half-mile 'dogathon' through the grounds.

Jim and I roll with the able-bodied walkers, and everywhere there are dogs, dogs, dogs. The route winds through ancient stands of majestic trees. It passes the Air and Space Museum, the Hall of Champions, the San Diego Zoo and the Reuben H. Fleet Science Center. At one stage Jim pauses, his gaze fixed on something across the street from where we are walking.

He points. 'That's the Vietnam Memorial Wall. You know, like they have in DC. It's the travelling version, like a mobile memorial.'

'Wow. I didn't even know they had one.'

'Uh-huh. You mind if we go take a look?'

'No. Let's go. Come on, Napal.'

We cross the road. Jim rolls slowly along the wall, his gaze seemingly scanning all of the names, and I can sense that he is searching for something or someone. Finally he glances back at Napal and me.

'I'm just checking. My brother was in 'Nam. I'm just checking his name's on the wall.'

'Your brother was in 'Nam?'

'Uh-huh. Here we are. S for Siegfried.'

Jim studies the wall for a long second. It's an emotional moment, and I don't know quite what to make of it. Did he lose his brother there? Is he one of those still listed as missing in action? The moment passes. I tell myself that I should have asked Jim what happened to his brother. But, then again, if he had wanted to talk about it, he'd probably have volunteered the information.

We roll across the dogathon finish line and gather for the talks. Mine is headlined 'Salute to Veterans' – a CCI initiative to make more wounded warriors aware that the dogs exist and that they can apply to get one. I feel honoured to be able to spread the word, but I'm sick with nerves as I roll up to the podium.

I've planned my talk and I open with this: 'I am Staff Sergeant Jason Morgan, and this is my service dog, Napal. Napal, give the crowd a wave.'

Napal does as instructed, and the audience seems instantly mesmerized. My nerves start to evaporate as my dog wins the crowd over. I begin by telling my story as simply as I can – from airborne warrior to wheelchair-bound paraplegic, the years of trauma and pain that followed, and the joy of finding Napal and how he's turned our lives around. I can tell that Napal is hanging on my every word. He's only got eyes for me, which boosts my confidence hugely, and as for getting stage nerves, my dog is a total natural.

I do a couple of demos, just to illustrate what I've been saying. I drop my keys and Napal retrieves them. I have him tow me back and forth across the stage, which really gets the crowd going. As my confidence grows I manage to crack a joke. I tell the audience I taught my dog to play poker, but every time he has a good hand he wags his tail – kind of a giveaway!

During the dogathon Jim told me how he'd taught Napal to bow: chin on the ground and butt high in the air. When our time is up I give Napal the command: 'Bow.' Napal goes down real low on his front haunches, head to the floor, kowtowing to the crowd. They love it. They go wild.

I was so worried about talking about life before the chair. But strangely enough, having done so I feel empowered. I feel a sense of mission: maybe this is what I am here for. Maybe this was why I didn't die in the Ecuadorian jungle, so I could go out with my miracle dog and tell our story. Maybe there's a lesson to be learned here. The way you deal with your life is your choice; nothing is impossible.

Afterwards the CCI people ask if we'd be willing to do more such appearances. I tell them the truth: anytime, anyplace, anywhere. All they have to do is call.

As we're saying our goodbyes to Jim Siegfried, he shares a special moment with me. Even after I let Napal off the leash today and gave him the 'Release' command, he never once ran to Jim's side. The other dogs that Jim raised weren't like that:

whenever they met up with him again they couldn't wait to rush over.

He and Napal spent eighteen months together – the formative time of the young dog's life – and Jim was worried that Napal wouldn't be able to break that bond and accept his life companion – me. But amazingly, it seems as if he needn't have been concerned. Napal definitely recognized Jim; a dog never forgets a person's smell. But he's not once been tempted to break away from my side and run to Jim's.

As Jim points out, Napal's loyalty and his love are humbling. He's a dog in a million. And, needless to say, Jim Siegfried is a guy in a million too.

Napal and I fly home, mission accomplished. We chill by the TV, sharing a takeout and a movie with my boys. My couch has a button on a side console. If you press it, a motor whirrs away and tilts it back to a near-horizontal position. It's important for me both to minimize the back pain and to prevent pressure sores from forming. The movie's not up to much and I want to change the channel, but no one's able to find the remote. I don't want to have to clamber off the couch and into my wheelchair in an effort to locate it. I figure maybe Napal can do the job.

'Napal, get the remote,' I tell him. 'Find the remote.'

He snuffles around beneath the sofa and comes out with several long-lost objects: an old sock, a pair of slippers, a couple of the boys' toys, some ancient half-eaten food items - which, incidentally, he does not try to scarf down. He just adds them to the growing pile of detritus. Finally he backs out from under the couch with the remote gripped in his jaws. We flip channels for a while, until we find something we all want to watch.

Small things – but these are the things that make a family.

My boys think Napal is a superhero. So do I.

I start feeding him fish-oil supplements. They make his coat even shinier and glossier. I figure if my dog and I are going to represent CCI, he has to look his very best. I learned in the military how much appearances matter. There's not a lot I can do about myself. Fish oil doesn't cut it. My hair is greying, and as a result people joke that I look like Richard Gere. I pretend to be annoyed. *Richard Gere? But he's pushing sixty!*

I decide to dye my hair. It'll be a younger, more dashing version of Jason Morgan that people get to see on stage. But the results don't work for me. I've gone prematurely grey due to all the pain and the stress, yet it kind of suited me. I guess I appear best when the dye starts to wear off and I'm caught between the two looks.

It's Napal who has the next big idea, or rather it's his actions that inspire me. Not long after our Oceanside talk we're at Baylor Hospital, in Frisco, for a routine check-up. I joke that I'm the million-dollar man. But in a way it's no joke at all. I've had dozens of surgeries. I've spent years in hospital. I figure the medical costs must be pushing a million dollars, and I owe my life and my limited mobility to the wonders of medical science.

I guess it's only right that Napal and I give something back. Among other things, Baylor treats acute cases – those requiring brain surgery, cancer treatment and the like. Many of those sharing the waiting room are in for life-threatening operations. They have no idea if they'll make it through and neither do their families.

As a service dog, Napal's not supposed to be petted. But I let people do so when we're going nowhere and waiting around. I give him the 'Release' command, and I notice that Napal is acting as an informal therapy dog. It's not just the kids who are stroking and playing with him as they count down the dreadful minutes, it's adults facing life-or-death operations.

I see Napal nuzzle a worried hand and wag his entire rear end encouragingly. He allows a patient to curl their fingers in the wiry hair of his rear quarters, where he just loves being scratched, and the expression on his face speaks volumes. He can sense what these people are here for and he knows what his presence does for them. His eyes say it all: *See, don't worry. It's really not so bad . . . You're all gonna be OK.*

I notice the familiar, easy, distant look that appears in the gaze of a patient as he pets my dog. He's far away from all of this now, sitting by his fireside with friends and family, plus his ever-faithful dog.

After my appointment we ask if we can volunteer. Can Napal and I form a team to help cheer and comfort those coming in for surgery? Baylor has never done anything like this before and at first no one seems particularly interested. The lady on the front desk explains that they have an in-house director of volunteers named Robin Jacks. She organizes a daily rota, from five o'clock in the morning through to four in the afternoon, so every arrival for major surgery has a volunteer greeter. I ask for five minutes with Robin Jacks. Five minutes, just to pitch what Napal and I could do.

She puts a call through. 'Robin, there's this guy here called Jason Morgan and he wants to talk about volunteering. Yeah, as a greeter. Oh, and he's got a dog. And . . . well, you'd best come see.'

It's the end of a long day and Robin clearly isn't up for this. But that's before I tell her the basics: I'm former military, I served in special operations, I was injured on a mission, and Napal is my service dog. Her demeanour changes completely. I can tell that I've hit some kind of a nerve, and Robin soon reveals why.

Robin's son serves in the 3rd Special Forces Group, the same outfit I was with. She hasn't heard from him for three weeks and she's dead worried, as he's out on active operations. I tell her that isn't so unusual. I tell her how my folks often didn't hear from me for months on end. I put her mind at ease, and Napal works his magic: soon she's stroking and cooing at my dog.

Robin decides she loves the idea of a wounded warrior and his service dog forming a Baylor greeting team. And so Napal and I get a regular Monday-morning slot to ease the suffering of those stepping into the unknown. You might think I'd spent so long in hospitals that I'd never want to set foot in one again. But that's the amazing thing about Napal – he can make the most unpleasant of experiences hugely rewarding. That's exactly what he does with the Baylor patients over the months of volunteering that lie ahead.

One little girl sticks in my mind. She had such a badly injured face that she couldn't talk. She was a picture of suffering. But then I dropped my wallet 'by accident' and I had Napal pick it up for me. Her face lit up with joy. She pointed at something else she wanted me to drop – and then kept doing so, smiling and laughing the entire time, until I'd run out of stuff for Napal to retrieve.

You know what she did next? She started tearing off little scraps of tissue from the box by her bed, and she threw them down for Napal to fetch. That's how keen she was for my dog to stick around. In effect, we were acting as a therapy dog team. I owe a huge debt to the medical profession – the debt of life. This was one small step towards getting that repaid.

It's around this time that Grant and Austin – who are seriously getting into their football – decide they want to do the Crape Myrtle Fun Run, to up their fitness levels. It's a five-kilometre race, one of many held in the area at weekends. I tell them that if they're going to do the Crape Myrtle, then so am I.

At the start of the race there are a couple of guys in chairs, but neither is anything like mine. I'm sitting in my regular around-town chair. These guys have sleek racing models – low-slung and lightweight, with cambered rear wheels, and a third wheel set at the front for greater thrust and balance.

'You know, you should get yourself a racing chair,' one of the guys remarks.

We chair racers are allowed to set off first. The guys in the racing chairs pull ahead of me and it isn't long before the boys overtake me as well.

I yell after them, 'See you at the finish . . . I hope!'

With Napal beside me all the way I make it – just. It takes me thirty minutes to roll five kilometres. I sure do need that racing chair! I get one from the VA. It is six feet long and low, which allows my hands to remain on the wheel rims all the way round, transmitting maximum power. The technique with a racing chair is to punch around the rubber rims, which are set an inch outside the wheels. If you try to hold on to the rims, they move too fast and your hands end up caught up in the mechanism. You have to wear special sticky gloves, which rely on friction with the wheel rims to get them moving and keep them going.

I practise hard to master the technique. I warn the boys: *Now I have a racing chair, they're toast.*

The next five-K race I complete in twenty-four minutes, and the boys are only ever a few steps ahead of me. I train even harder, and that's the last time they beat me. The very next race I start first and they don't see me for dust!

Rolling in that racing chair with my dog at my side is a fantastic feeling, something close to the freedom of running for real. The more I train, the bigger my arms and shoulders get, and the more power I can transmit through the wheels to the road. One time I even flip the chair over when trying to start too quickly.

The boys, Napal and I get into the habit of rolling and running a race, then heading out for some fast food. I know it doesn't make great sense to feast on junk food right after rigorous exercise, but that's how the Morgan clan does things – never the norm. I love the way the running and rolling and the fast-food blowouts bond us. With my dog, my racing chair and my training, I can be the dad my boys need me to be. I'm getting there, with my dog at my side.

But one time we end up in a Taco Bell where we've never been before. I roll through the entrance with Napal at my side and we're all four of us starving hungry. Most of the local takeout staff are used to us by now, but not here.

A guy tries to block the way. 'Sorry, sir, no dogs. We don't serve dogs.'

I don't even break my stride. 'Oh, that's OK 'cause he's not eating.'

Normally, people tend to leave it at that, but this guy's extra-double-whopper stupid. 'No, sir, you don't understand. We don't serve dogs.'

The guy just won't let it drop. He tells me that Napal and I have to leave. I guess because it's Napal he's attacking I let him have it with both barrels. I'm used to experiencing prejudice because of my chair, but with my boys and my dog I am very, very protective. I tell him in no uncertain terms that under the ADA it is a federal offence to deny access to a service dog. I tell him if he wants us to leave he can call the cops and see what they make of it.

At the mention of the cops the guy backtracks fast. He says he didn't know Napal was a 'handicap dog', despite the fact that he's got a bright-blue service harness on, with a CCI badge, plus the words – I'M WORKING. PLEASE DON'T PET ME.

My boys hate the word handicap. Rightly or wrongly, in America it's become associated with disabled people begging on the streets – cap in hand. Now it's Austin's turn to unload. 'Will you stop using that word handicap with my dad! You don't even know what it means. If you knew, you'd never ever use it for my dad.'

'You know, I've been called a cripple before,' I tell the Taco Bell guy, 'but handicapped, that comes a close second . . .'

He realizes that he's well out of his depth and makes a run for the kitchens. We order tacos and burritos and try to put the unpleasantness behind us. But as ever the stress has brought on the pain, and the boys can see me wincing and twisting in my chair as I try to hold in the cries.

Worse still, the pain kills my appetite. I cannot eat when I am in pain. In spite of my hunger my meal lies untouched before me, and all because of an ignorant server who didn't know how to welcome a guy in a wheelchair and his service dog. But the worst of it is this: I know Napal gets it. He's torturing himself because of it.

Napal understands when he's not welcome, or when his presence causes me grief – and with his discomfort comes a massive spike in my pain. And with the pain comes something else – another deeper layer of darkness. Almost inevitably the pain takes me back to my injuries, the source of all my hurt. That in turn takes me back to the jungle and a Chevrolet Blazer doing a violent series of somersaults down a swampy mountainside.

When I'm as happy as Napal can take me, I have further to fall. Those are the inevitable highs and lows of life with my best buddy, my dog.

# CHAPTER 26

It's a few days prior to Christmas. I have a million things to do: mostly presents to buy for the boys, plus I've got to find something special for Napal. I'm in my chair, zipping about getting ready to hit the stores. I head for the garage and call Napal. 'Come on, buddy, we gotta go!'

I hear this big, long, lazy 'YAAOOOWWOOWWL.' He's unwinding from the sofa, where he was having a real comfy time. I've realized something about my dog: he runs on what I call Mexico time. He's not lazy; he's not trying to make me late. This is just his pace. My dog is mellow, slow and easy all the time.

I sit by the garage door clapping my hands but, no matter what, my dog will not be hurried. And you know something? *It's good for me.* It takes the edge off. Slows me down. Makes me less Bruce Willis, more Richard Gere.

I scoot around the mall, easing my way through the Napal encounters; even during the Christmas rush people just have to stop and marvel at my dog. We reach the checkout, basket perched on my lap and piled high with what the boys have asked for. It's a Best Buy store and I've loaded up on video games for

Austin and Grant, plus an alarm clock that Blake specially asked for. I figure it's maybe $300 worth of stuff.

I have my military patches sewn onto the rear of my chair: those of the 10th Combat Weather Squadron plus the SOAR. I pass Napal my wallet and give him the 'Up' command so that he can hold it out to the cashier.

It's then that I feel a tap on my shoulder. There's a big guy behind me. He smiles at my dog, points at the basket and says, 'I'll get that. Let me get that.'

I tell him thanks, but he doesn't have to. I let the last items ring through. It's over $350 in total. I tell him it's a lot of money and that he doesn't have to.

Regardless, he hands the cashier his credit card. 'I got this. I got it.'

I try to find out the guy's name so I can thank him properly or even just send him a Christmas card. He's alone, with no family or a wife or girlfriend to show off to. He's done this out of the goodness of his heart, and he clearly wants to remain anonymous.

He leaves me with this: 'I got it. Y'all have a great Christmas, and thank you for your service.'

It's amazing. Such encounters lift me so high, and with Napal beside me things like this just keep happening. People notice me because of Napal. He attracts the eye. Then they notice the military patches and they can tell I'm a wounded warrior. I could be in a chair for so many reasons, but they come to the right conclusion because of my dog.

In recent days the communication between Napal and me has moved onto a new level. Before, it was all 'Napal, get this' or 'Napal, pull that.' I was using the verbal commands taught me at CCI. But recently I've stopped doing that. I've realized he doesn't need words any more. We've spent every second of every day together for the last few months, and Napal simply knows.

Mostly, I don't have to say a single word. He's there, a split second ahead of me, doing whatever I need whenever I need it most. It's like we have an invisible silken thread slung between us, one that links our minds directly. That's how he can sit in a superstore surrounded by people getting petted and wowed – the absolute centre of attention – but remain tuned to my every need.

Here's an example. Napal may run on Mexico time, but not when I am in pain. I smoke a cigar when I am hurting because it helps take the edge off. But I'll only smoke outside the house – mostly in the backyard. I can be out there smoking, and Napal will pop his head through the doggie door. Not his entire body, just his head, to check. He can be fast asleep on the couch, but still he'll sense my pain. Somehow it cuts right through Mexico time. If he sees I'm real bad, he'll come right through his door to be at my side. But if I'm mostly good, he'll throw me a look through the doorway – *Oh, I get it. False alarm* – and he'll go straight back to snoozing.

Christmas is a big time for the Morgan family. Tradition has it we gather on that most magical of nights, Christmas Eve, at my folks' place. It's several years after my accident now, and my dad's business has come good. They've bought a plot of land among the wilds and built their dream home. It's out near Lake Texoma, where we took family vacations when we were kids, and where I first presented myself to my father in my chair, on his sixtieth birthday.

The house is bounded by trees on one side, embraced by the wide sweep of a golf course on the other, and it overlooks the water. They have a swimming pool that cascades over a natural rock face, which at night reflects the lights off the lake. Bobcats often wander past their garden fence. It's a magical place, and God knows my parents worked hard for it. I'm so happy for them.

My boys, my dog and I drive out there for Christmas. We pile inside the house, arms clutching piles of presents. I go to use the rest room, and there's a commotion outside. The boys are yelling that Napal's looking for me. I call to him, and he uses his nose to open the bathroom door. He glances over at me and I can see he's got something gripped in his jaws. It's my car keys, and I didn't have the faintest clue that I'd lost them. I must have dropped them without noticing and somehow Napal realized. He made sure I was safely inside the house, then went back to find them. What a dog.

We gather on the patio at the rear. My dad has lit the open fire in the semi-covered barbecue area, and it's toasty enough for me to be out there in my chair, even in December. There are still a few people out shooting a last round of golf, and a bunch of guys in golf carts stop to play the nearby hole, the last.

My dad's an incredibly sociable kind of a guy. He leans on the fence and engages them in conversation. One of the guys has a black Lab, a female by the look of things. She can clearly sense Napal. She tears up and down the fence, barking and scuffing up the grass, trying to attract my dog's attention.

I can't go over to the fence, because my chair won't roll on the thick grass, plus the ground isn't very level. We're restricted to the patio, my dog and I. As for Napal, he just sits there, cool as a cucumber, glued to his post by my chair. Not even the proposition of a bit of flirting with a damn fine-looking lady black Lab can unsettle Napal.

The guy cracks a joke about his dog: 'You know, this is how I walk her, from my golf cart!'

'She's a beautiful animal,' my dad replies. He nods towards the patio. 'My son, Jason, is a wounded warrior, and that's his service dog, Napal.'

'Wow! That's one fine animal you got there. How do you get him to be so obedient? So well behaved? I mean, look at Dotty goin' wild here.'

Before I can answer my dad does. 'You know, he's a CCI service dog – that's Canine Companions for Independence. They spend two years training the dogs. They're even taught to pull your socks off for you . . . They have fifty separate verbal commands they understand.'

'Dad, it's more like sixty, with the extra ones I taught him,' I chime in gently.

'Oh. Right. Yeah, sixty. Dog ends up costing $40,000 by the time a wounded warrior gets one.'

'Dad, it's more like $50,000.'

'Yeah, fifty. Fifty. Well, CCI, it's just one amazing organization. Just a cotton-pickin' minute. I got some literature in the house if you'd like to take a look . . .'

Dad hurries inside and returns with a stack of CCI brochures. He hands them across to the golfer.

'Make 'em your Christmas not-for-profit,' he urges. 'There's none better. No more deserving cause.'

The guy says he will. He wishes us a merry Christmas, then mounts his golfing cart and motors off, his dog charging after him.

As tradition has it, that evening my dad dresses up as Santa Claus to hand round the presents. The boys don't know it's him, of course; they know him simply as Big-Big when he's in his Santa outfit. But tonight he's got a serious rival for star of the show. My mom has managed to rig up a Santa costume for Napal. It's got a floppy red strap-on hat, a red Santa jerkin and even a big white bushy beard. Napal takes the whole Santa suit thing real Mexico-time easy. He passes around the presents my mom has prepared for him to deliver, one mouthful at a time. It makes for a best-ever Christmas for the boys.

The new year rolls in. Napal and I have been together for nine months or so, and looking back I realize something important: I have lived three lives. Life before the chair. Life after the chair. And now life-after-getting-Napal.

First there was a life in which I could walk and run and leap out of aircraft. Amazing. Second, there was a life in which I couldn't do any of that. It was defined by what I had lost, and it was pretty low and dark.

And now, there's a third life, in which the void created by all the loss has been filled by one incredible dog.

# CHAPTER 27

The racing with my boys proves addictive, especially as I have Napal at my side all the way. There's a part of me keeps thinking about the big one – coming good on my promise to complete a marathon. I'd pledged to Colonel Funk and my special ops buddies: *You know what I'll do? I'll run a full marathon . . .*

I can't run one, that's for sure. But, who knows, maybe I can *roll* one?

CCI get in contact once more and ask if Napal and I will do another show for them. I tell them we'll be there. This time I come up with a little extra theatre. I figure we'll make a dramatic entrance: I'll have Napal pull me onto the stage. That's how we'll arrive.

We do just that and it goes down a real treat. I open with the story of how I was injured. I run through how Napal turned my life around and all the commands that he understands. But then I get to the heart of the matter: I tell them how my dog has changed my entire life on a far deeper level. I explain how it's not so much the visible, physical support that matters – it's the psychological. The companionship. The loyalty and the love.

'My dog knows when I am sad. He knows when I am in pain.

And he knows how to take me out of all that and to make me smile again. He's never in a bad mood and he always makes people laugh, and that can't fail to make me happy. There were long periods of my life when that didn't happen much. I pretty much forgot how to smile. After Napal, I'm smiling and I'm laughing all the time.'

There doesn't seem to be a dry eye in the house.

For some reason the pain peaks just then, and for a moment I lose my thread. The pain does that to me: it can block out all conscious thought. But I decide it's best just to be as honest and as natural as possible with this audience.

'Oh, hey, just a minute. My pain's real bad right now. Just a second . . . OK. It's dropping off. So, as I was saying, when you laugh the whole world tends to laugh with you. And with my dog at my side, I've learned how to find the joy in life again . . .'

After the talk CCI make a very special request to me and Napal: they ask us to be their national spokesteam. It will mean more travel and giving media interviews, which will take me away from the boys, but I know how much they love what I'm doing. They're proud of me. They're proud of their chair-bound dog-struck dad.

That July 4th I don't need to worry so much about the fireworks taking me back to that dark and fateful tumble through the jungle. Instead, I'm gathered with my folks around the TV watching Napal and myself give a series of interviews. In every one he's got his forequarters right up in my lap, and he stays like that all the way through. I see him react as the interviewer speaks his name – 'So, this is the famous Napal?' – and I know that he knows he is the focus of the show.

Right now he's glued to the TV like the rest of us. *Hey, who is that? That's one handsome dog!*

Through speaking for CCI I meet a disabled veteran who advises me to learn to scuba-dive. 'Trust me, it's the only way you can get complete freedom. You get in the water in your dive gear and you don't need a chair any more. Try it. It'll set you free.'

He tells me about the Cody Unser First Step Foundation, an Arizona-based not-for-profit that helps improve the quality of life of those with paralysis. Among other things it funds them to learn to scuba-dive.

I figure I'll give it a whirl. But I decide that if I'm to try it, then it is something I have to do with all three of my boys. We'll make this a family affair. Well, almost a family affair. Sadly Napal can't come diving. As far as I know, no one has invented scuba gear for a dog. For once he'll just have to be happy watching from the sidelines.

We train and get certified at the Clear Springs Scuba Park, in nearby Terrell. The only difference between what my boys and I wear is that I have these special webbed gloves because I can't use fins on my feet. The guy who advised me to try this didn't even get close with what he said. It is truly mind-blowing. This is the nearest I have ever felt to being normal again, to being like everybody else. It's also the closest yet I've got to being on a level with my boys – the same as any 'normal' dad.

Needless to say, Napal goes woofing wild every time the four of us go in the water. We do our final checkout dive at a local spring-fed lake, and no one looking down at the four of us in the water would ever know that I am paralyzed from the waist down. It is utterly wonderful to be able to move and to swim and to play with my kids, and to hell with the chair.

I feel every man's equal – almost. It is incredible. I can go anywhere. It's pure delight. My eldest, Blake, sums it up in an interview he does for a local newspaper on the scuba-diving experience. 'My dad makes it look so easy,' he tells the reporter. 'He sets such a great example. If he weren't my dad he'd probably be my best friend.'

I figure the ultimate would be to head down to Florida to dive, and there's no reason why Napal shouldn't come. But I don't know if it's possible for me. Wheelchairs can't cope with sand or rocks, so getting into the sea might be something of an issue. I squirrel the thought away in my mind as something for later. Diving in the Gulf of Mexico, plus rolling a full marathon: I'm drawing up my bucket list. But I don't want to do any of this if I have to leave my dog behind. He does so much for me. It's a two-way street. It's a bucket list for the both of us.

I swear Napal is semi-human. I've been in bars and I've dropped my keys and without a word he's just scooped them up in his jaws and placed them in my lap. Just like your buddy would. People find it incredible. It never ceases to amaze. I don't know how many times people have said to me, 'You know, that dog of yours is *human*. He looks at you in a way that you just know he gets it. More than any dog, he just *knows*.'

Napal even seems to get the somewhat warped Morgan family sense of humour. We're forever winding each other up, and we don't just restrict it to family. One time I'm at home messing with my boys. They've got into the habit of rolling around in my chair and deliberately leaving it out of reach. It's a good-natured wind-up, but I always have to get Napal to fetch my chair.

This time, stupidly, I stretch for it myself and I fall awkwardly. I know instantly that I've broken my leg. It's my top bone – my femur – and I feel it go. The bones in my legs are weaker and more vulnerable due to all the inactivity. But I can't feel a great deal more pain than usual, so I figure it's no big deal.

I call Napal and we drive to the nearest hospital. I guess I should have called an ambulance, but that never even crosses my mind. I'm on the examination bed by the time the doctor arrives. He confirms that the femur is broken and that they'll need to set it. He asks me where my folks are, so he can inform them. I tell him that I came alone. I see him do a double-take. I realize then that he doesn't know that I'm a paraplegic, and he's wondering how on earth I got there with a broken leg.

'So, erm . . . how exactly did you get here?' he asks.

I give a deadpan response: 'Oh, you know, I drove.'

His eyes are popping out of his head. 'With a broken leg? With all the pain? *You drove?*'

I give Napal a sly wink and let the doctor sweat a little. 'Well, no, not completely alone. I had my dog, obviously.'

I swear Napal is laughing. I swear he gets it.

I tell the doctor that I was in special forces, and they build us pretty tough. Finally, I let him know that I'm kidding. I tell him that I'm a paraplegic; my car has hand controls and I don't feel much below the waist.

But in truth breaking my leg turns into something of a drama. I've spent enough time in hospitals and I don't need any more, plus there are all the things that Napal and I have to do. We've got our regular Monday Baylor therapy dog visits. We've got events stacking up with CCI, and after our first TV appearances there are more interview requests. It seems like an age before the hospital finally releases me, with my leg bound up in plaster. On the drive home I stop at a gas station. After several days of hospital food I'm craving a real, genuine Coke and maybe some fries.

I roll inside and make my way towards the drinks counter, when some guy stops me. 'Hey! No dogs! Sorry, no dogs!'

I tell him what should be obvious – that Napal is my service dog and he's allowed everywhere I go. In response the guy comes out from behind his counter and orders us to leave. He's Arab-looking, and I know that Muslims can be hypersensitive about dogs, but that doesn't mean the law isn't the law.

I try to make a virtue out of necessity, and to educate this guy on the rules regarding service dogs, of which he's clueless. But he's just not listening. He keeps yelling at me that my dog is not allowed. Things are getting pretty heated, and I can see Napal cringing as the aggression zips back and forth.

Finally I pull out my cell phone and tell him I'm calling the cops. It's then that he relents. I grab myself a Coke and wheel myself towards the checkout, but the smell from the hot-food counter proves irresistible. I do a ninety-degree turn and it's now that the guy behind that counter starts to freak.

'Get back! Away! No dogs! No way can we have a dog anywhere near the food!'

I lose it. 'What's he gonna do? Lie in it? Pee in it? Poop in it?'

The guy blabbers on about food hygiene. I'm about to dial 911 when I get this message direct from Napal. I hear it, just as clearly as if he's spoken to me. He can sense my tension spiking, my pain peaking, and he knows what harm it's doing to me. To us. He throws me this look: *Let's just get out of here. Let's just hit the road. OK?*

We drive home in an exhausted silence. In the culture of the guys in that store dogs are supposed to be unclean. But their beliefs do not override the law, as no one's ever should. This is the United States of America. We fought long and hard for the freedoms we enjoy, including those of minorities like the disabled.

But of course, my dog has called it right. All I've achieved is to put myself in a whole world of pain. And you know something? When I feel pain I believe Napal does too. I believe he actually *feels* it. And when he takes my pain away from me, I believe that he takes it into himself. I sense that he takes on a massive load, and I do not want to burden my dog.

Julie, my twin sister, has just got herself a dog, having been inspired to do so after meeting Napal. She managed to get a CCI animal that failed to graduate – a change-of-career dog as they call them. She's a beautiful white Lab called Laurel, and she had far too much desire to chase and run to make it as a service dog.

Laurel is truly phenomenal. Or at least she is until Julie sees her next to Napal. She knows her fifty-odd commands – she pretty much mastered them all – but she was only ever 95 per cent focused on the job. The other 5 per cent of the time she was focused on chasing squirrels! Napal is 101 per cent focused on me 101 per cent of the time, and that's what makes him special.

But it also means that he feels my every emotion personally, in his heart. So when I pick a fight with a gas station attendant, or a waiter in a fast-food joint, I may be doing so for us, for our rights, but is it ever worth it? It's exhausting enough just being Napal, and remaining 101 per cent on-task all the time. Add in the odd fight like the one we've just had, and it's debilitating.

We get home, I remove Napal's CCI vest and he drapes himself right across me. When Napal's not in work mode he reverts to being the Morgan family pet, and this is him in slacker-dog mode. This is Napal saying, *Hey, I need some real attention here, some grooming, just so I know you appreciate me.*

It's fair enough. He's a big heavy hound, and having him up there hurts, but he deserves this. He's more than earned it. During his eighteen months with Jim Siegfried, Napal was rewarded for good behaviour with treats. That's how he was trained. But I can't do that. I need him to go wherever I go, and I can't always be feeding him. So mostly the only rewards I can offer are affection, praise and love.

I pet him and talk to him, apologizing for picking a fight, but I tell him I was doing it for us. He throws me a look that says it all. *Why go there? We've got each other. It's enough, isn't it? It's as good as it gets.*

Napal is right. It is as good as it gets. But there is one thing my dog cannot do for me, and that's cure me physically. As much as he's transformed my life, the fight against the medical complications is an endless one. I decide I'm not up to rolling a full marathon. Not yet. But I take a massive first step. I sign up to try for the Warrior Games, the US military's version of the Paralympics. I'm looking to compete in a raft of track and swimming events, as well as playing for the air force wheelchair basketball team. If I do well in the games and go on to roll my first marathon, I'll be able to sit tall in my chair, having come good on my promises and more.

It's highly competitive getting selected for the air force team, but I make it and I feel like I have rejoined the family. They even have a warm-up suit with the air force logo displayed on the rear side. I'm not back in uniform exactly, but it sure makes me feel a part of the military again. For the first time since receiving my 'permanently retired' letter I feel as if I've been invited back into the armed services that I love.

I'm hopeful about the coming games, especially as the training with the air force is so rigorous. I've also not given up on the dream of walking again. In fact, I still exercise my legs just about every day, and training for the Warrior Games can only boost my chances of getting some movement back again. Since the nerves were cut to reduce the pain, feeling is gradually returning. It's as if the nerve pulses have rerouted and discovered new pathways. I'm back to just about where I was after Dr Kao's surgery, and I cherish the thought of walking again.

But for now I've got the Warrior Games to train for. I'm offered sponsorship by the not-for-profit Wounded Warriors Family Support. They've heard me speak at CCI events and read interviews I've given to the media, and they offer to cover my costs. It's a hugely generous gesture. With their financial support I hire a personal trainer to really get me in shape. She's called Melissa Cussano, and she's tall, blonde, slim, fit and strikingly beautiful.

Of course, she falls instantly in love with my dog. One day I give her a lift to the gym. She needs Napal to make some space so she can get into the car.

'What do I say to get him to move?' she asks.

'Tell him to scoot over.'

Melissa does just that: 'Scoot over, Napal.'

He does as asked.

Melissa is awestruck. 'That's amazing! I can talk to your dog!'

I'm the first guy with paralysis that Melissa has ever trained. The nearest she's come before are guys with shoulder or knee injuries. But they're well on the road to recovery, with her training programme designed to aid that process. With me it's a little different, and there is no manual entitled *How to Train a Paraplegic for the Olympics*.

Melissa works out of a gym called Frisco Fitness Guy, which is run by a former marine. Most of her clients are middle-aged guys with busy business lives and families, who want to lose a bit of weight and get in shape. Even if it isn't what they came to her for, Melissa sets them all a goal: to run a half-marathon. Most laugh when she tells them, but little by little as the fitness regime begins to bite, they start to see that maybe it is possible. Melissa aims to be inspirational, and having me join her programme gives her something to really motivate them. *See that guy in the wheelchair? He's training to roll a full marathon. So quit complaining.*

Every day Napal and I are in the gym, pushing the limits. Or we're at the pool, me thrashing through the water, dragging the deadweight of my legs behind me, my dog trotting excitedly at the poolside. Every day Melissa gets me to sit on one of those big, blow-up balls. I have to keep my balance as she tries to shove me off. It's hard to win that kind of battle when you have no use in your legs, and especially when Melissa so loves to win.

But I guess all the fighting does the job. When I start training with her I wear a medium-sized shirt. By the time the games are approaching my shoulder, chest and arm muscles have bulked out so much that I've moved up to an extra-large. I feel fitter, happier and more confident than I have done in an age. I guess Napal does too.

They say that emotions run up-leash and down again, and it's never been truer about a man–dog duo than it is for us. I know it sounds cheesy but Napal is falling in love ... and so am I. Or rather, Napal's head over heels and long gone, whereas I'm easing my way into a new and unexpected kind of relationship.

With Napal it's all so easy. He's fallen for Julie's dog. Laurel has the loveliest nature you ever could wish for, and she only failed training due to her incurable need to chase squirrels. Laurel just can't say no. That's just how it is with some dogs and why shouldn't it be? Labradors have been bred for centuries as hunting dogs. It's in their nature.

In Napal's eyes Laurel is perfect. She's spirited, funny, wild and beautiful, and best of all she lives at my sister's place, which means there's a huge backyard to tear around in. Julie lives a twenty-minute drive from us. She and Scott have a beautiful house with a good two acres of land. In summer you can barely see the neighbours through the trees. Since moving into Julie's place Laurel has had the time of her life dashing after rabbits and squirrels. But whenever she actually catches something, she has no idea what to do with it.

One time Julie's daughter, Meghan, opened the back door

to find Laurel with something in her jaws. 'Mommy, there's something in Laurel's mouth.'

Laurel came inside wagging herself half to death. She was as proud as a new mom. Meghan prised the bunny free. It was a baby and it was completely unharmed. They carried it up to the far end of the yard and placed it back in its hole – or at least what they hoped was the bunny's hole. There are a lot of them up there.

Whenever we set off for Julie's house – and we visit often, especially in summer – Napal seems to know from the get-go where we're heading. He gets his nose stuck out the window, scenting the air, eyes gleaming excitedly. I can't resist a good tease: 'So, boy, off to see your girlfriend, eh?'

He ignores me. He's too excited to care.

Julie's kids have thought up a much better name for Laurel. They call her Humus. A few days after getting her, Julie and her kids were in the kitchen snacking on humus and pita bread. They joked that Laurel was so enthusiastic and loving she'd respond to just about any name.

One of the kids called over: 'Hey, Humus! Come here!'

Laurel bounded over, tail wagging wildly and knocking over the breakfast stools. The name stuck. But recently Laurel's earned a new nickname: Napal's Girlfriend.

Arriving at Julie's place is about the only time that Napal truly loses it. He throws his service-dog duties right out the window. We drive across the quaint little wooden bridge that leads into their front yard and he's practically elbowing me out of the way. We park by the garage and I've barely uttered the 'Release' command before Napal takes a flying leap out the door.

He races Humus across the front yard, around the side of the house to be first into the swimming pool. Napal always wins. He takes a flying leap out over the water and bellyflops right in, with Humus only seconds behind. Napal finds the combination of a hot Texan day, the pool and Humus simply irresistible. I'm barely into my chair by the time he's splashing and snorting and having the time of his life.

Laurel is a tiny bit more ladylike as far as hitting the water is concerned. She wants to be in there beside her beau, but can she really allow herself to be so easily tempted? A lady has to play a little hard to get. She puts one paw on the step into the pool and sniffs at the water. Napal's out there, kicking deep and trying to lure her in. The next moment she's taken an almighty leap, seven feet or more across the water, and landed right on top of him. This is the cue for all humans to leave the vicinity. It's complete chaos in the pool, and anyone who wants to stay dry has to hightail it out of there. We leave them to it, two young dogs deep in love.

A while later we see them tearing back and forth across the grass paddock that adjoins Julie's house. They fly up the slope, make a circuit around the outdoor fire-pit area, and they're play-fighting and lunging at each other, rolling over and over down the hill. I call Napal to me. I've spied a bunny at the top of the yard. I point it out and he goes completely rigid. He stares at the rabbit, unmoving. I know he won't go for it unless I give him the word.

'OK, go get the bunny! Go get him!'

Napal dashes off, and the moment Laurel sees what he's up to she goes tearing after. But together they are hopeless at stalking anything. They run around in crazy circles, chasing after each other's tails and pouncing on shadows, before finally realizing that all the wildlife has vanished.

*What, no bunnies? They never want to play. Why don't they ever want to play?*

People say that dogs grow to look and act like their owners, or is it vice versa? Like so many things my dog and I do, we've found romance at about the same time. It's almost as if Napal sensed how well I was doing – that I was ready to start a relationship with my trainer, Melissa – so he struck out in that direction too.

*Hey, it's open season! If he can, so can I!*

Like me, Napal's a dark-haired guy who's fallen for a gorgeous, sandy-haired blonde.

It's priceless.

# CHAPTER 28

Napal and I head up to the Olympic Training Center at Colorado Springs, to do some pre-games training. We've been there for a week when the air force ask me if I will be one of the co-captains at the army versus air force football game – West Point against the Air Force Academy. The army have a wounded warrior representing their team, and the air force figure they should have one too.

Napal and I will do this, along with the Hollywood actor Cuba Gooding Junior. The two of us – three, with my dog – will go out for the coin-toss at the start of the game. I figure it'll be a fabulous experience if Blake can make it too. Recently he told me that he might want to join the air force when he's old enough, and his big dream is to play football for something like their academy.

I buy him a ticket and a friend takes him to the airport, to catch the flight to Colorado Springs. The morning before the game the air force have a very, very special surprise for us. They've sorted it so Blake and I can go riding on horseback through the foothills of the Rocky Mountains. Julie used to keep horses, so I have ridden a good deal, but of course I've never even dreamed of getting on a horse since my paralysis.

The air force guys reassure me it'll be OK. They have a special ramp that they roll me up. The horse is brought to the end of the ramp so I can transfer onto its back. I settle into the saddle, but with no feeling or strength in my legs it's not as if I can use them to grip, which is basically how an able-bodied person remains in the saddle.

They've given me the slowest, most docile horse imaginable, but I'm still having trouble keeping my balance even when we're stationary. They decide to tie me on. They rope my feet to the stirrups, which helps with the balance issue, but what if I fall or the horse takes a tumble? Roped on, I will definitely break some bones, brittle as they are.

I glance at Blake. He has never ridden before, but he looks so excited to be in the saddle and about to start a horseback hike through such majestic scenery. What a wonderful adventure this is going to be. There's no way I can flunk this. We set off, and I soon realize what an incredible experience this is for the both of us.

Ever since my paralysis I have been almost completely restricted to hard concrete, sidewalks, or solid floors. Everything nature provides is too soft or overgrown to negotiate on wheels. But on horseback I can make my way through a forest, climb a hill and traverse wild ground. For the majority of able-bodied people, it's a given that you can stroll through woodland feeling the crunch of pine needles beneath your feet, the smell of tree sap fresh in your nostrils. That's what you do. For me that had become an impossibility. Yet the horse sets me free. And you know something? The way the animal moves beneath me feels almost as if I am walking again. The rolling, rhythmic, up-and-down motion is the closest I've come to the feeling of being able to walk once more.

I am awestruck, and ahead of me Blake looks so incredibly happy. But my steed is definitely the slowcoach. She's moving extra carefully with me, as if she's been ordered to, and as a result we start to fall behind. Then she decides enough is enough: she's going to put on a spurt of speed to catch the others. She breaks into a trot. This is not good. I am hanging on for dear life as my mount surges ahead. But to be able to share this special moment with my son makes it worth the risk. Happily at the end of the ride I've just about managed to avoid taking a bone-crushing tumble.

We head from there direct to the football game. Blake gets seated alongside the air force team, and for him this is his dream day of days. I roll over to the sidelines, Napal keeping pace beside me. The pitch is Astroturf, and it feels soft and squishy under my wheels. I'm in great shape due to all the training for the Warrior Games, but even so it's going to be tough to wheel myself, especially as it has started to snow.

I turn to Cuba Gooding. 'Hey, you know, it's real hard for me to roll on Astro. When we get called for the toss, just go slow for me, OK?'

Cuba flashes a broad smile. 'Sure. No problem. OK.'

I guess this gets forgotten in the excitement of the moment.

We get the call. Cuba and the air force guys set off at a fast jog. I set myself rolling and try to keep up, but I'm sweating my ass off as the wheels dig deep. There is no way I can ask

Napal to assist me. No dog in the world could pull a guy in a chair through this. I reach the centre of the field just as the team captains shake hands and the coin goes flashing through the air. I have told all my friends and family to watch out for me and Napal, as the football game is being televised nationally.

I rejoin Blake in the stands and get an avalanche of text messages.

'Hey, we saw Napal, but no sign of you!'

'Well . . . your dog looked great!'

'Go Napal!'

I figure they're trying to wind me up, so I ignore them and concentrate on the game. The air force team comes from behind to win. It's a perfect day. Blake, Napal and I fly home together. I have recorded the game and we flick on the TV. Sure enough, the opening minutes show the two captains shaking hands and the coin-toss, with Napal's handsome-as-hell head right beneath the handshake. But of me there is no sign: I am out-of-frame completely. Once again it is my dog who takes the limelight.

I gesture at the screen. 'Hey, Napal! Can you believe that? They got you, buddy, but there's no sign of me. Can you believe that?'

The boys are in fits of laughter. I suppose I've just got to get used to it: my dog's going to steal the show every single time.

But it's just when we're up so high that my physical condition decides to kick me in the teeth, big time. I guess it's due to all the training, but I develop a pressure sore. It's at the base of my butt, where the skin rubs against my racing chair. I get admitted to a VA hospital so they can treat it. Napal tries to cheer my spirits, but there's not a lot he can do to lift me right now, and

I can't look after him properly when confined to a hospital bed.

Every day I spend in surgery is a day less training. Melissa visits. So do my folks. But that's about all. When I'm in hospital I don't invite all comers. I don't want their sympathy because I'd rather be out there living life and doing what we do. With the CCI appearances, the media interviews, plus the Warrior Games coming up, I feel like we're on a mission. We've got work to do. But instead, I'm stuck in hospital due to a freakin' pressure sore.

It's made worse by the fact that the doctor doesn't even ask my permission to open up the pressure sore, and once it's open he does nothing to treat or close it. As far as I'm concerned I've had it. I check myself out without telling anyone. The doctor calls my folks. He warns them that I have an infected sore and that the poison will work its way through to the bone. It will kill me, in a similar way to how such an infection contributed to the death of Christopher Reeve, the *Superman* actor.

He gives me six months to live.

Meanwhile, I've quietly checked myself into Baylor, the hospital where Napal and I volunteer. It's never occurred to me before to use a non-VA facility for surgery, but I'm ready to try anything. I see Dr Lemmon, a surgeon who just happens to be a reservist in the military. He's also known as something of a medical genius. He even made someone a new tongue using a graft from their arm tissue.

Dr Lemmon takes one look at my pressure sore and says he'll deal with it. He figures he can get the infection to heal sufficiently to allow him to go in and do interior and exterior stitching, to close the wound completely. But as luck would have it, the only available slot he has for the operation is on the morning of Christmas Eve. He just doesn't know if he can make it happen, because everyone is scheduled for time off over the Christmas break.

Dr Lemmon gathers his medical staff. He explains that he's planning on doing an operation on me on Christmas Eve, and that he needs volunteers to come in and assist. He declares that he's drawing a line in the sand, like they did at the Alamo. All those who are willing to volunteer should step forward.

Someone asks, 'But who's Jason Morgan?'

'He's the guy with the dog. Napal. The wounded veteran with the service dog Napal.'

At the mention of my dog every single member of staff steps forward to volunteer.

The surgery goes ahead. The staff get a Christmas tree erected in my room and they invite my boys and my folks in for a special dinner. Over food and drink the story does the rounds. Mom thinks it's priceless.

'Hah!' she teases. 'I've been known as Jason's mom for so long, this is sweet. Now you're known as the guy with Napal!'

The surgery is successful. I'm released into the real world and the life that I love. With Melissa's help I train like my life depends on it. I head back to Colorado Springs as the Warrior Games are about to start. Swimming is one of my strongest sports, and in the backstroke I'm neck and neck with this other guy. In between gulps of air I can hear Napal woofing out barks of encouragement from the poolside.

'AAAROOUGGHHH!'

My folks are there to cheer me on and it's a photo finish.

The timing pads indicate that I was one seven-hundredth of a second behind the other guy, but the judges check the photos and I've actually won. When my name is announced in first place, Napal goes woofing-wild. That's one medal won for the air force and I feel so proud. Napal joins me on the podium as I get my gold, and his bark of joy echoes around the four walls.

The big one is up next, the one I've been training for ferociously: the 1,500-metre wheelchair race. Melissa's been driving me hard, and when the heats are done I've made it through to the final seven. I'm pumped up to go all out to win. I'm hoping for at least a bronze but I need to roll a great race.

It's especially tough because I'm competing with double amputees, who carry thirty or forty pounds less weight. More to the point, you can be a double amputee and still have lost none of your mobility or muscle use above the amputation level. You can rely on pelvic, back and stomach muscles to help push the chair. As a paraplegic I can barely harness any of that core power; it all has to come from my arms and my shoulders.

The racer in pole position is the one to beat. He's an army guy, and I know from chatting during the heats that he rolls full marathons. We're at 6,000 feet here and the air is thin. We have four laps of a 400-metre track ahead of us. I know I am up against it.

The starting pistol fires. Three pull away at breakneck speed, led by the army guy. I try to stay with them, and I'm thinking, *Surely they can't keep this freakin' pace up for the full mile?*

By the end of lap two I know I cannot stick with the lead guys. If I try to, I might not even finish, which would be the ultimate ignominy. I decide I have no option but to roll my own race. By the start of lap four my shoulders are burning and I'm soaked in sweat. I can hardly catch my breath. The army guy rolls past me, lapping me. I feel totally humiliated. I struggle hard with that final lap. Ahead of me three guys roll across the finish line. The winner has done it in the upper four minutes mark, which is insanely fast. By the time I crawl across the line I'm a full two minutes behind.

I'm in fourth place, which means I have failed to win a medal. I feel as if I have pushed myself to the limit and beyond, and all for . . . nothing. I roll to the end of the field utterly racked with agony. I come to a stop with my nerves on fire. I feel embarrassed and emotionally devastated. I bury my head in my hands and for some reason I start to cry. It's weird. I don't usually tend to show my emotions. The military taught me to hold my feelings in. I can't fathom why this has so got to me.

I guess I feel as if I have let myself and my team down – which means the entire air force. My mom and dad and sister, plus my nephew and niece have all flown up to watch me race, only for me to fail to win a medal. I hunch deeper, head down, trying to catch my breath and to hide my tears. That's when I see Napal running across the track towards me. Melissa has had him, but he can't wait to see me. He must have broken away from her and dashed over because . . . he knows. My dog knows exactly how much I'm hurting right now.

I have my head hunched low over my lap but Napal's having none of it. He nudges himself in there, thrusting his muzzle between my face and my thighs. *Come on, buddy, let me in! Let me in there!*

He gets his fine head deep in – no licks and no messing – thrust cheek to cheek, skin-close to mine. I throw my arms around him. I let my tears fall onto my dog's face, and it is just so incredibly comforting. For several long seconds we stay like that, communicating silently, my dog speaking to me, as always. *I'm here for you, buddy. You did fine. You did good. I'm here for you, just like I always will be.*

I can hear Napal's voice inside my head, as clearly as if he's talking in my ear. His tone changes. *But why didn't you let me pull you in your chair, you amazing, lovely, stubborn-as-hell human? We'd have won that race as well!*

If I'd let him – if the rules allowed it – Napal would have dragged me to victory. He'd pull me all the way to hell and back if need be. Something strikes me right then. It's a lightning bolt of revelation. I haven't won the race. But hell, I have the best battle buddy, the best life companion a guy could wish for. And this moment – this simple truth – means more to me than winning ever could.

I tell Napal exactly that, and I manage to lift my head and dry my tears.

One of the most surprising things about the Warrior Games is that I'm about the only guy there with a service dog. Very few wounded warriors seem to know that such dogs exist, let alone that they could get one. Napal and I spend much of our time spreading the word, and it just reinforces to me the scale of the need.

For these guys, seeing Napal use his nose to open the doors to the Olympic Center, or calling the lift for me with his paw is such a big wow. As ambassadors for CCI this is absolutely where we need to be. I call Corey Hudson, CCI's director, and tell him about my experiences. We decide this needs action. He suggests a lobbying trip to Washington. If we can get Congress to legislate that the VA has to publicize what service dogs can do, that would be a start.

I know what one dog, Napal, has done to turn one life around. Imagine what a score of dogs could do for these guys.

A photo of me in my racing chair makes the front cover of *The Airman*, the magazine of the US Air Force, with the headline NEVER SAY IT'S IMPOSSIBLE. After the shock letter I received invaliding me out of the military, I feel as if I've finally been let back in again. I may not be able to serve or to jump out of aircraft, but that doesn't mean that I can't play a part.

Off the back of *The Airman* article I get an invitation to visit my old unit at Keesler Air Force Base, where I spent a year in weather school on my way to combat weather training. I tell them I'd be happy to oblige. When I pass back through the gates, I guess they've invited me here to meet and greet a few of the old hands.

Far from it.

After a tour of the school they take me into the squadron mess. Before me are ranks of guys in full-dress uniform – practically the entire intake for that year's combat weather school. They rise and stand to attention, and I'm amazed and touched by this honour that they've extended to me.

I'm asked to talk about my life in the military and my injuries. I choose to tell them mostly about life-after-getting-Napal.

And mostly, of course, they're all dying to meet my dog.

# CHAPTER 29

Napal and I attend a couple of CCI fundraisers, plus we do a big chunk of filming for National Geographic, telling our story as part of their *Extraordinary Dogs* series. I don't know it yet, but this will have unexpected consequences for both me and Napal. However, that's a way in the future.

I take a call from a lady called Deanna, who sits on the McKinney YMCA board with me. She's seeking a speaker to talk to some youths in an inner-city school – they've got themselves involved with drink, small-scale crime and drugs. I've never spoken to such a crowd before, but she figures my story and the message it embodies might well prove instructive. It's also to mark Veterans Day, so it fits.

I turn up and I get the usual caution. 'Ten to fifteen minutes,' she warns me. 'That's about all they can handle.'

I tell her we'll see how it goes.

I've got a special show lined up for today. I open by telling them that Napal is my service dog, and I've been taking him to acting classes. I hold my finger and thumb out like a pistol and shoot: *Bang!* Right on cue, Napal 'drops dead' on the stage. He lies on his back, legs in the air and paws curled over, unmoving.

The kids hold their breath. They're spellbound. I can hear the collective sigh of relief when I bring him back to life again.

'Napal, come alive! Napal, come alive!'

He springs to his feet and takes a bow, and the kids are laughing and smiling. Napal and I have them in the palms of our hands (paws). Now that I've got them captivated I tell the basics of my story: how I ended up in a wheelchair, but that now I compete in the Warrior Games. I tell them how we can all overcome unimaginable adversity, especially with a loyal buddy by our side. Then I try something new. I tell them about my war with pain and how Napal helps me win my battles. 'So, I don't know if he'll do this, but let's see.'

I double over and cradle my head in my hands, as if I'm having a real bad pain attack. Napal steps across and puts his head in my lap to comfort me. You could hear a pin drop. Some of the kids are close to tears. Then I hit them with the message – something I figure will be far more powerful than a cop saying, 'Don't use drugs 'cause they're bad and you'll go to jail.'

'So, if you think it's cool to take hard drugs and that it doesn't hurt anyone, think again. Just think of me and my dog. Say I know this guy in a wheelchair and he'll never walk again, and all 'cause of drugs. Use me as your excuse. Just think of me and Napal. My dog and me, hold our image in your minds.'

Deanna comes up to me afterwards, all teary-eyed. 'How do you guys do that?' she sniffs. 'How do you do that? And I don't even like dogs!'

Through Deanna I meet her sister, Joanna. It turns out that she's got two asthmatic boys and they can't have dogs in the house. But for Napal Joanna can't help making an exception.

She invites us over. We meet her husband, Dave, and they're both totally smitten. Joanna and Dave will become two of our staunchest and most generous-hearted supporters. If ever I'm away with Napal and the boys need looking after, I'll always be able to count on them.

Joanna offers to take on the role of my personal assistant. She thinks that the work Napal and I are doing is so important that I need to be 'properly managed', and she says she'll find the time to help. And it's Dave, her engineer husband, who'll care for my boys when Napal and I are away at those events that his wife has helped organize.

The first time that Dave comes to help us he's in for a surprise. He arrives at our place expecting the house to be a real mess and the boys to be out-of-control tearaways. *No mom at home. Dad in a chair. It's going to be some kind of a nightmare.* Not a bit of it. He asks my youngest, Grant, how they've learned to be so good at caring for the place, and themselves.

Grant smiles a little self-consciously. 'That's easy – there isn't a woman around to do it for us!'

Joanna helps organize our first-ever visit to the nation's capital, Washington DC. It's April 2012 and I take a call from a guy called John Libonati, a business executive. He explains that they're holding a Washington fundraiser for CCI, and their intended speaker has just dropped out. CCI has proposed me and Napal as a replacement. I tell John that I'd be honoured to attend and I hand him over to Joanna to get the travel details sorted.

In due course Napal and I board the flight to DC. He curls up neat and comfortable beneath my seat, snoozing away on Mexico time. Unless you looked very closely, you wouldn't even know that he was there. My chair is packed out of sight in the rear, and the guy who takes the seat next to me clearly has no idea that I'm a paraplegic.

We spend the entire flight chatting and we get on well. We touch down in DC and he gestures for me to get off first.

I shrug my apologies. 'Thanks, but I gotta wait for the aisle chair to get me off the plane.' The aisle chair is narrow enough to pass down the aisle. A normal wheelchair is just too wide.

'Oh, why's that?' the guy asks.

''Cause I'm paralyzed from the waist down.'

He smiles. 'Ha ha. No, really, why?'

'I am. I'm paralyzed. And that's why I got my service dog with me. To help.'

'No way. There's no way . . .'

I call to Napal, and he unwinds lazily, acknowledging that for now at least Mexico time is over. He yowls-growls and pokes his nose out. *You called?*

The guy stares in open-mouthed amazement. 'No way . . . Man, I never even knew. I never even had a clue you had a dog down there.'

I kind of like pulling tricks like that. I like seeing how the able-bodied react to being teased by a person in a chair. It's funny, but people kind of expect it from an able-bodied person, but somehow not from someone who's wheelchair-bound. Most people just don't know how to take it. I wonder why that is. Does sympathy for my disability mean that humour can't be accommodated too?

This guy takes it all with good grace. And I figure we have

surely made a impression and hopefully recruited another convert to the cause.

John Libonati is there to meet Napal and me at the airport, with a limo and driver he's hired for our entire time in DC. As sometimes happens, we hit it off right away. It's hard to describe, but everything just seems to click. John Libonati is another guy like Jim Siegfried: both are firmly on the side of the angels.

A former US Secret Service agent, for twenty-three years John looked after world leaders and presidents. He was on former president Ronald Reagan's security detail, and after retiring from the USSS he took a job with Owens Corning as vice president for government and public affairs. Most of those invited to this evening's CCI event are either former Secret Service types, or they're John's present-day business colleagues.

John tells me his aim is to raise $10,000, which will be enough to name a CCI dog after his friend who fell from a horse and ended up disabled. Working closely with CCI, he's also arranged for Napal and me to do a lobbying visit to Congress. Plus we'll be going to Walter Reed hospital, the main facility wounded warriors are sent to, so we can spread awareness about the availability of service dogs.

John has put the fundraiser together via his personal network, relying entirely on volunteers and sponsorship in kind. Owens Corning has underwritten the main costs. A buddy of John's who works at Home Depot has provided the venue; another guy who works in the drinks industry has provided all the alcohol; a third guy who owns a store across the street has donated free valet parking. And so on.

'Long-winded black-tie events are a dime a dozen,' John tells me on the drive into downtown DC. 'They're not my style. This'll be short and focused, and very much all about CCI. There'll be a video, then your speech, plus a relaxed mix-and-mingle. I'll try to talk as little as possible and let you and your dog speak for the cause. There'll be no direct request for money or hard sell. People can give what they can. That's about it.'

John mentions that the director of the VA – another former USSS guy – will be there, as will other key people on the VA board. Clearly it's vital that Napal and I are on top form tonight.

The evening opens with Corey Hudson saying a few words, which lead into the CCI video. It's then time for John to introduce Napal and me, after which I have my dog pull me into the centre of the stage. That has become our standard means of entry to events, and it sure does tend to grab people's attention. Having done a little theatre, we get serious. I tell the audience in detail about the events that led up to my injuries, my long battle to recover, my pain and my bouts of depression. I tell them how I lost my reason for living, and then I speak about getting Napal. I tell them how I feel as if I have even more purpose in life since getting my service dog than when I was serving in special forces. That is how this dog has turned my life around.

The audience is welling up, which doesn't exactly help me fight back my own tears. What I've said about having a purpose in life was on the spur of the moment, and it's the first time that I've actually put that thought into words. It's surprised even me. Tonight is a defining moment in my life, and it was all totally unscripted and unplanned.

I finish by getting Napal to do his bow, long and low, and

there's tumultuous applause. When it's died down enough to hear myself speak, I ask the audience a last question: 'Hey, after all of that, don't you think Napal deserves a treat?'

The audience agrees that he does.

'Napal, go get your treats. Go find your treats.'

I've placed a bag of Cesar Softies on a table at the back of the room. Though he rarely gets one, Napal has come to love these small, paw-shaped savoury treats. Tonight's bag is a Cesar Softies Medley, a selection of his favourite flavours. Napal can smell a Cesar Softie a mile away, and I've given him a sneak preview of where they're hidden.

'Please move aside to let him pass, and don't pet him – he's working!'

Locating them in this dark room causes Napal not the slightest problem. He weaves his way through the crowd, puts his paws on the table and grabs his bag of treats, returning to me on the stage so I can feed him one.

It brings the house down.

At the end of the evening John Libonati announces that they've raised approaching $20,000, double their funding target. That means they can sponsor two dogs. One will be named after John's disabled friend. But the other, John announces, will be named Jason Morgan. I am astounded and deeply honoured, and I'm unable to hold back my tears now.

In a private moment John tells me there is something else he wants to do for us. He's going to see about making my dog and me honorary members of the Secret Service. I can just see it: *Agents Jason Morgan and Napal, at your service.*

John takes us out to dinner at Bobby Van's Steakhouse, a

fine old-style restaurant in downtown DC. My pain is pretty minimal right now, which is good because it means I can enjoy the food. I tell John that at tonight's event I shared details of my life that I have never really spoken about before. I delved deep into life-before-the-chair and it's been emotional.

John thanks me for my candidness and honesty. He tells me that it inspired people to give with such generosity. And in return he begins to tell me about the special journey that brought him to CCI.

'I come – proudly – from a blue-collar New York family. My dad worked as a NY sanitation guy. In fact, most of the time he did several jobs back to back, to keep the family. In spite of that, plus dropping out of school during tenth grade, he had an amazing approach to life. He cared about those less fortunate in almost every way. Plus he never uttered nor would he ever tolerate the slightest racial slur.

'He worked three, sometimes four jobs, but still found the time to coach my and my brother's league team. We never owned a home, but he never missed dinner with the family: 6 p.m. every night, regular as clockwork. If he saw a homeless person on the street he would go to them, get them coffee and comfort them.

'One time my brother and I were the victims of a gang assault. The gang leader was arrested. My dad saw his mother sobbing in the courtroom because she did not speak any English and had no bail money.' John pauses. 'You know what my dad did? He provided her with the bail money, then drove her and her son home. I mean, who does that? Whoever does that?

'But a while back my dad was diagnosed with a neurological disease – one that would slowly paralyze him. The exact cause took years to work out. Spinocerebellar degeneration, they called it. A very slow, debilitating disease. And in 2009 he finally lost his ability to walk.

'That's when I began to research service dogs, in the hope that one might be of use to him. My research told me that CCI was the best provider. Their Northeast Regional Facility is only forty miles east of my parents' place. I went to visit and I fell in love with CCI and its mission. I decided to hold a fundraiser for CCI when I returned to Washington. That was today.'

I'm all but silenced by John's story. Hearing it has been hugely emotional. But one thing I feel compelled to ask: 'So, is your dad getting a CCI dog?'

John shakes his head. 'We never did apply. His age and living conditions didn't make him a good candidate. Plus we know he doesn't have long left. But he loves dogs. We had one when I was growing up – part golden retriever and part Labrador. She was a family dog, but really my dad's. They were inseparable. She was put down when she reached fifteen and he cried for weeks on end.'

I can tell how emotional this is for John. 'My dad's confined to bed and he's suffering', John continues. 'A CCI dog just wouldn't help much. But I wish he could have met you guys. You and Napal, you are such an inspiration. He'd have been glued to your talk, and though he doesn't have much he would have insisted on giving generously.' He glances at me. 'So, tonight, I guess it was also for my dad.'

Wow. John Libonati. He's another Jim Siegfried. What a guy.

Later, Napal and I are in our hotel room getting ready for bed. It's been a long and very special day, but it's also been emotionally draining. Another day of days, one of so many in life-after-getting-Napal. There is a knock at the door. 'Room service.'

*That's odd. I didn't order room service.*

I open up. A guy in hotel uniform wheels in a trolley. 'Complimentary. On the house.'

He whips off a domed silver lid to reveal two metal bowls. One is part-full of Evian mineral water. The other is piled high with . . . dog biscuits. Eukanuba, by the smell of things. And there is nothing – *absolutely nothing* – for me!

The following morning – my dog very well fed and rested – we head over to the Congress Building on Capitol Hill. As well as John, a fantastic woman called Deb Dougherty accompanies us. She's the director of CCI's Northeast Regional Facility. Deb's been instrumental in getting this lobbying trip organized. She and John have executed a pincer movement, securing appointments with everyone we need to see. Napal and I speak before several Congress members and their staff, and I give them a potted version of our story. I relate my experiences at the Warrior Games, explaining how almost none of those present had any idea about service dogs. I reinforce how vital it is that we let veterans know about the dogs and what they can do. I point out it was only by luck and chance that I learned about service dogs, and hence got Napal.

One congresswoman says she worries that more awareness will create a tsunami of needs, and that we don't have the dogs to cope. As politely as I'm able, I tell her the obvious: that is no excuse to keep wounded veterans in ignorance and in suffering. We point out that federal funding has been allocated to the service dog programme, so falling short isn't justified on any grounds, not even financial. More dogs can be trained to fill the need.

It's hard to argue with a wounded warrior and a dog like Napal. By the end we've got an agreement in place: all VA facilities will have to stock and promote service dog literature and videos. It's a fantastic result. Far more than we'd ever dreamed of.

From Capitol Hill we head across town to the Walter Reed National Military Medical Center, which provides care for injured military personnel from across America. I wheel my chair from bedside to bedside, Napal sticking close, as I chat to the wounded. Most of the guys appear to have lost limbs in combat – Iraq and Afghanistan – and I am moved by the sheer number facing life-altering disabilities. But I see few signs of self-pity. I see so much spirited, positive, go-getting attitude. Many of the guys can't move much, but they call Napal and me over with their eyes. They're so keen to hear about my dog and how he might help ease their disability.

I try to communicate how much easier it is to face an unknow-able future with such a dog by your side. I explain the ways my dog has revolutionized my life and how he has given me back the will to live. It's difficult for guys like us to be always asking for help, but it's no sweat to ask it of your dog. These are intensely private moments, ones of high emotion, forging real, visceral connections. And I know that Napal and me are exactly where we need to be.

We're there for a good ninety minutes at least. At one stage one of the hospital officials suggests to me that it's 'time to move on'. I tell the guy that I'll find time for every wounded warrior who calls to me. My dog and I are on a mission and we're not going to be sidelined by some hospital bureaucrat.

'There are always guys like that in the system,' John remarks. 'Leave him to me.'

I've been asked not to talk to the veterans when they're getting their physical therapy sessions. But I see one guy, who has had his arm amputated, working on his PT with his partner by his side, and she seems fascinated by Napal and me. I lie to our guide, saying the guy and I have served together, which gives me an excuse to say hello. I roll up to the pair of them. Within minutes he and his partner are hooked by my story of life-after-getting-Napal. That guy and I will stay in touch and he'll end up getting a CCI dog, which will revolutionize his life.

One thing is crystal clear to me following this visit. Lack of awareness among such guys about the availability of service dogs is widespread. There are so many veterans to reach and so much work to be done.

Before leaving DC John tells me there is a final, very special visit he has lined up for us. He's put a call through to the then director of the Secret Service, Mark Sullivan, and we've been invited to visit. We drive over to the USSS headquarters, situated on H Street, between 9th and 10th. It's a relatively new building, having only been completed a year back, but the reception we receive is vintage stuff.

Mark Sullivan rolls out the red carpet for me and my dog. First we're taken to the command centre, where we get a full briefing about the USSS. Then we're taken to see the Wall of Honour, which commemorates all those agents who have fallen in the line of duty. Last but not least the director declares that we are being adopted as two of the USSS's own. I am handed a special USSS challenge coin. As for Napal, he gets a blue collar threaded around his neck. On it is stamped the USSS's logo, plus WORKING FOR THE UNITED STATES SECRET SERVICE.

Wow. He really is *Special Agent Napal.*

John drives Special Agent Napal and me to the airport. He gives a mini-speech of goodbye and of thanks. He talks about how after this visit we will be friends for life – the three of us. He describes Napal and me as one of the most impressive duos he has ever come across, in two decades of meeting numerous heads of state and world leaders.

'None compare to you guys. You are genuine, inspirational and positive, and you remain undeterred by all misfortune. If ever I think I have cause to complain about my lot in life, after these few days I will think again. You never give up and you never stop giving back.

'You are special,' John tells Agent Napal and me. 'There are few like you in the world. Don't ever forget that.'

# CHAPTER 30

So Napal is now in the US Secret Service. Of course, this doesn't mean that there's anything particularly more secretive about the way he comports himself, as matters are about to prove.

It's close to Christmas and I've got a carol service to attend at the local school. Blake is both a football stud and he sings in the choir. How cool is that? He's really pleased to have me see him perform. Before the service commences the music teacher says a few words.

'I want y'all to listen real hard and experience the music. So I'm gonna dim the lights, and if y'all can be real quiet now, I'd appreciate.'

The room goes dark and the air is electric with anticipation. We're all expecting the first notes of the first carol to strike up when instead, a monstrous, elongated 'YAOOOOOUUUUU-WWWWWWLLL' reverberates deafeningly around the hall. It's Napal of course, doing his when-is-this-all-going-to-be-over act. But it's pitch dark, Napal is a black dog lying beneath a row of shadowed chairs, and every head has turned to stare in the direction of the sound: me.

I can hardly shout out, 'It's not me! It's my dog!'

He's totally invisible. They'll obviously think, *That guy in the chair is a real wacko. He's even got some make-believe dog!* But my boys, bless them, see the funny side, and it's even funnier now that our dog is Special Agent Napal.

I've learned to accept that Napal comes as an indivisible package. Without the quirky, laid-back side of him, I wouldn't get the 101 per cent laser-focused loyalty and love. I figure Napal needs his Mexico time as an antidote to his utter devotion and ability to take my pain away. He's earned his Mexico time ten times over, for my pain is one hell of a burden to have to carry.

It's about now that I receive a surprise email. The National Geographic series *Extraordinary Dogs* has aired worldwide, and a British author, Damien Lewis, contacts me. He says he saw us on TV and feels that Napal and I have an incredibly inspiring story to tell. Have we ever thought of writing a book? I tell him it never even crossed my mind, and I wouldn't have a clue how to start, but I know we love to tell our story.

The Brit author promises to send me a previous book that he wrote with a warrior and his dog, and we can take it from there. I speak to Corey, the director of CCI, about the idea. He says it's unlikely that it'll ever happen. There are always guys saying they want to write a book. Very few ever come to anything.

I figure he's probably right, so I'm surprised when I receive a package in the mail. The book – *Sergeant Rex* – was co-written by Damien Lewis and Corporal Mike Dowling of the US Marine Corps. It tells the story of Dowling and Rex, his bomb detection dog, and their 2004 tour of Iraq. I start reading and I'm gripped.

I invite Melissa and the two little girls she has from a previous marriage on a trip to the zoo, together with my boys. It's kind of a celebration that life can be so good, but I also want to run the book idea by her. I tell her that this crazy Brit has been in touch wanting to write about my dog and me. She's immediately enthusiastic. A book would be a great way to get the message heard. Melissa backs the idea all the way. I feel heartened by her enthusiasm.

Napal and I roll around the zoo knowing we're gonna have some real fun here. The animals are used to being stared at by humans, but Napal – he's a totally different proposition. This big, burly lion comes bounding over. He collides with the glass, glaring at Napal from barely inches away, and is that *hunger* I can read in his gaze? As for Napal, he is in denial. He plonks his butt down with his back to the window: it's his hear-no-evil, see-no-evil, scent-no-evil stance. *If I can't see it or smell it, it's not there.*

I pull him up into my lap. I reassure him: 'Good boy. You're OK. You can take him on, can't you Napal? You'd get him, wouldn't you?'

Napal takes a peek at the lion, but he's not so sure. *Woahh! Big pussy cat! What is that? Shoot, this thing wants to eat me!*

Blake has come with us, and he gets down on a level with Napal, eyeballing the lion. He does his special, growly like-a-dog voice: 'Grrrrr . . . I can take you on! Grrrrr . . . I can take you on!'

Melissa and her girls are in fits.

Next we head for the monkey enclosure. As soon as the primates lay eyes upon my dog they start jabbering and screaming and dancing about in a rage. Clearly they do not appreciate having a dog around. As for Napal, he gets his paws up on the railing and stares into their enclosure, as cool as a cucumber. *Weird looking kind of an animal. Wonder if it's good to eat?*

The cheetahs are next. They're lounging around in the sun, paying not the slightest attention to anyone, and then they spy my four-legged companion. They come bouncing across to us, the pair of them pacing backwards and forwards before the glass, hissing and pawing.

I get Napal to give them a show, towing me this way and that in my chair. Melissa and her girls are on the floor, they're laughing so much. As for Blake, he's got that cute, far-away, dreamy smile on his face that he reserves for my dog when he's involved in some of his classic Napal antics.

After the zoo visit I mull over the book idea some more. I call the author on Skype so we can talk it through. I tell him I'm doubtful. I tell him there is a lot I simply cannot remember. Big chunks of time are shrouded in shades of grey. He reassures me that there's a whole universe of a story here that we can explore, and maybe in doing so we'll uncover more of the memories. I tell him what seems to me to be obvious: he's got to meet Napal. He'll only know for sure if he gets to meet my dog. We decide either Napal and I will to fly to the UK, or more likely he'll come to to visit us in Texas. We sign off agreeing to explore some travel options.

I take a call from John Libonati. After the Washington visit we speak almost weekly now, and he's really got the bit between his teeth. He tells me he's trying to sort Napal and me a visit to the White House, using the influence of some senior USSS colleagues who work on the president's security detail. He figures it would be a great opportunity to push our message about what CCI dogs can do for the wounded and the disabled.

I tell him we're ready. He just has to make the call.

I get contacted by Wounded Warriors Family Support, the organization that sponsored me to attend the Warrior Games. Having seen how I competed, they wonder if I'd be willing to roll a full marathon. If so, they'll sponsor me to do so. They mention that the iconic Marine Corps Marathon is coming up in October 2012, in Washington DC. That's only six months away.

There would be no more fitting race to train for as my first marathon. I barely need time to think about it. I remember the pledge that I made to my special operations buddies not long after I came out of the coma: *You know what I'll do? I'll run a full marathon. How does that sound?*

I tell Wounded Warriors Family Support I'll do it.

I redouble my training. Every spare moment Napal and I are in the gym, driven hard by Melissa. We study the route of the Marine Corps Marathon and realize how hilly Washington DC is. I'll need to boost my upper-body strength and my stamina big time. Melissa gets a special brace made with the help of Justin Meaders, a guy who's become a good friend of mine. Justin was injured in a motorcycle accident and is also a paraplegic. He's gone from there to competing in the US Paralympic Triathlon Team.

Justin helped me design my racing chair. We place his brace on the floor and slot my chair into it. It's now positioned with the rear wheels on a treadmill and hard against the friction drum, to simulate rolling up some serious uphill stretches. Downhill presents almost as big a challenge: the last thing I can afford to do is let my chair roll away with me in it.

We intersperse the gym sessions with live training on the roads; we can't use the sidewalks because if I hit a kerb at speed it could wipe me out. Melissa rides ahead on a bicycle to make sure the intersections are free. We start by cycling/rolling five-mile stretches, and we build it up gradually. By June we've pushed it to a regular ten miles, which means we're well on course for hitting the eighteen-to-twenty-mile mark by September. Melissa doesn't want to go beyond twenty miles. If I can roll twenty, she argues, I can roll the full twenty-six.

Napal loves my regular gym sessions. For him they are a golden opportunity to indulge in some serious Mexico time. While I'm pushing myself to exhaustion, he sprawls at my side, snoozing. Unlike Blue, my Australian shepherd, Napal has never been much of a snorer, but boy does he dream. I figure he makes up for all the animals he's not had the chance to chase in life by doing so in his sleep. I'm there punching my wheels against the friction blocks, and Napal is splayed on the floor, his legs twitching as if he's running. His mouth and lips tremble as he makes excited little yelp-bark-growls deep in his throat, never quite letting the sound truly fly. His eyelids flicker with the thrill of the hunt.

*What is he after?* I wonder? *Bunnies? Bobcats? Coyotes? Who knows?*

We're in the midst of one of these training sessions when I take a call from Jim Siegfried. He has some simply amazing news to tell me. Tatiana, Napal's younger sister and the puppy Jim Siegfried raised next, has just won one of the American Humane Association Hero Dog Awards. Less than a month after Tatiana graduated from CCI she saved the life of Christina, a young disabled woman from Florida.

Christina suffered progressive hearing loss as a teenager, complicated by asthma and Ménière's disease – an inflammation of the inner ear which can cause people to fall over, faint or black out. Tatiana was trained as a hearing dog, so she would nudge Christina in the leg if there was a noise she couldn't hear – for example, the bleeping of a pedestrian crossing.

Christina got Tatiana in June 2012. Not long after that she realized her dog had another amazing skill. It wasn't something taught by CCI; it was innate. Whenever Christina was about to suffer an episode of Ménière's disease Tatiana would nuzzle at her anxiously. Christina put two and two together and learned to read the signs. From then on, whenever Tatiana gave the warning, Christina would get somewhere safe – lying or sitting down – to prevent herself from falling over and getting hurt.

One evening they went to sleep in Christina's room, with Tatiana up on the bed. In the middle of the night Christina went into full respiratory arrest and stopped breathing. Tatiana jumped off the bed, dashed across the corridor and woke Christina's parents. 'What's going on, Tat? What's wrong?' The dog practically dragged them back to Christina's room. They immediately called 911. The paramedics said that if they'd reached Christina a minute later she would have died.

Christina sent Jim an email, explaining all that her dog had done. She rounded it off: 'Tatiana has not only become my ears and my best friend, but she has also become my heroine and guardian angel. Simply put, she is priceless ... To her, and to everyone involved in her training, upbringing, and ultimately her placement with me, I owe my LIFE!'

Jim had driven to Los Angeles to attend the AHA Awards, in Beverley Hills. By chance he pulled into the parking lot at the same time as Christina. As soon as Tatiana laid eyes on Jim, or more likely scented him, she all but bolted, but at the last moment she held herself back, remaining faithfully at Christina's side. Christina had given Jim a card. On it was written, 'Tatiana: interesting facts. Has brown eyes, was the 2012 AHA Hero Dog Award hearing dog finalist . . . and the 2012 Animal Hero Kids Caring Canine Award. And beware of her helicopter tail!'

After the ceremony Jim and Tatiana got to talk for a while, just the two of them, which was good, since things hadn't been easy for Jim over the past few months. He had been hospitalized with a pressure sore. It had happened during the last few weeks of raising Tatiana, so he hadn't been able to hand her over at her CCI matriculation. Another puppy raiser had had to step in to do so, and I could only imagine how hard that must have been on Jim.

As if that wasn't enough, once he was out of hospital Jim decided it was time he finally got himself a CCI service dog. He was given a yellow Lab called Delmar, but after a couple of weeks Delmar had started limping. Jim got him looked at, and it turned out that Delmar had developed arthritis in his leg so Jim had had to hand him back to CCI. Jim had found the parting so emotional, he didn't even know if he could handle getting another service dog.

I could sympathize. I could utterly relate.

I couldn't even begin to imagine losing Napal.

# CHAPTER 31

Much as I might fear losing Napal, it's actually myself I need to worry about right now. I develop a pressure sore on my right heel, most likely from where it has bumped against the chair during training. I don't worry about it a great deal. I don't want anything to bring me down.

The boys and I do some diving at Crystal Lake, a local spring-fed stretch of water, and some algae gets into the wound. It becomes infected. I get it cleaned and dressed at the hospital, but it doesn't improve much. One day Melissa and I are out training, and I go over a kerb too fast and bump my heel. The wound breaks open. I leave Napal with Melissa and head for the emergency room in Baylor. They refer me to Dr Nicholson, a foot specialist and another army reservist. He tells me that the pressure sore looks infected. He says they'll need to do an MRI scan to check if the infection has gone through to the bone.

I ask him what he'll do if it has. He tells me they'll cut out the infected part, put a flap of skin over it, and in a week or so I should be good to go with no major interruptions to my training. With the MRI done he discharges me. I've got to return in a couple of days to get the results. I train hard for two days, then return to Dr Nicholson. His expression is grim and full of foreboding.

'It's much worse than we ever expected,' he tells me. 'The infection must have been in the bone for a long time. You have contracted osteomyelitis in your right leg – the foot or the heel. We can try and treat it, but that will mean months or even a year in hospital, with no guaranteed results.'

I ask the doctor what he proposes.

'I'm sorry, Jason,' he tells me, 'but my recommendation would be to amputate your lower leg.'

I am in total shock. From right out of the blue: *amputation*. This is the last thing I was expecting.

I ask Dr Nicholson for a few moments alone with my dog. I pet and hug Napal as I try to get my head around what on earth is happening to me. *To us.* Ever since my injury I have nurtured the dream of walking again. Of standing on my own two feet. Of getting out of my chair, even if only temporarily. Those first words I uttered when I came out of the coma have stayed with me: *Sir, I am going to walk again.* So much of my life has been focused on doing just that. Hearing that I could lose my right lower leg is a terrible blow. It's shattering, psychologically. Or it would be, were Napal not here with me.

I sit in the examination room and talk it all through with my dog. If I have to choose between a year in hospital with no guaranteed outcome or the amputation, I figure I'll opt for the latter. Hospitalization will kill me. It'll kill my spirit dead. Plus the infection could spread even further and might become fatal. And there is no way Napal could ever stay with me. Being parted from my dog for a year or my leg for life? I figure it's a no-brainer.

I reach down and caress him, sinking my fingers deep into his soft, glossy hair. 'So, buddy, this is the moment. This is the crossroads. I can either go back into the dark place and spiral into the worst kind of depression, or I can look forward and face the challenge. I've always wanted to do this marathon; it will give me something to live for. We need this. We need it. What do you figure?'

I stare into the wide-open eyes of my dog. He's got what I call his Puss-in-Boots look on his face right now. It says, *Sometimes you just got to face up to the worst and say, 'We can do this.'*

'You know what, buddy, you're right. Let's get this done. But on one condition: we're still gonna roll this marathon. I don't want to go back to the depression. We can either go back there and feel sorry for ourselves, or carry on living our dreams. So, what do you say?'

I can tell that Napal is with me. Together we can get this beat.

I call Dr Nicholson back in. I ask him if we go ahead and amputate can I still compete in the Marine Corps Marathon? He does a double-take. He looks at me like I'm mad.

'I really wouldn't advise it. You'll need to concentrate on recovery and getting fitted with a prosthetic limb.'

I tell him I don't need a prosthetic. I'm going to roll the marathon sitting in my racing chair – no prosthetic required – plus training hard will be my best route to a speedy recovery.

'OK, OK.' He throws his hands up in a gesture of mock surrender. 'Shoot. If you really want to, then I guess you can.

If it heals properly, I guess you can. But the surgery, the blood loss, the healing time – it'll set you back months.'

We cut a deal. I'll go with the amputation, if he'll do all he possibly can to get me out of the hospital and back into training as soon as possible. The infection is so bad there's no time to delay. We need to get this done right away.

I put a call through to Wounded Warriors Family Support, to warn them. Their immediate reaction is to tell me not to worry about all the money we've invested so far in my training; I just need to concentrate on getting well. I have to tell them three times over before they start to believe me: I am still going to roll this race. I call Melissa and tell her everything. At first she thinks I'm joking. But when she finally understands that I'm not, she backs me all the way. *She knows.* She knows that if I don't have the marathon to aim for, the darkness and depression might take me. She knows that we have to do this. We have to roll that marathon; it will give me something to live for.

The morning prior to the surgery I have to have some tests, to check that the infection has not gone to my organs. They're especially worried about my heart. If it's taken hold there I might not survive the amputation. The tests are done at another hospital, and Julie volunteers to keep me company as we await the results.

Needless to say, we're on tenterhooks. I keep taking calls from my mom and dad and brother John. They're all asking the same question: *Have you got the results?* The nurses in the waiting room are sweet. They bring Napal a bowl of water and fuss over him. Eventually, they tell us that the heart specialist is ready to see us, and we're ushered into his office.

A guy comes in, a file of papers tucked under one arm. He glances at us, then does a double-take as he spies my dog. Without a word he turns and leaves, slamming the door behind him. Julie and I exchange glances.

'Was that the doctor?'

'Who was that? Slamming a door like that?'

He was an Arab-looking guy, and with a sinking feeling I sense this is going to be a re-run of the gas station incident: *No dogs! No way can we have a dog anywhere near the food!*

It is one o'clock in the afternoon by now, and my surgery is scheduled to start at two. We do not have the time to mess around. A nurse knocks and enters. We repeat the question to her: is the guy who stormed out on us the heart specialist?

'I'm afraid you need to leave,' she replies.

'Was that the doctor?' Julie repeats. 'Was that the doctor?' She can be fierce as hell when she needs to be.

The nurse looks utterly wretched. 'Yes, it was. But he's said he won't see you unless you get rid of the dog.'

I am twisting in my chair as the stress makes my pain spike. Napal can sense it, and he's hurting with my pain. He sits up and nuzzles at my hand, trying to de-stress me, but in a situation such as this that's all but impossible.

'All we want is the results,' Julie tells the nurse. 'And we're not leaving without them.'

The nurse says she'll see what she can do. A few minutes later the doctor returns. He was angry when he slammed the door. Now he's shaking visibly, either with fear or with rage. I'm also in a bad way. It's only Julie's presence beside me that enables me to hold it together, and to hold my tongue.

Julie reaches out a hand. 'Just give us the results, please, and then we'll leave.'

He replies to Julie, but his eyes are fixed on my dog: 'No. I will fax them through to your surgeon. I'll fax them through.'

'I don't think you understand,' Julie counters. 'My brother has surgery scheduled for two o'clock today. That's an hour from now and we need the results. It's not a simple surgery – he is having his leg amputated. We need to know that his heart is OK. Can you just tell him that?'

'No. Like I said, I will fax the results to your doctor.'

I feel like flattening this guy. 'Jeez! I just need to know! A team's waiting to amputate my leg!'

He shakes his head. 'I will not speak with you until the dog is gone.'

Julie glances at me. I can see the frustration and the hurt burning in her eyes. 'Do you want me to walk Napal down the stairs for a moment, so you can get the results?'

'No. No way. I do not.' I turn on the guy. 'My dog is allowed to go wherever I go. Under the ADA that's the law. Don't you even know that?'

'It's . . . it is unsanitary to have a dog in my office.'

'You know I could . . . You know what I could do? What you are doing is so against the law!'

Julie gets to her feet. She announces that we're leaving. As she walks and I roll towards the door, the doctor starts to backtrack a little.

'You know, I am sorry, but I just had to get the dog—'

We slam the door, which cuts off the last of his words. Frankly, I don't give a damn what he has to say. Under the law, we could sue Dr Hate-the-Dog's ass off. As we leave, a number of the staff accost us. They are deeply ashamed of what has happened and almost as angry as we are.

'You know, you can sue.'

'Under the ADA you can sue.'

'You should do that.'

Of course we could sue him ten times over for what he's done today, but we're just not that kind of people. And anyway, the priority right now is my health. My life, even. It has to be.

Julie drives us back to Baylor. We reach the hospital to find the results have been faxed through. The infection has not gone to my heart. The surgery can go ahead as planned.

My folks gather for the operation. My brother scrawls on my lower right leg in black marker, 'If found, please return to . . .' with my phone number and contact details.

My sister writes, 'I'm too sexy for my leg.'

As we did before, we use humour to help get us through. But in truth nothing can prepare me for what is coming. Even being chair-bound I was still *complete*. I hadn't lost any parts of myself. There was always still the promise – however slim – of getting back on my own two feet. But after the amputation . . .

Towards the end of the operation one of the nurses comes to tell my folks how it's going. The surgery has gone well, or as well as can be expected when you're cutting half of someone's leg away. She's an older lady and she seems to share the Morgan family's sense of humour. 'I gotta tell you something . . .' There and then she starts to sing, 'I'm too sexy for my leg. Too sexy for . . .'

'Oh, you saw that.' Julie laughs. 'That's so funny.'

'You know, when we took the covers off and saw what y'all had written, the entire staff were in stitches. We were laughing right before the surgery. But don't you ever tell Jason that, you hear? He doesn't need to know that!'

When I come round from the anaesthetic at first I cannot see anything so very different, because six inches below my right knee is a thick mass of bandages, covering everything. But there comes a time when they have to change the dressings, and that's when I first get to see the stump where my lower right leg used to be.

I cannot bear to look at it. I turn my head away. My mom leaves the room in tears. For a long time Melissa sits with me and holds me as we both cry. When it's dressed again I keep the stump covered with a blanket, so I can't see.

I'm released from hospital on the 4th of July weekend. I plan to spend the time at my folks' place on Lake Texoma, together with my boys. We head out in my parents' boat so we can spend the evening on one of the islands, but then we realize we've somehow got to get me off the boat onto dry land without the aid of a landing jetty. It's easier said than done, especially as my right leg is heavily bandaged and incredibly delicate.

There are some folks on the island preparing for their own 4th of July festivities. The men in the party volunteer to carry me. And so I'm lifted across the shallows in my wheelchair and deposited gently on the sand. These are people that we've never met before. This is the kindness of strangers.

We have some big fireworks to unleash, and I will not be left out of things. Despite everything – or maybe because of it – I need to be in there, lighting fuses from my chair. The trouble is my chair absolutely will not move on sand. Grass is difficult, but sand is impossible. All I can do is hope for the best as everyone else runs, and the fireworks go off in my ear.

People keep yelling, 'Jason, don't stand so close when they go off!'

I yell back, 'Hey, I don't have any choice! My wheels are stuck in the sand! Anyhow, I'm not standing!'

Eventually the fun and games are over and on Sunday I head home. The first thing I do when I get to McKinney is visit Walmart and make for the pet counter. It's Napal who's helped get me through this amputation, and I figure he's earned himself a treat.

'There you go, boy,' I tell him. 'Choose your toy. Go get your toy.'

Napal walks up and down the aisle a few times, eyeing the squeaker toys. Finally he places his jaws gently around a rubber duck and plucks it off the shelf. We head for the checkout, Napal grabs my wallet and pays and then we move out towards the car. But as we make towards the parking lot I notice that my dog is limping. It was Thursday when the hospital let me out. Today is Sunday. I figure we'll train tomorrow morning, after which I'll take Napal to the vet for a check-up. I really hope he's not getting sick. It doesn't escape my notice that it's his right rear foot that is hurting, which equates to the limb I have just had amputated.

I lie in bed that evening, brooding. There is no hiding any more. Alone in my bedroom is where it hits home. My mind becomes fixated on what I have lost. A part of me has been cut away and disposed of, and the loss wounds me. Deeply. My curtains remain closed and my mood is dark. It's the worst it's been since I willed an airliner to fall out of the sky.

It's Napal who pulls me out of it. I've lost count of how many times he's been into my room, realized I'm not ready to face the day, sighed and left disconsolately. But one time he comes in and refuses to leave. Instead, he gets onto the bed and does something he has never done before. He gets on his hindquarters, puts his forepaws around my shoulders, and my big black Labrador gives me the longest and tightest bear hug a man could ever wish for.

I hug him back, like I'm holding on for dear life.

Napal must have sensed that something extraordinary was needed, and he's delivered. My dog has a very special aura. You can feel the softness and the kindness shining out of him. You can see it just as soon as he enters a room. No one has ever asked me if it's safe to pet my dog. You just know instinctively this dog is all about caring – he couldn't harm a fly.

And today, with his loving embrace, he's pulled me out of the darkness and back towards the light.

# CHAPTER 32

After Napal's beautiful, magical bear hug, from somewhere I find the will to get up and face the day. It's four days after being released from hospital, and we head to the gym to restart my training. Of course, the amputation means we face a raft of new challenges.

I am used to rolling the racing chair with my legs tucked up under me, kind of kneeling in it. Melissa has to figure out how to do this now with one leg tucked under me and one – the stump – thrust out in front. We have to strap the stump down so it won't bang about, plus my balance is off, with one side of me sitting marginally higher than the other. But with Melissa's help I muddle through. We start with a three-mile road session, and it feels good. If we can work it up from here, there is still no reason why we can't make the Marine Corps Marathon as planned.

We finish training and I take Napal to the veterinarians. If anything his limp seems more pronounced, as if he's somehow injured his paw. The vet thinks Napal looks hale and hearty, as always, but he takes some blood and runs some checks anyway. The news that he delivers to me comes as a real shock. It turns out that Napal has a cancerous tumor in his right rear paw, and they're going to have to amputate.

It's nothing like the entire paw, thank God. We've caught the cancer in the very early stages and the vet figures there's little danger that it's spread. They'll only need to cut out the tiny infected part. But my dog is going to lose a part of his body that mirrors my own loss, and at almost exactly the same time.

I am devastated at the thought of Napal having cancer; at the possibility that I might lose him. The vet reassures me that they've found it well in time and that there is nothing much to worry about. The surgery goes ahead almost immediately. Napal getting part of his paw amputated wounds me almost as much as having my own limb cut away. I've felt for a long time as if we share a life force, my dog and I. This seems to prove it.

I take a call from John Libonati, who's heard about both amputations. It's an emotional conversation. I share with him my real worry: what if Napal has to lose half of his leg, as I have? I tell him that even if he does and he cannot be a service dog any more, I am determined to keep him. I don't need any service dog; I need Napal. I only want Napal.

Yet I keep circling back to the same question: *What if I lose him?* John is a great listener and he is hugely encouraging. He tells me my concern for my dog is greater than my concern for myself, and that just proves the depth of the love between us. He tells me not to worry. Our bond is forged of a love that cannot easily be broken.

But having my lower right leg amputated has been a lot tougher than I ever imagined it would be. When I get into the shower and see the stump it makes me feel physically sick. It feels close to the shock of my paralysis. The difference is that now I have Napal. He gets me through it.

This will become a key message when I speak at CCI events. Even though my dog and I have both lost a part of ourselves, we've lost none of our belief in the mission. It's not the size of the dog in the fight that matters; it's the size of the fight in the dog.

Together, Napal and I work on our recovery and we train hard. There's a lady who uses the gym called Carol Long. She's just retired from a senior position in the Coca-Cola Company. We get talking, and she is so inspired by Napal that she volunteers to become a CCI puppy raiser. By the time we're getting close to the date of the marathon, she's been given her first CCI puppy to raise.

By now I'm too fast in my chair for training on busy roads; Melissa can't hit the intersections quickly enough to make it risk free. So we head to the Texas Motor Speedway track, which has a five-mile loop. Four laps makes twenty miles.

Melissa mounts her bike and we're off, but oddly it's her who now seems to have the problem. She's working her butt off but the bike seems to be going nowhere. After the first lap she's close to exhausted. We stop to check her bike, and it turns out that the brakes are jammed on. She's just cycled five miles with the brakes on!

'Yeah, I saw that from the start,' I tease her. 'I saw you working your butt off. I just didn't want to say anything.'

Melissa cracks up. 'I am so relieved! I knew I wasn't that unfit!'

We free the brakes and together complete the rest of the twenty-miler. Melissa declares that we're ready. The Texas track is all on the flat of course – the Marine Corps Marathon will be a very different baby – but we're about as good as we're ever going to be.

We fly up to Washington just prior to the race. Team Morgan consists of Melissa, Bill Stender – the former marine who runs the gym where we train – and his wife Tisha. The day before the race we study a map and the lie of the land. Bill, Tisha and Melissa hire bikes to ride the course and they do a pre-race recce. The ride goes so well they decide to keep the bikes for the day of the race. Generally I can roll faster than most people can run, especially on downhill stretches. The bikes will enable them to keep up with me, as my support team. But increasingly the fates seem set against us.

Hurricane Sandy is blowing in, and there are tropical-force winds and rain forecast. Pushing my chair for twenty-six miles in those kind of conditions will be sheer hell. I decide to go for it, anyway. Melissa loads up energy bars, drinks, wet-weather gear, spare gloves and spare tubes – in case I blow one on a downhill stretch. She stuffs it all into a bulging backpack that she will carry as she cycles.

The day of the race dawns grey and sullen. Napal has to remain in the hotel room as he's not allowed to run the race with me. John Libonati has agreed to fetch him and bring him to the finish line, so my dog can be there for me when – if – I make it. I say a fond farewell, then head for the lift in my regular chair. Melissa, Bill and Tisha follow, pushing my racing chair. Once I'm under way, they'll retrieve their bikes from the hotel and catch up.

I transfer into my racing chair and Melissa straps my right

leg down in its new position, poking out front. I'm as ready as I'll ever be.

From the start the race is hellish. The wind is in my face – fierce, wet and cold. The first uphill stretch seems to last for ever, but the downhill is gone in a flash, the friction wearing through my first set of gloves. I need another pair, or I won't be able to push my rims round with any degree of speed. I'll grind to a halt. But when I look for Melissa and the others at our first scheduled RV, they're nowhere to be seen.

I reach the mile-five marker and I send a text message: 'Where are you guys? Need gloves. Urgent.'

I reach the mile-seven marker and I send another, more worried text. 'Where are you guys? I need you!'

I reach the mile-ten marker and I'm getting desperate. The rain is sluicing across the race route in thick, grey curtains, and it's washed the sticky spray off my wheel rims and gloves. On the uphill stretches I'm losing all grip and traction. Much more of this and I'll be at a standstill.

I hit the steepest incline yet and my shoulder and arm muscles are burning up. I've practically stalled. A runner overtakes me. He offers to help push me to the crest of the hill, but I refuse. Either I do this thing by the book or not at all. If only I knew where Melissa and the others have got to. I steel myself to go on: alone, unsupported, my gloves slipping and sliding against my slick rims.

I crawl towards the mile-thirteen marker. I am almost at the halfway point and still no sight of Team Morgan. I have no idea what can have happened to them. I wonder if I can go on. I remind myself of my promise: *I'll run a full marathon.* I force myself to keep rolling, but I'm desperate for fresh gloves, sticky spray and an energy drink. I can't keep going if I can't grip my wheels, and I can't keep the muscles pumping if I run out of energy. I curse myself for being so stupid. Why didn't I carry some of this stuff? I'd just presumed my support team would be with me every step of the way.

I send a text: 'Nearing mile 13. No sign of you. WTF?'

It's not like me to curse. I'm Goshman, remember. It just goes to show how desperate this is becoming.

Unknown to me, my support team has hit the mother of all problems. En route to the hotel to get the bikes the road was blocked due to a bomb scare. The diversion sent them a long way round, and they ended up running along an eight-lane highway to reach the hotel. Finally, they got there and jumped on their bikes, but then the real dramas began.

A diversion sent them across a field. Maybe it was a park, but right now it was knee-deep in muddy water. Hurricane Sandy had landed, and the wind and rain were ferocious. There was no way to pedal through the floodwater, so Melissa, Bill and Trish were forced to dismount and push their bikes through the deluge. They made for an overpass on which was a mass of runners. Somewhere towards the back of the pack they hoped they'd find me, hunched over in my racing chair, hurting and soaked to the skin but still somehow rolling. The question was, how to get from the flooded field up to the level of the overpass?

They saw a sidewalk that looked promising. It led to some steps, but for some reason they stopped short of the road. The only option was for Bill to climb up the last twelve feet, hand over hand. Somehow they managed to pass the bikes up to Bill, who dumped them on the sidewalk, after which Melissa and Trisha had to clamber up and join him.

They found themselves at the mile-twenty mark. The last message they had from me was 'Nearing mile 13. No sign of you. WTF?'

Melissa had to presume I was behind them. That was the call she made. She set off running, telling Bill and Trisha to head with the bikes in the other direction, towards the finish line. That way they were sure to link up with me one way or the other.

'He can't be this far!' she yelled. 'He needs us! He needs what we have in the backpacks!'

By now I'm approaching the mile- sixteen marker. The wind is gusting in my face, trying to force me backwards, the rain pummelling into my exposed skin like an ice storm. I've been hunched in my chair for the best part of three hours, and I have jolts of agony shooting up my spine, like lightning. I realize now how much the amputation has set me back in my training, taking time away that I could never get back again. My gloves are in tatters, and my arms and shoulders feel as if they are on fire, yet at the same time I feel chilled to the bone with the cold.

It's crunch time. I've pretty much given up on my support team, and I wonder if I really can go on. I glance ahead into the stinging, icy, wind-blown grey-out, raindrops cannoning off the highway like machine-gun fire. The road rises towards an overpass. Another freakin' hill for me to climb, and I have almost no grip left. A stream of dirty water gushes down the gulley at the roadside, gurgling down a grated iron drain as if to mock me.

*Roll a marathon! Who was I kidding?*

And then I see it. Up ahead of me is a bizarre apparition. A crazy figure is elbowing her way through the throng, going against the flow and seemingly running the race *the wrong way*. She has a mop of bedraggled blonde hair atop an expression that is utterly desperate. I spy her about the same time as she sees me.

I've rarely been so thankful to see anyone. Melissa is full of apologies. She unloads her backpack and wraps me in a windproof. She has fresh gloves for me. She covers my wheel rims with sticky spray galore. She feeds me gooey energy gel, which I suck down greedily. And she reminds me that at the end of the race my dog is waiting.

I set off once more. Melissa runs beside me, blurting out a breathless version of what happened: bomb scares, diversions, hurricanes, wading through a flooded park with the bikes and scaling an overpass laden with them. In spite of everything I can't help laughing, but I also tell her how hard it's been for me. It's so much hillier than we anticipated; the weather has made it sheer hell. For the last few miles I've been going against the wind. It's so much harder to push a wheelchair racer into the wind than it is to run into it; the chair itself creates so much resistance.

Melissa runs the last six miles with me. At mile twenty-three we link up with Bill and Tisha, who boost me even more. The wind and rain are worse than ever, but Bill yells out fantastic words of encouragement. A crowd lines the route, and Bill's words fire them up to support me.

'Wounded warrior coming through! We've got a wounded warrior coming through!'

Their cheers and applause drive me on. The last mile is excruciating. It is uphill, the surface rough and uneven under my wheels, but the crowd goes wild as they see me inch painfully towards the finish.

They buoy me up and from somewhere I find the strength to go the last few yards. I thrust out my chest as I roll across the finish line. It's over. I get a medal hung around my neck, and someone throws a Marine Corps Marathon windcheater around me as I shiver with exhaustion and cold. Then I pretty much collapse.

The pain hits me like a tidal wave. Melissa can tell how much I'm hurting. It's rarely if ever been this bad. I've spent over five hours hunched in a chair, and my back is killing me. I need to get out of the chair and into the prone position, or I'll black out with the pain.

There's a medical tent at the finish, but I do not have the strength to lift myself out of the chair and onto one of the cots. The medics don't seem to know what to do with me.

Melissa yells, 'Get him out of his chair and onto a stretcher! Get him onto a stretcher!'

They lay me flat on a cot and Melissa ices my back. Slowly, painfully slowly, the waves of agony recede and my mind clears a little. I lie there thinking, *I've done it. I've done a full marathon.* Not on my feet, as I'd promised, but I've come as close to my promise as humanly possible. *You'll never walk again. You'll never get to do a full marathon.* Well, I have now.

I check the race computer, which has kept a record of my times. Some miles I've completed in four minutes or less. When the hurricane was behind me, I could have just put out my hands and got blown along. But my slowest mile has taken me nearly thirteen minutes, uphill and into the teeth of the wind. You can walk it faster than that.

John Libonati finds me. He tells me the good news: I've placed fifth in the wheelchair racers. All things considered that's something close to a miracle. We celebrate. We rejoice in the simple fact that I have proved all of the naysayers wrong. Most people said it would be impossible to roll a marathon after the amputation, but my folks never faltered; my boys sure didn't; and Melissa and John have remained 100 per cent behind me. I could not have done it without them all.

But mostly, as I tell him, I could not have done it without my dog. Napal puts his fine muzzle close to my face, as I lie on that cot racked with pain and exhaustion, and with ice packs pressed against my spine, and he speaks to me: *I knew you could do it. I knew you could. Together, we've done it. We've done it all.*

I look back on everything I've achieved since the injury, and, you know, my dog is right: we have done it all. I did walk again: I walked those 250 steps. I've ridden a horse. I've learned to scuba-dive. I competed in the Warrior Games and, in truth, I did the air force proud. And now I've rolled a full marathon. I figure only one thing remains on my bucket list, the greatest buzz of all: to jump from an airplane and free-fall to earth.

But I guess there are some things that are beyond what's possible, and will always remain so.

# CHAPTER 33

That night we have a celebratory dinner. John Libonati tells me something really touching. He's started writing a storybook for children. The basic theme is that, contrary to what most humans think, dogs are fully aware of the world around them. They also know they only have a short life – ten to fifteen years – so they live it to the max. Which is why they are always happy, loving and playful.

'I want to teach humans – kids – a lesson through the attitude of dogs,' John explains. 'Dogs are amazingly loyal, always. They are always happy to see you. You can leave them for five minutes, return, and they're overjoyed to see you again. They're only ever mean if taught to be mean by a human. The smallest things make them happy. And Napal, he epitomizes all of that.'

My dog is beneath the dinner table getting some much-needed Mexico time. De-paining me after the marathon sure took it out of him.

'They have no need for lavish possessions,' John continues. 'And since they realize how short their lives are, they have to cram in as much loyal, loving happiness as they can. We humans see the decades stretching ahead of us and we take life for granted. We become petty and forget what's truly important, which is being happy, loyal and helping others. Dogs never lose sight of that. We can learn so much from a dog's approach to life.'

He smiles at me and glances beneath the table. 'It's inspired by Napal.'

John Libonati – he's some kind of a guy. As for his story, I figure he's captured the special magic of dogs in a few choice words. And next up where John is concerned, my dog and I are off to visit the White House.

It takes a few days to recover from the epic race. I use the time to primp Napal. I scrub his teeth with his foul-smelling doggie toothpaste, scour out his ears with cotton wool, shampoo his coat and brush it until it gleams. I've got into the habit of sending him to my local PetSmart once a month for a treat, but they are always so reluctant to return him. 'Can't we just keep him for a while longer? *Please?*' No one ever wants to part with my dog.

Napal groomed, I figure we're ready. There is an old saying in John Libonati's line of business: 'You never leave the Secret Service.' Today he'll more than prove it.

We head over to the White House in a limo. We sweep through the gates and it drops us at the West Wing door. Napal gets to press the entrance button with his nose. At every turn the Secret Service guys keep checking my dog's credentials. 'Oh yeah, Agent Napal. This is one very special dog. He's one of us.'

We're hoping to meet President Obama so we can talk about service dogs, but as bad luck would have it his schedule won't stretch to it. That means we won't get to see inside the Oval Office, which is something I've always wanted to do.

I get Napal to help me roll my chair right up to the rope and bollards, which close off the Oval Office. I lift my foot off the chair and sneak it inside the rope. At least now I can say I set foot in the Oval Office.

One of our Secret Service escorts thinks my dog needs the same honour too. 'Hey, shoot, your dog's gotta get into the Oval Office. He needs to be in there.'

I 'accidentally' drop my keys on the far side of the rope. In a flash Napal dashes under the barrier and whips them up in his jaws. He drops them in my lap, tail thrashing and half knocking the bollards over. Now my dog's had his paws in the Oval Office, just like me.

I guess there is one shortcoming with Napal, as the ideal service dog: he is extremely fussy about where he goes to the bathroom. CCI dogs are trained to pee and poop just about anywhere, on command. A lot of the time there won't be grass or a tree around for a service dog to relieve itself on, so they're trained to go on open tarmac or concrete.

But Napal hates doing that. He insists on holding it in until he can find a patch of natural vegetation. That's seen as a weakness in a service dog, for it can seriously inconvenience its life companion. Likewise, the dogs are taught to wolf down their food so as not to hold up their handler. Napal never has a problem gobbling up his chow. But peeing and pooping – he's real particular about that.

Washington DC isn't the best of places for such a dog, the White House even less so. I can sense that Napal has to go. I tell the Secret Service guys my dog needs to use the bathroom and ask if there's any patch of grass that he might be able to use.

The guys glance at each other, mischief in their eyes. 'The Rose Garden. It's all yours.'

'You're kidding, right?'

'No, siree.' They nod towards the doorway that leads to the famous Rose Garden. 'Number one or number two, Agent Napal has the freedom of the White House.'

So it is that Napal gets to be one of the few dogs – maybe the only dog – ever to have had a pee in the Rose Garden. I figure that's a rare honour for my four-legged companion. Before we leave he also gets to open the famous press-room door – the one that leads into where the president holds his media briefings – using his nose on the disabled button. It's too bad we don't get to say hello to the president, and to exchange a few words about the importance of service dogs but, all in all, Washington has been fantastic.

Bill, Trisha, Melissa and I say goodbye to John, until the next time. Napal gets to give him a kiss and a hug. We fly back to Dallas Forth Worth, knowing that we have achieved the seemingly impossible: *I did roll that marathon.*

Back in McKinney we hit our favourite bar, an Irish pub called Delaney's. We celebrate the marathon long into the evening. Napal is such a regular here most people know him. We leave late, and I'm rolling down to the disabled space in the parking lot when some idiot in a pickup goes tearing by. He's doing close to fifty and he practically takes our noses off.

I yell after him, 'Hey, ever heard of a speed limit? Slow down!'

An instant later the truck skids to a halt in a cloud of burning rubber. The guy slams it into reverse and does a crazy, weaving slalom back towards us. Luckily I've got backup – three guys from the bar. Mr Angry jumps from his vehicle and starts to rip into my buddies verbally. He stinks of alcohol, and I can see some poor woman cowering in the truck cab.

It looks as if it's about to come to blows, so I decide to intervene. 'You know, it was me who shouted for you to slow down 'cause you almost took my dog's nose off.'

I figure it may defuse things. No one goes for a guy in a chair, right? Unbelievably, he turns on me. His language is foul. He seems out of his mind. My buddies crowd in and eventually he backs off and leaves.

I ask the guys to hang around until I've got myself safely into my vehicle. I hit the road, but I've not gone far when I meet a red light. I see a pickup screech to a halt behind me, and I just know it's Mr Angry. He's been waiting in a side street for me to come by.

I see him punch open his door, pound down the street and then he's reaching through my open window to unlock my door. If he gets it open and pulls me out I'm done for. Napal is in the back and he's freaking out. I have a split second in which to make a decision. What do I do?

I lean back as far as I can, grab the door handle with my left hand and, using that as leverage, propel myself forward, sticking him in the nose with my right. It's the last thing he's expecting – to get hit by a guy in a chair! I whack him with all the strength I can muster after training to roll the marathon. He stumbles away from my vehicle and I stamp my foot on the gas.

I run the red light, but it's past three in the morning and the streets are deserted. I do a circuit of my block several times just to make sure that I've lost him, then pull into my driveway and kill the engine. It takes an age before my pulse returns to something approaching normal.

But for every one of life's downers there are so many more good times. I get given a sponsored truck with a hook and winch system in the truck bed that lifts and lowers my chair, so there's no need to disassemble and rebuild it every time I go somewhere. There's also a camper shell that rises and lowers like a clam, to keep my chair dry. Motor oil manufacturer Pennzoil has teamed up with racing-car owner Roger Penske and the Paralyzed Veterans of America to fund the truck. I'm hugely grateful for their generosity and support.

I go to the NASCAR races in Phoenix, Arizona to get it and to do some media and promotion. I drive it home to show my boys. We roll to a halt and Napal lets out one of his biggest-ever *ARROOOUFFFS*. He's letting them know we've got the wheels and we're home. The boys pile out the front door and gather to admire the truck's cool lines, plus the fold-out winch system. I can see that the boys' minds are racing, especially as the summer vacation is just around the corner.

It's Austin who pops the question: 'So, where we gonna go for the summer? We can go anywhere!'

'Let's go to the Rockies,' says Blake. 'Let's go camping.'

We've had this conversation many times before, and each time I'm forced to pour cold water on my boys' excitement. I hate doing this. The Rockies are a great idea, and I have never been camping with my kids, or at least not when they were old enough to remember. But, sadly, I still can't manage it now.

'I can't, guys. My wheelchair. I can't get through gravel or rough ground, remember.'

'Well, let's go to Florida!' says Austin. 'Let's go to the beach.'

I feel like a total Mr Killjoy. 'I can't. The wheelchair. It won't go through sand.'

The Pennzoil truck is great – it will make life so much easier for us – but it will only take a dad in a wheelchair so far.

Shortly after our visit to the White House there is a state election, and Napal and I head out to cast our vote. It's a bright and sunny Texas day and I've got sunglasses on, plus Napal is at my side, as always. I join the line of waiting voters, but this female helper pulls me to one side.

'I'm so glad you're here,' she tells me. 'We've got these brand new voting machines that have never been used. Come right this way.' I think this is weird because there were loads of people in line before me, but I follow anyway. She holds open a door to a pristine new booth. 'Go right on in. It's all yours.'

Inside I find a machine that allows people to vote in Braille. The woman seems to have presumed that I am blind, in spite of the fact I've followed her a good way through the voting facility. By now I've learned from Napal not to sweat the small stuff, and I remind myself this was done with no ill intent.

'Erm, you know, I don't read Braille,' I tell her. I try a joke: 'Oh, and my dog doesn't either.'

Napal and I are pushing three years into our partnership by now. These days I've reached the stage where I can pretty much laugh at most of the prejudice and idiocy that's thrown at us. I've lost count of the times we've got out of the truck and someone has asked, 'Gee, is that your seeing-eye dog?' This suggests that I can somehow drive my truck blind.

'Yeah, he's good, isn't he?' is my standard response. 'It only took a week to teach him to drive.'

Shortly after the Braille incident my spirits are lifted by a couple of phone calls. One is from CCI telling me that the dog named Jason Morgan is doing great with his puppy raiser. They plan for him to graduate on Veterans Day 2014, and they ask if I'll speak at the event. I tell them that I'd be honoured to. The other is from a veteran called Dana Bowman. Dana is fellow ex-special forces and a double amputee. He's formed a not-for-profit organization called HALO for Freedom, and he wants to invite me to a forthcoming event at Mineral Wells in west Texas, so I can talk about service dogs and CCI. There's also going to be a helicopter hog hunt and a couple of other fun things.

Wild hogs are a real menace in Texas. The population is out of control – they breed so fast numbers double every few years – and they rip up farmland and wildlife habitats. Each female pig has on average twenty-four piglets a year. The population is exploding. Culling them is the only way to keep the numbers down.

My talk with Napal at the HALO for Freedom event goes down a storm. This year's big deal – the airborne hog hunt – is scheduled for the following morning. On the spur of the moment I ask if it might be possible for my eldest boy to come with me on the helicopter ride. Dana Bowman tells me he's more than welcome, as long as there's room. I get Joanna to factor it all into our schedule.

I phone Blake and tell him to get his act together: we're going helicopter hog hunting. I get in my sponsored truck and drive the two-hour journey home. I collect a very excited Blake and we drive right back again, leaving Austin and Grant to stay with their mom, who's kindly agreed to have them. I wish all three of my boys could come, but there just isn't room on the helo. It's late by the time Blake and I get to Mineral Wells, but the long drive will prove more than worth it. Tomorrow will turn out to be a day that I will always cherish, and my son will too.

While serving with the SOAR – a helicopter assault unit – I was taught how to shoot from the air. It's far from easy. You have to aim *behind* the target, to compensate for the helo's forward motion. They start the flights early, but Blake and I hold back. I don't want my son to unwittingly take the place of a wounded warrior. We're scheduled for the last flight, but as luck would have it a news camera crew needs the ride. There isn't room for Blake and the camera crew, so my son is forced to sit it out. We take off and I spot the first hog. I figure the quicker I can shoot this thing, the quicker the pilot can take us back, and I may just get Blake airborne.

I put seven shots into the hog, and it goes down – the camera crew filming over my shoulder through the open door. A lot of the wounded warriors who go before me have never shot from a moving helicopter at a running target, and it takes them several clips to down a pig. But we make it back in double-quick time.

The helicopter pilot just happens to be a former SOAR guy. He's seen the badges on my wheelchair, and he's realized that my son has not had a flight. The pilot's yet to power down and he signals something to those outside. I see Blake get rushed across, and a moment later he leaps inside.

The pilot jerks a thumb in our direction. 'Get your son

strapped in real good 'n' tight! Let's show him what the SOAR can do!'

What a relief. I so wanted Blake to get to fly.

We take off, and the pilot gives me and my son the ride of our lives. He brings the helo down so low it kicks up the dust as he swoops over bushes and weaves through trees. It is a much a better flight for Blake to be on than the one from which I shot the hog.

'See how we're dodging around the trees, sticking to the cover?' I yell at him. 'That's just how we did operations in Ecuador – down real low where the bad guys couldn't see us. Awesome, huh?'

After the flights there is a golf match for the wounded warriors. Golf was my sport prior to getting injured, but I've not been able to play since. Dana's sorted some motorized all-terrain golfing chairs which use hydraulics to lift you to your feet. In one of those I get to 'stand' and play golf for the first time since my paralysis.

Napal keeps trying to run after the balls to fetch them, but even so it is fantastic having him there. The golfing event has been sponsored by a familiar figure, former president George Bush Junior. I guess I shouldn't be surprised when he can't seem to resist saying hello to my dog. While he's petting Napal, I grab the opportunity to tell him all about CCI and what service dogs can do.

The grand finale of the HALO for Freedom event comes as a total surprise. There is a not-for-profit called America's Huey 091 Foundation (it's since changed its name to the Independence Corps), which was founded by former Huey helicopter pilots.

They've donated an all-terrain electric wheelchair, which comes complete with camouflage paint, four-wheel drive, chunky tyres and even headlights!

This chair represents the promise of ultimate freedom to someone who cannot walk. It will give that person the ability to move off-road on all kinds of terrain – stones, gravel, beach, grass.

I am utterly blown away when Dana Bowman presents the chair to the world's luckiest wounded warrior: me.

# CHAPTER 34

Dana has a slogan which sums up what the HALO for Freedom foundation is all about: 'It's not the disability; it's the ability.' It chimes with a phrase that I use a lot in my talks: 'What really changed my life was when I focused on my ability, not my disability.' That's kind of become my catchphrase.

With the gift of that all-terrain chair, my ability has just been boosted big time. It gives me and my boys the freedom we have so long craved. I could never have afforded to buy a chair like that. The $25,000 price tag is way beyond my means, and the VA doesn't provide them because they're classed as a luxury.

Blake and I say our goodbyes to everyone at the event, but it's Napal who gets to say the longest farewell of all. There were thirty wounded warriors there who just got their first sight of a service dog in action. None of them had any idea you could get such a dog or knew about CCI. Seeing is believing, and it's seeing Napal in action that makes every scrap of difference.

One guy is especially struck by my dog. Mark Fucaril was a victim of the Boston Marathon bombings. He wasn't even competing; he was a spectator. But he ended up as a single amputee and in danger of losing his other leg too. Of all the victims, he spent the longest time in hospital. As with so many, Mark had no idea service dogs existed, let alone any notion of what they do. He's more than a little reluctant to part with Napal.

'Oh no, that's not your dog. That's my dog now. You're not taking him home. You're not taking him anywhere. He's mine.'

I glance at him. 'Mark, don't make me get out of this chair now. 'Cause if I have to I will, and then it's getting serious.'

I head home with my son and my dog, and with that all-terrain wheelchair strapped into the rear of our truck. I can't wait to break it out and hit the wilderness with my boys. But first off it means we can go to the beach, something I've been dreaming about for over a decade.

I load the boys into the truck, strap the all-terrain chair in, and we head to Florida for a summer vacation. It's a twelve-hour drive and we do it pretty much in one go, arriving around midnight. I'm exhausted from the drive, but I'm so excited that I can't wait to hit the beach. I park, unload the chair, set it rolling, and we head onto the pristine white sands. It's a fine moonlit night, plus I've got the chair's headlights to blaze a trail.

Previously I've always had to watch my kids from a distance when they're playing anywhere like this, never being truly part of things. Now, we throw a ball in the magical light right through to dawn. Right through to sun-up I roll around in my all-terrain chair, and the boys run and yell and tumble beside me.

Napal too is in seventh heaven. My freedom is his freedom. Prior to this he's always had to stick with me. Tonight, as the moonlight glints off the water on a totally deserted beach, I let him off the leash and watch him run free. He dashes for the ball, racing to be the first. I do an extra-long throw towards the sea, and Napal gets ahead of my boys, a dark arrow lancing through the moon shadows. He runs right on past the ball and out into the water. He's hot from playing and needs to cool off, but he's spooked by the roaring, churning chaos of the ocean. He keeps dancing back and forth in the shallows. It's hilarious. And so heartening.

I love my boys – all four of them. I guess I don't show it much. I'm not a guy who wears his heart on his sleeve. But this magical night on this moonlit beach – this is what it means to be a dad and a family. For some reason I feel ready to tell my boys what happened to me. I've never let them hear the details before now. All they know is that Dad got injured in the military.

I sit them down and tell them most of my story – or at least what I've pieced together from the few witnesses and my recovered memories. I guess I've wanted to shield them from the darker truths until they were – until we all were – able to deal with them. I guess we've come of age.

Later we head for a beachside restaurant where we've heard the food and the atmosphere are fantastic. There is only one downside. I can't park my chair anywhere near where we want to eat because the furniture consists of long benches and tables, and I can't get through. Still, I manage to slide along a bench and make myself relatively comfortable.

The food *is* fantastic. At the end of the meal my boys go to fetch my chair, which is parked to one side of the restaurant. There's a guy with his family on an adjacent table, and he asks me to take a photo of them. He hands me the camera and I oblige.

He checks the photo. 'Hey, buddy, you figure you could take it from just over there, so we get the beach and stuff in the background? That'd be real neat.'

'You know, I'd love to, but I can't. I'm in a wheelchair.'

The guy thinks I'm joking. 'Come on, buddy. How about it? Just for me and my folks.'

I try a smile. 'No, no, you don't understand. I'm in a wheel-chair. I can't move.'

He laughs. 'Come on. The joke's wearing thin. Just go take the photo.'

'Buddy, I can't. I'm paralyzed from the waist down.'

'It's just one photo, that's all.'

The boys return, wheeling my chair. I look at it and shrug. 'Pretty much as I was saying . . .'

He looks aghast. 'Oh my gosh. I am so sorry. I mean you look . . . I mean above the table . . .'

I try and make it easier for the poor guy. I call Napal out from under the table, where he's been lying silent and unnoticed. 'Yeah, and this here's my service dog. You even get to pet him, just to show there's no hard feelings . . .'

And so I've learned not to sweat the small stuff. My dog has taught me well. And now I've rolled on a beach, recapturing some more of what was lost. Every day I win back a little more with my ever-faithful dog at my side.


Joanna has booked Napal and me for a gig in New Orleans. It's been organized by the Automobile Association of America, and they're auctioning off a Harley-Davidson motorcycle to raise money for CCI. Napal and I do our usual show and tell, and at tonight's event I figure I want to focus on the ability, not the disability.

I speak about what a difference Napal has made to my life. I tell the audience that I've spent approaching three years in total being treated in hospital, but that Napal and I are regular volunteers at Baylor, a major heart and brain surgery venue. I tell them how we start at seven in the morning every Monday, greeting patients and their families in the waiting room. These folks face maybe losing a loved one, but for the time we are there Napal takes their minds away from all of that. That's the magic of my dog. That's something only a dog like Napal can do. I list all the things that I've achieved since my injury, but tell them I could have done none of them without Napal. I say this all the time and I mean it from the heart.

But then I lose my thread. I've told myself that if I ever forget where I am – if my mind wanders mid-talk – I can always resort to the head-in-the-hands nose-pinched look. I can hold if for fifteen seconds and no one will flinch. My talks are always emotional and there are always audience members in tears.

'I just need a moment,' I tell them. 'The pain is real bad right now.'

Often it is, but more often than not I just need a few seconds to remember where on earth I am in my story. Since my paralysis my memory is far more fractured and indefinite; my mind can drift easily. So I have learned the little tricks that buy me the time to remember, without discomfiting anyone in the hushed, expectant crowd.

I finish by telling this New Orleans audience that the famous Napal is going to give them a bow. 'You know how famous he is? He's the only dog that has ever got to pee in the Rose Garden!' I relate the story of our White House visit, and it raises the roof.

After the talk the organizer tells me she is smitten. 'Your story, your journey – it's amazing. And your work together, it's so inspirational.' She books Napal and me as speakers for their gala fundraiser for the next three years.

We drive back to McKinney. Napal and I are chilling out at home. The boys are at their mom's place for the weekend. I want them to spend as much time as they're able with her. It's good for them to know their mom. I lose one of my sneakers under the low coffee table that sits in front of the TV. I ask Napal to get it, but it's right underneath and it's a tough one, even for him. He works at it from one side, then another, and it's a good five minutes of snuffling and pawing before he finally wiggles it free.

He brings it over to me triumphantly. I go to pet and praise him, but he backs away from me and heads for the kitchen. This is weird. Since when did Napal refuse a cuddle? I feel unworthy of my dog, like maybe I've upset him. I know I am utterly blessed to have him, and maybe I've taken him for granted?

He pads in a few moments later with a bag of Cesar Softies in his jaws. My dog has actually opened the pantry door, found his treats on the shelf, grabbed them and brought them over. He thrusts the bag towards me. *Here. Come on. That – what I did just there. Sometimes cuddles just aren't enough! That deserves a Cesar Softie!*

I figure my dog is dead right. I feed him a few and we cuddle up together on the couch into the early hours of morning. My mind drifts to something Dana Bowman told me at the end of the HALO For Freedom event. HALO stands for High Altitude Low Opening – an elite forces parachute insertion technique that gets soldiers fast and unseen onto target, something I was familiar with from my time in the military.

Dana said that for the next event he plans to get wounded warriors airborne, so they can actually do a HALO jump. He asked me if I'd be up for it. I'd go out tandem – strapped to an able-bodied jumper, falling together under the one chute. I told him that I'd love to. It's my ultimate dream to jump again. And so Dana promised to get Napal and me scheduled for the next HALO for Freedom event.

Before that can happen, we get invited to ride in Scott Turner's car in a Veterans Day parade. Scott's running for Texas state representative, and he'd like Napal and me to be in the front of his convertible, with our names and US AIR FORCE VETERAN on the vehicle's side. I agree. Scott sits high on the trunk with his feet on the rear seats, where the crowd can see and cheer him. He's a former NFL guy, having played for both the Redskins and the Denver Broncos. He's also been hugely supportive of CCI. But the funny thing about the parade is the effect my dog and I have on the crowd. Or, you guessed it, just my dog really.

Napal sits upright on the front seat, perched on my lap, his head and forepaws resting on the open window, nose in the air. He has this look on his face that is so classy and sassy: *I am the famous Napal. Which of you two-footed fellows is going to vote for me?*

As the car passes the crowd applaud. Then they catch sight of my dog and the noise changes immediately to long drawn-out oooohs and aaaahs. That reaction – that gooey outpouring that a people resort to when they see something utterly cute – follows our vehicle all down the promenade.

Then someone yells, 'Hey! I'd vote for the dog!'

I guess I don't blame him. If you met Napal, maybe you would want to nominate him for president. Which gets me thinking: *Hell, Napal and me, maybe we do have enough in our life together to make a good book!*

I email and Skype the British author, and we explore the idea some more. Finally we agree to meet so he can spend some time with my dog. He arranges to fly into Dallas Fort Worth in a couple of months. In fact, he'll arrive on the Sunday after our forthcoming HALO for Freedom jump.

Joanna volunteers to come with us on the jump event, to help organize everything. Carol Long also volunteers to come, along with Jazz, the CCI puppy that she's raising, so they can help spread the word. My folks will be there too. They can't wait for me do the jump. In truth, neither can I. This honestly is the big one. If I can pull this off we will have done it all. With Napal at my side I'll have slain every last demon.

At this year's event there will be three Medal of Honor winners – two from Vietnam and one from the war in Afghanistan. There will also be scores of wounded warriors who very likely won't know about service dogs, or how they can transform their lives. Hopefully, I'll get some to sign onto CCI's waiting list there and then.

The mission continues. That's what we're here for.

# CHAPTER 35

The day of the HALO jump dawns. Everyone is briefed that this is my first jump since I was injured over a decade ago, when I parachuted into the Ecuadorian jungle as a combat weatherman serving with the SOAR.

I roll out to the waiting aircraft. Joanna is there with her camera, waiting to catch it all on film. The guys lift me out of my chair and load me in through the cargo door – the same one that we'll be leaping out of once we're at altitude. Paul, the tandem master, straps me on, and we prepare to pile out of the aircraft's open door at close to 10,000 feet of altitude.

We talked a lot the evening before, so Paul knows my story. He knows my legs are brittle and he knows the risks of me breaking something. But he understands why I have missed doing this so much, and why I'm willing to take the risk now. He straps my legs into a harness to hold them clear during the landing . . . and we're ready.

The green-for-go light blinks on. I cross my arms over my chest so as not to snag on anything, and Paul pushes me ahead of him out the door. Together we plunge into the whirling void. I am overawed to be here in this moment, doing the impossible.

We plummet earthwards, the wind roaring in my ears.

I let out an adrenalin-fuelled, ecstatic scream: 'AAAAAHH-HHHHHHHH!'

'YEAAAAHHHHHHHH!' Paul echoes.

You just gotta yell your head off in the free fall.

It is even better than I remember it. The rush of the free fall, with the wind roaring in my ears, brings it all flooding back – the memories, the thoughts and the emotions of who and what I used to be. But I don't feel bad any more. I don't regret life before the chair, or try to deny that was me.

Somehow, I feel complete.

Paul pulls the chute, and in an instant our world goes from a blast of howling wind so fierce you can barely hear a word, to utter serenity and calm. He begins the series of tight turns, which end up throwing us out almost horizontal to the 'chute, as we spin around its axis. It's crazy, and the G forces are extreme, and of course I love every second. This wild ride towards earth is all I ever hoped it would.

I hit the ground and my adrenalin spikes off the scale. I am as high as life can take me. I seek out Napal and tell him what he knows: *We did it. We made it. We climbed the highest mountain; we scaled the tallest peak.*

I speak to Paul and the others about a crazy thought that has just occurred to me. Since I managed this, is it possible that I could jump solo, in my wheelchair? Could I get jump-certified in my chair? If so, I could free-fall into events such as this. If I could land in my wheelchair, now that would be making an entrance!

Paul figures I'd need to get a specially made chair, one fitted with shock absorbers and tested in a wind tunnel. But he can see how cool it would be.

Today's HALO jump has been videotaped, and they play a clip at that evening's black-tie gala. I couldn't remember what I said right after the jump – I was buzzing so much – but when the video clip plays it brings tears to my eyes. My family and friends are there, and we talk about how the last time I jumped was over a decade ago on that mission into the Amazon. We talk about what it's been like to wait all these years, dreaming of being able to fly again, and now, finally, that dream has become real.

Napal is far too smart to mistake my tears for sadness. He knows I'm the happiest I've ever been – well, ever since the day he and I found each other. He goes to get into my lap for a hug but, oddly, he seems unable to get his front paws up. It's almost as if he's too weak to get his big, heavy torso onto my chair. This isn't like my strong-as-an-ox six-year-old black Labrador.

This isn't like him at all.

Later, in my hotel room, Napal seems strangely exhausted. I call the vet on his private number and talk through my concerns. We saw him two weeks ago, for Napal had a stubborn cough. It seems to have gone now, but I can't understand why it has left him so weak. The vet tells me to bring Napal in for an examination just as soon as we're home.

The following morning we go to check out of the hotel, but as we're waiting for the lift Napal has a pee in the corner. This is so unlike him. He has never had an accident before. I load him into the truck and we set off for the journey home. Normally my dog loves to drive. He sits up front, his head against the cracked-open window, his nose in the wind and ears flapping, loving every minute.

But not today. Today, he climbs onto the back seat and falls into a deep, deep sleep. He's curled around himself and he seems dead to the world. As I drive my mind drifts to that HALO jump and the idea of doing it with Napal in my chair.

'So what about it, boy?' I ask him. 'Fancy making the jump?'

There is zero response. I eye him in the rear-view mirror. He's sprawled across the seat so flat out I cannot even tell if he is breathing.

I call out his name: 'Hey, Napal.'

Nothing.

'Hey, Napal.' Slightly more insistent now. 'Napal. Hey, Napal. How you doin', buddy?'

Still no response.

'Napal. *Napal.*'

Still nothing.

'NAPAL! WAKE UP, BUDDY!'

Finally he shifts his head a little and opens a groggy eye. Thank God. But a moment later he's drifted back into that same exhausted sleep. That moment when I feared I couldn't wake him has scared me to death.

It's a little over an hour's drive to reach home. I wake him upon our arrival, but he almost seems to need my help to get down from the truck. He's never been like this before. It's not as if I can call my boys for assistance. They're away for a week with their mom, skiing in Colorado, leaving me free to work with the British author guy.

We get into the house, and for the first time I see Napal

blunder into something. It's like he can't walk straight or keep his balance. Or maybe he's not seeing properly.

I'm worried sick, but there's not a great deal I can do about it right now. I'm exhausted from the drive, and over the last two days I've had a bare few hours' sleep snatched here and there. It's late on a Saturday, and Napal's veterinarians will be closed for the weekend. I call the vet again, and he tells me to get Napal in to see him first thing Monday morning.

So we crash out, my dog and me, on the same bed. And we sleep. But even now he's different somehow.

Normally, we'd have fifteen minutes on the bed cuddling, and then he'd shift about and grumble – making his Mexico-time ruff-ruff-ruff bark-moan: *Hey, I love you, buddy, but I'm not really comfortable*. And then he'd jump down and wander out-side to use the bathroom. He'd pad back in and flop out on the doggie duvet I keep right next to my bed. Duty done, time to rest. That's Napal's bed. He loves sleeping there.

But tonight there's none of that. He stays on my bed all night long. And he's pulled himself in real tight. It's almost as if he can't bear the thought of not being close to me. Almost like he's scared.

There's a moment when I relive the fear that I experienced on the long drive home, when I didn't seem able to wake him. He's in such a heavy slumber, barely moving, his breath coming in such deep, slow sighs and sloughs, that a moment comes when I fear that he's gone. Slipped away.

But why am I so worried?

Why do I fear that death is stalking him, my boy?

Two weeks back we were at the vets. They ran all sorts of

tests on him. They didn't find anything. So why am I lying here sleepless in McKinney and worried sick about my dog?

Tomorrow the British author's coming to work with us on our story. He's flying in from London, and I was feeling so excited to have him finally meet Napal. To see the dog everyone goes wild over. But right now I don't even feel as if I can take Napal to the airport. I can't manhandle him into my vehicle, and he doesn't seem to have the energy to get in there of his own accord.

Things don't improve a lot with daybreak. Napal's reluctant to leave my bed. I heap his bowl with Eukanuba, but he doesn't seem able to eat. He's off his chow. I have never known this before. Sure, he has a sensitive digestive system, famously so. If he ever gets fed human food it tends to upset him, and we've had a few bouts of diarrhoea in the past.

But not to eat his Eukanuba, that's unprecedented.

I let him out to go use the bathroom. When he's done I call him back in, but he seems unable to find me. He comes back through the door, yet can't seem to work out where I am. I call him from my chair, but he's unable to either hear or see me. I have to roll over to get him. This is scary. This is role-reversal territory. My dog is no longer looking after me. Instead, I'm the one who's trying to care for him.

I let Napal spend the morning resting. Sleeping. He doesn't seem capable of anything more. I wonder if it's just that the HALO days have exhausted him. He was there doing his CCI ambassadorial stuff and I didn't for one moment see him falter. We've got a bunch of wounded warriors – maybe even a Medal of Honor recipient – who now say they're going to get a CCI dog. They're signing up to the programme having seen Napal in action. My dog has worked his magic, and maybe that's what's wiped him out – giving so much to everyone else as always, so there's little left for Napal. But then I remind myself of what we've done before.

We did an east- to west-coast three-city tour of the USA once, in three days. It was practically non-stop. Napal loved every minute. He was in the aircraft alongside me with a seat of his own, sitting up and watching the movies. He was born to work, to perform and to care for me. You might even say he was bred for it.

The normal graduation rate for CCI dogs is around 30 per cent. In Napal's litter and line it is 70 per cent. Phenomenal. They just don't come any better.

That afternoon I head to the airport. Napal is still sleeping, so I leave him on his bed – he's not up to going anywhere. I park in the wrong garage at the airport and hope I can roll through from one to the other, but it seems so wrong being here without Napal. I never go anywhere without him. That's who we are. He can be slow about getting going – all grumbly as he shakes himself into action. *Hey, what's the hurry, man? You're hardly speedy, so I got plenty of time to get rolling.*

But right now I'm trying to get from one massive multi-storey car park to another, and without my assistance dog. I feel . . . disorientated. Out on a limb. Vulnerable. Only now that I do not have him do I realize how closely we are grafted together. It's like Napal has become another limb. A part of me. Part of my body and my personality. Something I can't go anywhere without.

Yet today I've had to.

I make the terminal late due to the parking fiasco. Thankfully, the immigration queue is massive, so I figure the author guy will be snarled up in there somewhere. I check, and that's what the airport staff tell me. I try to relax into the wait, but my mind remains troubled.

The guy appears. I recognize him from his photo on his website. He waves at me from the arrivals gate. I wave back, then scoot forward in the chair to greet him. We shake hands.

'Jason Morgan. Hey, they finally let you through.'

'Damien Lewis. Yeah, it took a while. Great to meet you and put a face to a name at last.'

I see him looking for my dog. He knows we go everywhere together.

'Oh yeah. Napal's back at the house. He's kind of not feeling so good right now. I left him there to rest.'

It's a typical me comment. Understatement. No betrayal of the emotions or turmoil I'm feeling inside. I come from a long line of Morgan men like this. Strong and inscrutable on the outside. Never show your emotions or your fear. So I tell Damien that Napal is just a little tired, whereas in truth I'm scared to death that he's on the brink of something really serious. Not eating. That's bad. But I don't say that to the guy who's come here to help us tell our story.

The pain in my right leg, the one that I've lost half of, is really bad. It's jabbing up into my backbone and brain, like sharp spear tips. My mother is convinced that it's psychological; the pain has been triggered by the emotional turmoil that's twisting my guts up tight like a knotted blanket.

We drive home and I find that Napal's been up and about,

which is encouraging. He gets to his feet to greet me. I stroke him and show him love. I check his food bowl but he's barely eaten. I grab a frankfurter from the fridge. I never give him human food, but this is an emergency. I try to feed a broken piece to him. He can't see that it's there. He can't even seem to smell it. I have to get it right under his nose to get him to take it. I feed him the whole thing. But with each chunk it's clearer and clearer that somehow he can't see.

Damien and I talk about Napal. Damien agrees it's really worrying. I call the vet's cell phone and fortunately he answers. I apologize for disturbing him on a Sunday evening, but I explain what's happened. The vet offers to opens up at eight sharp on Monday so he can see Napal early. I go to bed and Napal gets up there with me, although I have to ask Damien to help lift him, as my dog hasn't got the strength.

And this is the second night that Napal spends comatose, curled up as close to me as he can possibly get, as if he's desperate not to let me go.

# CHAPTER 36

Napal's breathing is so deep and so slow there are times when I fear it's stopped completely. It reminds me of myself when I spent those months in the depths of the coma. The very thought freaks me out.

I'm sick with worry, and my stress levels peak to where they've not been in an age. The pain returns with a vengeance. It's worse in my right leg, and from there it shoots up my backbone direct to my brain. I spend the entire night with the TV blaring out white noise and blue light. It's a cover for the groans and the cries as I twist and writhe.

Come morning I've barely slept. I know I won't be able to rest until I've got Napal sorted. Our life forces are so closely intertwined, and whatever his mystery illness is it has me wound up tight like a coiled spring.

Damien has to lift Napal into my truck. My dog is too weak to make it alone, yet he's far too heavy for me to think of carrying him. This is not what I invited the guy over for from England. I asked him here to witness Napal the wonder dog in action. Not this.

Worse still, I can see how tortured Napal is psychologically.

He keeps trying to do his stuff, to walk tall by my side and to care for me, but he just isn't capable of it right now. Instead, I have this weird, unsettling feeling that I have suddenly become the carer for my dog. Trouble is, being chair-bound I don't have the wherewithal. The *ability*. If it weren't for Damien being here, I couldn't even have got him into my truck. You can't lift much of anything – and certainly not a seventy-pound dog – when you're confined to a chair.

We arrive at the vet's surgery a good ten minutes early. It's only the second time that I've brought Napal to LazyPaw, as we've just changed vets. I gave a talk recently to a bunch of sixth-graders, something organized by Annette, a friend of my mom's. Annette advised me to switch to LazyPaw. She told me they have a very special connection to CCI service dogs. They care for several already. Napal and I have only made the one previous visit, but I've been hugely impressed by them so far.

We park in the disabled bay. A couple of smartly dressed young women turn up and unlock the office. I check my watch. I figure it's time to learn the worst. I get my chair ready, while Damien lifts my dog down from the rear of the vehicle. Napal stands there morosely, head hanging low, before he plods forward to try to take up his position faithfully at my side.

I take a long moment to pet him. 'It's OK, boy. Nothing to worry about. We're here now. We'll get you sorted.' I turn to Damien. 'Say, can you grab his harness and fit it onto him. It kinda just clicks around his chest . . .'

With Napal in harness I roll off, heading for the disabled ramp. I pause for a moment, figuring my dog should have a pee. I point him towards the grass, which is bleached brown from the cold winter months. The first hint of spring is in the air, and there's a gentle warmth in the sun that peeps over the McKinney skyline.

I give him the bathroom command: 'Hurry. Come on, boy. Time to use the bathroom.'

Napal takes one or two feeble steps towards the grass, but he's hardly left the sidewalk when he starts to pee. This is so unlike my dog.

I murmur something, speaking half to Damien and half to myself. 'See, that's not like Napal. He's always off finding himself a nice patch of soft ground to pee on. But this, he's barely stepped off the path.'

One of the receptionists pops her head out of the office door. 'We're ready when you guys are.'

'Just got the sprinkler going to green the grass,' I tell her, trying to explain why Napal is peeing so close to their entrance.

She smiles. 'Go right ahead. That's what it's there for.'

I let Napal finish, then steer him to the door. He's slow and unsteady on his feet, and I swear he can't see properly. I have to guide him by his lead every step of the way.

The receptionist shows us into a simple examination room. It's got a brown tiled floor, a wooden bench and a shelf full of vet's equipment. I park my chair in the centre and hunker down, pain rampaging through my guts. Napal flops down at my side. No sooner has his head hit the floor than he seems to drift into the deep, coma-like sleep of the night just gone.

Damien takes the bench and our eyes meet, worriedly, before we go back to staring at Napal.

'I don't think he can see properly . . . You see the way I had to guide him? I mean, what would cause that?'

Damien shakes his head. 'No idea. But he's not well, that's for sure. Let's hope the vet can get him sorted.'

We wait.

There's a faint tap at the door and Brent Bilhartz steps in. He seems like a tall guy to me, but then again everyone looks tall when you're in a chair. He's dressed in a checked shirt, faded jeans and cowboy boots. He's got kind blue eyes and an air of total integrity and compassion about him. He sinks to his haunches before Napal and reaches out to caress one of his ears.

'Say, it's the famous Napal. Always a pleasure to see you.' He glances up at me. 'So, Jason, I wasn't expecting to have you back again so quickly.'

'Yeah, well, me neither, but Napal's been real unwell.'

For a second Brent flicks his eyes across to the stranger in the room.

'This here is Damien Lewis,' I volunteer. 'He's a writer flew over all the way from England to work on a book about me and Napal.' I caress my dog's head. 'So, we need you well, buddy. We need to get going on the writing.'

'A book?' Brent smiles. 'Hey, that's real neat. No one deserves it more than Napal.' He starts to feel along my dog's underside, beneath his haunches and around his head and neck. 'How's it been with him since last time? Not so good?'

'He's just not himself. He's kind of exhausted. Sleeping all the time real deep. And he's bumping into stuff, almost like he can't see.'

The vet pauses what he's doing and goes to fetch a light. He shines it into each of Napal's eyes, taking a good long look.

He flicks the light off and glances at me. 'Well, he's responding to light like he should. He blinks when he should. But he's definitely not himself, that's for sure. This is the not the same dog I saw when you brought him in two weeks ago.'

I'm hunched over in my chair, fighting against the knives that jab and slice into my guts. 'No, it's not. But if he can see OK, why's he not able to find stuff? Like food. Plus I called him in from the yard yesterday and he just couldn't seem to find his way.'

The vet pauses for a second, taking a good long look at Napal. 'I just think he's run-down and exhausted and doesn't have the energy to look where he's going, or pay much attention.'

'But what would cause that?'

'I don't know. But we'll find out. You mind leaving him with us for a couple of hours? We'll work up some bloods and do some X-rays, and we'll reload in a couple of hours, OK? And don't worry; we'll get him all worked out.'

'Thanks. I appreciate it. This is Napal, after all.'

The vet nods. 'This is Napal. And we're very lucky right now 'cause it's the Easter break, and all the kids that grew up around here, they're home from college. We've got a load here right now on work experience. They're way better off doing that than a lot of stuff kids get up to these days! So, anyway, we're overstaffed, which means Napal will get the very best attention possible.'

'That's good. He'll appreciate it. You know how much he likes being around young people.'

I see the vet freeze for a moment. His hands are feeling under Napal's rear haunches. He delves around in one spot for several long seconds. Then he glances at me, and I can see the worry etched in his eyes.

'So, here's something . . . I can feel a real hard lump. Right here. Has he had this long? Under his back left armpit.'

I shake my head. 'He can't have. I'd have felt it when putting on his harness. I'd have felt that immediately.'

The vet nods. 'So I figured. I'd have felt it two weeks back. No way would I have missed that. So, we've got to figure that it's recent, huh?'

I hunch over even further, arms crossed over my stomach, pain arcing up my spine like bolts of lightning. 'I guess so. Well, I'm real glad we're with LazyPaw right now . . .'

I can't think what else to say. I thank the vet again and turn to roll out of the room. Napal tries to struggle to his feet alongside me. He's still determined to be there for me, in spite of everything. I tell him he's a good boy and that he's got to stay here with the vet; that I'll be back in an hour or two.

Brent leads Napal away, but he pauses at the door. He's eyeing my dog as he paces behind him so very slowly, eyes downcast and with a poise like his head's become too heavy for him to carry any more.

'You know, he was nothing like this when I saw him two weeks back. He's really gone downhill fast.' Brent glances my way. 'You know, I'm worried. I'd be lying if I didn't say I was.' A pause. 'But leave him with us, and we'll reload in an hour or so.'

He and Napal disappear through the door. I hear Brent call out to his assistants, 'So this is the famous Napal. Get him straight into ICU. I'll need bloods and—'

The door closes.

I'm left with Damien our visiting writer and no dog. We've got two hours to kill, and I don't know what on earth I'm going to do. We go outside and pause in the sunlight.

I glance at Damien. 'What we saw in there and what the vet said . . . you know, that scares me to death, it really does.'

'I know. It's worrying. But let's just wait and see what the tests show. Tell you what – let's leave him a book. It'd be a nice gesture, and he seems such a lovely kind of guy.'

'Yeah, that'd be good,' I tell him. 'Make sure you sign it. Brent would appreciate that. You got one in the truck, right?'

He tells me that he has. He hurries off to fetch it. I stare out over the rolling suburban skyline. I'm alone. The sun is well up and I can feel its warmth on my face, but I have never felt so cold or so desolate inside.

What Napal has experienced over the last forty-eight hours goes against everything he's ever known in his life, which is the joy of his duty. Now he can't do it and it's cutting him up. Torturing him inside. I can feel his pain, and it's messing me up real bad. Whatever it is that's wrong with him, I pray to God that Brent is able to get it sorted, and quickly.

We drive away from LazyPaw, and I put a call through to my mom on speakerphone. I tell her the basics.

'Oh my goodness . . . oh my goodness.' Mom is so upset she doesn't know what to say.

I finish the call as we always do: 'Love you, Mom.'

'Love you, Jason, love you. I'm sure it's gonna be OK.'

I ring off. 'My family and I are pretty close,' I tell Damien. 'They're what got me through everything really – well, my family and Napal . . .'

We head home. I can't think where else to go. We try to kill time, but the atmosphere around the house is brittle and tense. The very moment the two hours are up I put a call through to LazyPaw. I get the receptionist and ask her how Napal is doing. I'm told the tests are done and that they have a diagnosis.

'Well hey, that's a relief. What is it?'

'Jason, we're going to need you to come in. Brent wants to tell you in person, OK?'

'OK . . . Well, I guess we're on our way.'

I kill the call. I glance at Damien. 'They got a diagnosis, but they want us to go in to hear it.' A beat. 'That's not good, is it?'

I can tell that the poor guy doesn't know what to say. He flew in here only yesterday, expecting to spend a few good days with me and my dog. The plan was to drive down to Florida, where we'd been offered the use of a beachside apartment, so the three of us could do some storytelling by the sea. And now this.

We drive back to LazyPaw in silence. We're shown into the examination room. Brent enters, leading Napal after him with infinite gentleness. He lets my dog flop down exhaustedly by my side. I greet him with some ruffles around the ears where I know he loves it, plus a bunch of encouraging words. But he slumps down on the cool tiles and he's half-asleep almost instantly.

Brent goes down on his haunches, kind of squatting before me at my level. There's silence for a second or so.

Then: 'So, there is no way to sugarcoat this. Jason, it is not good news.' He glances at Damien, who's sitting on the bench against the wall. 'Is it OK to talk? I mean, you want me to tell you this alone . . .'

'Oh no. I mean, this guy's here to write our story, so he can hear everything . . . I mean, that's if the book ever happens . . . So, yeah, please go right ahead.'

'OK, so like I said there's no way to sugarcoat this. Napal is full of cancerous tumours. He's got a few weeks to live at most, possibly just days. Even with a full dose of chemo that's all anyone would give him, plus for half of that he'll be in hospital. This is a very, very special dog. We can pull out all the stops. But we can probably give him no more than that.'

Silence again.

I feel as if I have been kicked in the guts by a mule, while at the same time I've had a dagger thrust up to the hilt into the very centre of my spine. The pain saws through me, flaying flesh from bone and ripping out nerve endings. My entire body is on fire. Popping. Burning. There is a monstrous roaring in my ears and there is absolutely nothing I can think of to say.

'You want to talk to the oncologist?' Brent continues. His voice sounds as if it's coming from a long way away, like I'm falling down some dark and howling tunnel. 'I don't think she'll say anything that I haven't, but this isn't just any dog. This is Napal. It might help put your mind at ease, so you know you've done everything possible?'

'The oncologist? Yeah, I guess it wouldn't hurt.' I don't know where the words are coming from. This isn't me talking. It's some autopilot standing in for the real me. 'But I don't want him to suffer. That's the crucial thing.'

Brent gets to his feet. 'OK, let me go and shake their tree. See if they've got space for anything today.'

He leaves. I'm entombed by my pain. It's like a wall of fire is swirling all around me, cutting me off from the world. A while later Brent returns. I don't know how long he's been gone. I'm not even here any more.

'They're frantic today, but they're squeezing everyone else in real quick so they can—'

I glance at Brent, the look in my gaze silencing him. 'Tell me. If it was your dog what would you do?' The words fall like dark boulders into a still pond. They shatter the surface.

'Me? If it were my dog?' Brent is visibly shaken. 'Jason, this is always difficult with any dog, but Napal . . . My wife tells me if it ever stops being difficult, then that's the time to give up doing what I do. But I have to tell you, what I'm seeing here is the deep, deep fatigue of a terminal disease. That is what this is.' He glances at Napal, who's slumped next to my chair. 'I'm not gonna lie to you. He fell asleep back there and there was a moment when we saw him and we thought, *Oh my God, has he gone?* It was such a deep, deep sleep. So, if it were my dog, I'd euthanize him. That's what I would do if it were my dog.'

Someone says, 'I just don't want him to suffer, that's all.' I guess the voice is mine.

Brent eyes Napal. 'We might give him two months with chemo. We might. But they would not be good months. I think when we all look at him and see him lying there, here, lying on the floor like this, we know what we've got to do.'

'I just don't want him to suffer at all.'

Brent glances towards the door. 'What kind of day is it out there? We could do it in here, but if it's a nice day outside . . .?'

'It's a fine day. The sun is shining. It's warm. Napal loves to lie in the sun – no matter how hot, he loves it.'

'We can do it outside . . . Lay him on a blanket in the sun.'

'Napal would like that.'

'Outside for sure. Yeah, why not? If that'll make it any easier. I'll do anything I can. Go to any lengths. This is Napal, after all.'

Brent clambers to his feet. With great difficulty he rouses Napal. 'I'll need to get an IV into him, which will be difficult 'cause his blood pressure's real low . . . I'll just be a minute or two is all.'

As he leads Napal away for a second time, I can tell that my dog wants to stay. He wants to stay and to do his duty, to stick by my side until his dying day. *But today is that day.* Unexpectedly, unbelievably, ten years too early, today is his day to leave this beautiful world that we've shared together for all too short a time.

Napal is only six years old, so how can this have happened? We've done so much, but we have so much more to do: a whole lifetime of adventures and love and giving; so many more lives to touch and inspire. And I cannot – I simply cannot for one moment – come close to believing that I am about to lose him today.

Brent pauses at the doorway, waiting to hand Napal to his assistant. She is a petite blonde girl called Beth and she looks to be no more than in her early twenties. As she takes Napal's lead I can tell that she is on the verge of tears.

Brent turns back to me. 'I'll get him cremated, and we'll need a very special urn for him. A very special urn. There'll be nothing in the catalogue that will suit, not for a dog like Napal. So, there's this graphic designer friend I know and I'll get him to design something. Something that'll really suit . . . and don't worry, there's no charge for any of this. Not a cent for any of this at all today.'

I mouth some words of thanks to Brent.

I roll outside. Nothing feels real. I don't know what on earth to say to anyone. For a moment I wonder whether I should call my boys, but they're hundreds of miles away vacationing with their mom, so it's not as if they could make it here to say a last goodbye to the dog we have loved so much and cherished so deeply.

I figure there is one thing I really do need to do though – I need to call Melissa. If there's one other person who should be here at Napal's leaving, I guess it should be her. I make the call. I have no idea what I say. All I do know is that Melissa drops everything, and in a few minutes she'll be with us.

Damien and I find a patch of warm sunlight out of the wind. There are no words for where we are right now. I can tell he's struggling to hold back his own emotions, even though he's only known Napal for a day. That's the effect my dog has on people, yet in a few moments, somehow, unbelievably, Napal will be going to the place of his leaving.

Brent and his assistant join us. Beth has to steer Napal with gentle hands so he can find his way across the brittle, sunlit grass. Her eyes are brimful of tears. She mutters an embarrassed apology.

'I'm sorry,' she sniffs, 'but it's the first time I've ever met him. This is Napal . . .'

Brent spreads a blanket in the sun. Damien asks me if I'd like a last photo. *A last photo.* I never thought it would come to this. I tell him I guess I would.

Napal stands bravely by my chair. I can tell that the effort of that alone is almost too much for him. I know there's no chance of a final cuddle or a bear hug. Napal barely has the strength to remain on his four paws, let alone to climb into my chair. I cup his face in my hands and bring his forehead close to mine, and I whisper gentle words tight in his ears. I pour out my love and my affection, and I tell him how it's all going to be OK.

'Good boy. Brave boy. Not long now . . . You're being such a brave boy, you know that.'

I tell him if there is a doggie heaven he's sure to get there. I promise that I'll see him there some day.

A figure rushes over from the parking lot. It's Melissa. She falls at Napal's feet, brushing her fine blonde hair away, her face streaked with tears. Melissa sets everyone off. We do a group hug, her arms half around my dog and half around me. Napal knows it's her, and I sense somehow that he's glad she's here at his parting.

I lift Napal's head and give him a last lingering kiss on the nose.

I guess this is our final, final goodbye.

Brent eases Napal away from me. He lays my dog onto the blanket in the sun. Napal closes his eyes. I know he knows that he is leaving this world, and I can sense that he is ready. He is so utterly, utterly finished I cannot understand how I didn't see this before. It's as if he's been keeping it sharp and good for the last leg of our epic journey – getting me up and into the HALO and watching me jump – and then, when his task was done, when the voyage was finally complete, he allowed himself the time and the space to fall.

Beth arranges Napal's limbs so the vet can get the syringes

in. My dog is so trusting to the very last that he lets her do it with never a growl or a whimper of complaint.

'So, this is the first one,' Brent announces quietly. 'I'm putting in the general anaesthetic.'

He plugs the syringe in.

'OK, now the second.' He pumps in the longer dose.

For several long moments there isn't the barest sound apart from those all around trying to choke back their tears. I can sense Napal is leaving me. A moment later and I can feel his presence – his warm, loving, caring, gorgeous, loyal presence – fading. And then my life companion, my best friend, my son, my battle buddy – the person I've spent more time with in the last years than anyone – is no more.

Brent turns to me. 'He's gone.' A pause. 'We'll take care of him from here.'

I'm speechless. The tears are pouring down. What is there to say?

'Let's get him away before it starts to show,' Brent says quietly to Beth. 'Before he starts to change.'

Beth turns to me and holds out a tear-stained hand. 'I'm sorry. I'm so glad to have met you, even though . . .'

She leaves that last bit unsaid: *Even though no one could have imagined that this would be the day that Napal passed away.*

She turns to help Brent wrap my dog in the blanket. His death shroud. They lift him up, and the last I see of Napal is his shiny black nose poking out as they carry my beloved dog away.

'We'll take care of him from here,' Brent says again, as they go to turn the corner. 'We'll take care of him from here.' And I know in my heart that they will.

Melissa gives me a long, tearful hug. 'At least he spent his last days with wounded warriors,' she sobs, 'doing what he loved most, working and inspiring others.'

'He did. Just last Friday three guys signed up to get a dog, having got to meet Napal.'

Melissa wipes at her cheeks with the back of her hand. 'A star among stars.'

'A star among stars,' I echo.

Yet I still cannot believe that Napal is gone.

# CHAPTER 37

This day should never have happened. It's one of those can't-have-happened days. A parent should never have to bury their children. That's how I feel about Napal – as if I've been forced to do just that. Today should never have happened.

The hours after losing Napal are some of the most difficult of my life. I am down so low and I am entombed in my pain. But mostly I am so utterly, utterly lost. There are so many people I feel I have to tell. I call my boys on vacation in Colorado; the news is a bombshell to them. I call Julie on vacation in Mexico; she breaks down when she hears the news. I speak to Mom and Dad, and they are in pieces. It is so unexpected. It has hit us all like a bolt from the blue. Then there is Napal's vast network of supporters and fans, but I can't face speaking to most of them right now.

The one person I do call is Jim Siegfried. He answers with his customary 'Hey, what's up?'

Telling Jim that Napal has passed away is one of the hardest things I have ever had to do. Somehow, it's tougher even than breaking the news to my boys. Jim and I talk for hours, reminiscing about the dog that we loved so much. Our dog.

A dog that dared us both to hope, but who has left us so prematurely.

That evening I roll around my local Walmart. No one so much as notices me. I am back where I started – back in the limbo of life after paralysis. In a few short hours I have lost everything that Napal ever did for me – all the limitless joy, hope, love and the meaning that he brought into my life. And, mostly, this is what I will miss: I will miss the bridge my dog provided to the outside world. To 'normal' people. To life.

The most people seem to manage is to ask, 'Say, where's your dog? Where's Napal?'

It's as if I don't exist without him. I miss him more than I would ever have imagined possible. Napal has been with me every second of every day. My loss feels akin to losing one of my own sons.

That night I barely sleep. When I do drift off I quickly wake again with no idea why. For a moment I wait to hear the familiar jingle of Napal's dog tags, as he wakes with me just to check if I'm OK. I call for him. No answer. And then I remember: *My dog is gone*. It all comes flooding back to me. *Napal is gone*.

At some stage during the night my phone rings. I check the caller ID. It's been going berserk as word gets out that Napal has passed away, but I just can't bring myself to speak to anyone much right now. This caller is different. It's John Libonati.

It is an emotional call. We are grown men, yet we cannot stop the tears. At one stage I impress upon John how important it is that we honour Napal's memory. There needs to be some kind of a lasting memorial to this dog of dogs, this fabulous ambassador for CCI. John promises that he will get it done.

He tells me something to try to lift me: Jason Morgan, the CCI dog named after me, has just graduated. This past Veterans Day he was assigned to a disabled Vietnam War veteran. John tries to find a delicate way to tell me that CCI will want me to have another service dog, for I cannot be their ambassador without one. But who could ever replace Napal?

Come morning I wheel myself to my truck in the garage, and I call out for him: 'Hey, buddy. Come on, we gotta go . . .' And then I stop myself. *Napal is gone.* I have to remind myself over and over again: *Napal is gone.*

I end up in hospital, I am so racked with stress and pain. I need morphine to rein it in. I get so many messages of condolences, so many invitations to visit and to speak and to share my loss. Mostly, I can't. There are no words.

Oddly enough, having Damien with me proves somehow helpful. Together, we journey through the memories. I tell him that all things happen for a reason. There is a reason he was here for Napal's dying – so this book can be a fitting tribute, the perfect memorial to a four-legged hero; to a life lived so well. To the dog that gave me hope.

I can think of no better way to celebrate the life of this extraordinary animal, one who touched so many, than to tell Napal's story. To immortalize it in these pages. The day I met Napal was a truly extraordinary day. He turned my life around and very possibly saved me. He healed a family, and in our love and our special partnership my life's mission was born. He gave me hope. Hope – that is absolutely what defined this dog – hope and a boundless capacity to love.

Damien and I head out to my folks' place. We gather with

Mom, Dad and my brother John to share the memories. Mom pulls out a massive, dusty heap of files. I had no idea, but she has kept every last thing: every newspaper clipping, photograph, medical report, and even the faded yellow flier for the auction that raised the funds to get me to the Quito clinic for the nerve graft surgery.

My dad has kept the photos of the Chevrolet Blazer that rolled down the mountainside. I have never seen them before. It looks so crushed and broken up it's a wonder that anyone survived. There are days of tears and laughter . . . and rage – rage that Napal has been taken from us ten years too soon. But I guess for all of us this is also a time of healing.

I receive a call from Brent at LazyPaw. As gently as he is able to he lets me know that Napal's remains are ready for me to collect. I motor over. I get presented with a box made of polished redwood, complete with brass hinges and clasps, plus a golden padlock. 'Napal' is inscribed on the brass nameplate. I take the box, and the most surprising thing is how heavy it feels. I wonder whether it is the wood or the ashes inside that weigh so much. But then Napal was a big, weighty animal.

Brent hands me two plaster casts to go with the ashes. Napal's front paws are imprinted into them. The casts are so detailed I can see the fingerprint-like tracing marks all over Napal's pads, like the tiny spreading branches of a miniature tree. They are beautiful. Down the side of each is carved his name: NAPAL.

I hold the ashes and the plaster casts and I feel . . . over-whelmed. On the one hand I cannot believe that my dog has been reduced to this. On the other, what Brent has done is just so generous-hearted and uplifting. I cannot begin to think where I might scatter Napal's ashes. Maybe I'll just keep them for ever, close by.

The drive home is emotional. There are few rational thoughts in my head. I feel a deep sense of gratitude to Brent and the LazyPaw staff for making something so dark and difficult so much easier. Less painful. But at the same time I cannot believe that all that remains of Napal is a box of cold, grey ashes.

I take Damien to the airport. He's got to leave – flying back to England after a trip that was hugely challenging and emotional, and so unexpected. On the drive there I thank him for being here for me and Napal – and for my folks – at such a difficult time. I tell him again what seems obvious to me.

'You know, all things happen for a reason. I believe that absolutely. So, you were here just as Napal's time was done, and it was his time to leave us. That's no coincidence. Can't be. I mean, what are the chances? You're here so you can witness his end and help tell his story. Communicate the legacy. The memory.'

He shakes his head in wonder. 'Yeah, I mean twenty-four hours before Napal passed away. I'm still shocked from it. Reeling.'

'Like I said, you were here for a reason. We all are. You lifted Napal in and out of this vehicle for the last time. That makes you a part of this.' I glance at him. This guy has shed a good few tears over the past few days. It's been a hugely emotional time and we've grown close. 'Well, you're in it now. You're a part of Napal's story. No way you can't be.'

We say our farewells and I drive home. I tell myself the first thing I have to do is remove Napal's feed and water bowls from the kitchen. I can't have them there reminding me every minute that he is gone. I tell myself that in the dark at home and alone I'll find the time to properly grieve. I'll find the space and privacy to heal.

But, in truth, I still can't believe that Napal is gone. I just can't believe it. I am left alone with a wooden casket full of ashes. I am back in that dark chapter of my life after the paralysis and before getting Napal. I am in a lonely, empty place and I feel so lost.

It is CCI's director, Corey – he I have become good friends – who convinces me that the mission is far from over. Corey, plus some of the other fine people there. They remind me that my and Napal's work has only just begun. There are so many veterans, wounded warriors, plus young and old with disabilities of all kinds, not to mention hospital patients and school children, who are still to be reached. The mission continues.

I tell them there will never be another Napal. It is a cliché, but people say that only the good die young. Napal took me where I needed to go and achieved the seemingly impossible, and he died well before his time. There will never be another like him.

We get talking about how I'm going to need another service dog, and CCI assure me they'll start the search. They advise me it may take a good while to find the right match, but they'll work on it. And the hope of that, the promise of it, somehow makes my loss just that little bit more bearable. But only marginally.

For days on end I roll around in a daze. I feel so bereft without Napal. So hopeless. I feel naked without him at my side.

Some days later I take a call from CCI. 'We've checked with all the regions – Northwest, Southwest, Northcentral, Northeast and Southeast – and it looks like we may have found one in the Northwest region. I'm talking to the trainers later today. The dog is very high energy and extremely smart. I mean real high energy. I just wanted to make sure that's not an issue with you and your kids.'

'Hell no,' I reply. 'My boys are busy teenagers. They'd love nothing more than a high-energy dog.'

You know, the worst thing for my boys was coming home from vacation and facing the cold reality of our loss. There was no Napal to meet them at the door; no Napal to accompany them to school; no Napal to play ball with on the beach; no Napal to lift their dad up as high as he could take me.

So getting a new dog is also about buoying up the entire Morgan household.

# CHAPTER 38

It's six weeks after losing Napal when I fly up to San Francisco, to the beautiful Santa Rosa facility, CCI's national headquarters. It is built in a lush garden campus, on land donated by the Schultz family, the heirs to the Snoopy cartoons.

I meet the other hopefuls. I'm the only one here to get a second dog. They see me as an old-timer, a veteran, and they bombard me with questions. For my part, I can hardly wait to get introduced to the dogs. Among others there are Forester and Flicker, both yellow Labs; there is Chevy, a big, sturdy yellow Lab–retriever cross, and there is Rue, a small black female Labrador.

I have no idea which dog the trainers have lined up for me, but I sense it's going to be either Chevy or Rue. I work with Chevy one day and with Rue the next. I like big, strong dogs, and if anything Chevy is bigger even than Napal was.

I think to myself: *Probably not Rue*. She's like a mini version of Napal, and she reminds me so much of my loss, which is still so raw and so painful. I figure Rue is just too close . . . Too reminiscent of Napal . . . But, boy, does she have attitude.

Three days in we have the pre-match. I am expecting to get

Chevy. In a way he's similar to Napal. There's a Mexico-time side to Chevy, and he's far less of a bundle of energy. As for Rue, I figure she's got a pretty curious name. I ask where it comes from. Apparently she was named after the character Rue in *The Hunger Games*.

It is Rue I get matched with. The trainers decide that she is the one, and I'm not for one moment going to gainsay them. For the first time I take my dog to my room. It's been a long day, and after all the trauma of the last few weeks I tell myself that I will lie there with Rue – just as I did with Napal – and we will cuddle and we will bond.

But oh no, not this dog.

I take off her harness and . . . Rue goes wild. She does twenty crazed circuits of the room, tearing around the place, up over the bed and bouncing off the walls. *Uh-oh.* This is one rocket-fuelled dog. Am I really going to be able to handle her energy? Then I tell myself to man up. I'm no novice at this service-dog thing. You wouldn't want to put Rue with a greenhorn. But Jason Morgan, the long-time battle buddy of Napal? Hell, I should be ready for anything. In any case, CCI has pulled out all the stops here, and not in a million years am I going to go against what they've decided.

She tears around like she's just drained a whole barrel of five-hour energy drink. All she wants to do right now is to play. Rue is two different dogs: the one in the vest, when she's working; the one out of the vest, when she's a total live wire. Vest or no vest, Napal was just too cool and laid-back to ever bother much with crazy.

The first time we get to have our dogs on release time I know exactly what to do with Rue: I take her into this fenced-in area of grass and I let her fly. I throw a tennis ball and she brings it right back to me. But the second time she returns with a *football*. She's the smallest dog running with the biggest ever ball. I throw the tennis ball again, but Rue refuses to go for it. I hurl the football, and she's off like lightning – the smallest dog with the largest, craziest sense of adventure.

There's a teenage boy in our graduation class. I do not know exactly what is wrong with him, but his disabilities are so severe that he can only speak via a machine. It looks like a mini-computer. He punches keys, and it produces short sentences in a voice like a cyborg. 'Food is nice.' 'Your dog is good.' That sort of thing.

For some reason he's drawn to Rue and me. He starts to talk to me through her – as if he's using Rue as a conduit. But the most amazing thing is the way in which, over time, he begins to speak without using his machine at all.

'Does your owner like his food?' he asks Rue. 'Does your owner need some water?'

Rue reacts. She understands. And it's clear that he adores her. By the time he gets his own dog he's not bothering to bring the cyborg machine to lunch anymore. He has no need of it. It's incredible. He talks to me via Rue, and to the others via his own dog – his bridges to the wider body of humanity.

I'm asked to give the graduation speech on behalf of the class. I decide to scoot around and capture everyone's stories. One in particular captivates me. There is a couple here with a twelve-year-old boy who has severe autism. If they take him into an enclosed public space – like a shopping mall – he panics and cries, and tries to run away. As a result they've pretty much given up taking him to such places. But with his CCI service dog they're going to try again.

They are so nervous about going to the mall. They have dual leashes on the boy's dog – one that they can hold, and a second, smaller one to keep him close to his canine companion. And with his dog at his side the boy handles it all just fine. The dog has revolutionized what life will be like for them and their son. Truly amazing.

I'm warned that my speech can't be more than three minutes long. I try to cut it down, but I can't. I hand it to Flora, the head trainer, telling her that it's as short as I can make it. Any less and I'll miss the vital points. The magic.

'Well, how long is it?' she asks.

'About six to seven minutes,' I lie.

She reads it. 'Don't change a word. It's beautiful. Everything in it has to be said. Don't change a thing.'

Graduation is scheduled for the Saturday. My dad flies in that Friday, although Mom can't come as she's on a long-scheduled vacation with her girlfriends. I get him to wait in the lounge area and I lead Rue out to meet him. I give Rue the 'Release' command, and my dad kneels down to her level. He grabs her and hugs her close, and she licks away his tears. Dad tells me that he's crying for so many reasons: because his son has a dog at last, without which I seemed so lost; because he can see already that Rue and I are close; because he knows just what Rue will do for me, and for my boys.

But he's also crying because Rue is such an echo of Napal. The sight of us together brings memories of Napal flooding back, and reminds him of all that we have lost.

My dad – a big, gruff Texan who never shows his emotions – remains on his hands and knees for what seems like an age, letting Rue lick the tears from his eyes. It is instant love on my father's part. It feels so special to have my dad here with me – to share a moment that it so important in my life.

At the brunch before the graduation there is an open-mic session at which anyone is free to speak. My father decides he has to say something that only a parent can.

'I want to tell you that when you walk out of here with your dog it will not only affect the person getting the dog; it will affect everyone in your family. Every single one. Lives will for ever be changed. Jason's dog changed hundreds of other lives. Your dog will change your sister, brother, father, mother, cousins and wider family. These dogs change every life they touch . . .'

I go to shave and change into my military tuxedo. With my disability it takes me an age, and I'm only just ready in time for my talk. I start by speaking about how Napal changed my life and that of my boys – how he turned our family around. I say how Rue will pick up on the work that Napal and I started. I relate the tales of the teenager with the voice machine, and the twelve-year-old with autism – just two amazing stories from this graduation.

'It's up to you how much you want your dog to engage, but be prepared,' I tell my fellow graduates. 'Don't ever think you can run into the store real quick to buy some milk; it ain't gonna happen. And that is one of the greatest joys. You can roll out with confidence knowing that 99 per cent of people will welcome you with your dog, and not look at you askance because you're in a chair. Your dog will be your bridge to the wider world. Be ready.'

I finish with this: 'Don't ever put limits on what your dog or you can do together, as a team. The limits are boundless and I never would have imagined that I could do so much and achieve so much as I did with Napal. So too can you.'

A round of deafening applause fills the room. I go to leave the stage but Corey stops me. 'I want you to stay up here, Jason, 'cause we have something for you.' He hands me a plaque, a gift from CCI. It is inscribed, IN MEMORY OF NAPAL.

I am so touched.

As I roll off the stage with Rue's lead grasped in one hand and Napal's plaque held in the other, I know that Napal's memory will live on in so many different ways.

I tell my dad that I have brought Napal's ashes with me. I figure we should scatter them on the nearby shore of the Pacific Ocean, somewhere scenic and beautiful. Napal loved the water, so where better than somewhere with a view over the sea. I ask one of the CCI guys if he can suggest a suitable place – maybe somewhere along the coast road.

He glances around at the beautiful, sunlit campus. 'Hey, why not do it here? Here on the campus. This is where Napal started life, after all.'

He's right. It is. All CCI puppies are gathered here at the main campus, before being shipped all over the country to their puppy raisers. This was Napal's entry point into the world of service dogs. This would be perfect: the full circle.

My dad takes a walk in the grounds. He returns and tells me he thinks he's found the spot. He leads me to a rose garden, one that has a Snoopy statue in the midst of it. With the Schultz family having donated the land, there are Charlie Brown and Lucy and Snoopy statues all over the place. Snoopy is arguable the most famous dog in the world. The garden reminds me of the White House, where Napal got to pee in that most famous of rose gardens.

'OK,' I tell my dad. 'It's perfect. Let's do it here.'

He steps away so I can have a little privacy. It's just Rue, me and what remains of Napal. I say some words to Napal, but I'm looking towards Rue, and it's as if somehow I can speak to him through her.

'Thank you for being such a great friend. I cannot thank you enough for the way you changed my life. You brought me out of a dark world into a place where I could never have imagined being after my injury. Thank you for that. Thank you for your loyalty, friendship and for always being there for me – through the best and worst of times.'

I scatter the ashes with my right hand.

'What you and I started I'll carry on with Rue, continuing the work you began. I love you, Napal. I always will. No one will ever take your place. No one ever could. Even though you are not physically present in my life, you'll always be a part of it. I will never, ever forget you, Napal.'

I scatter the last of the ashes among the rose blossoms, a faint dust drifting through the sunbeams. Behind me my father has tears streaming down his face. I glance at Rue. She is watching real close, as if she knows how important this is for me. For us.

Our eyes meet and there is a special moment. I take her head in my hands and I speak to her, very directly.

'I think you know this – you probably already realize – but, Rue, you have some big paws to fill. I know you're up for the task, little lady. I know you are . . . I know you're not Napal. There will never be – never could be – another Napal. But you're your own dog and an amazing dog. Like I said, a dog with some big paws to fill.'

I give her the command. 'Let's go, little lady.'

We roll and walk towards my dad, and we've got the whole world ahead of us. For Napal, this is where we found a fitting ending. For Rue and me, this is where it all begins.

It's both an ending and a beautiful beginning.

# AFTERWORD

Jason Morgan enlisted in the USAF in 1989 and he volunteered for special forces in 1993. He didn't get Napal until November 2009, so several years after his paralysis and being consigned to life in a wheelchair. It took that long for him to hear about CCI, which just goes to show how great was – and is – the need to spread the word about what such dogs can do. It was October 2013 when Napal passed away; they'd had just a few short but amazing years together.

Since then Jason has continued with his work publicizing what service dogs can do for the disabled and in particular for veterans. Rue, his next CCI service dog, picked up pretty much where Napal left off. Today Jason regularly speaks to audiences of over one thousand, with Rue of course at his side. Jason and Napal – and now Rue – have raised hundreds of thousands of dollars for the cause.

Recently CCI set up a new regional centre in the Dallas area, working in conjunction with Baylor Scott & White Hospital, an initiative that Jason and his folks helped bring to fruition. Jason also appears widely on the media, giving interviews about the way Napal and Rue have changed his life, and he continues to raise three teenage boys.

In the course of writing this book I made several visits to Texas and the wider USA, to speak to Jason, his wonderful, welcoming family and his extensive network of colleagues and friends. I spent time with Jason and Rue, getting to know the service dog that continues the work that Napal started. Although there could never be another Napal, Rue is her own dog with her unique character and ways.

There could hardly be a better team to spread the message or to further the cause.

*Damien Lewis, Dorset, England, 2015*

# GLENART
## BRAVEHOUND

The value of Companion and Assistance Dogs for British veterans, particularly those with Post Traumatic Stress Disorder (PTSD), is starting to be recognised. Glen Art has established the BRAVEHOUND initiative to begin meeting this need.

BRAVEHOUND currently offers training and support for veterans and their dogs, as well as providing suitable dogs to help to transform the lives of veterans and their families in the UK.

In the future BRAVEHOUND will train Assistance Dogs.

Do get in touch if you would like to support our work or to find out more about BRAVEHOUND.

BRAVEHOUND is a Glen Art Initiative.

Glen Art is a charity registered in Scotland SC043908

www.bravehound.co.uk
www.glenart.co.uk

# Canine Partners

Canine Partners is a registered charity that trains assistance dogs for people with physical disabilities including civilians and members of HM Armed Forces.

The dogs are trained to help with everyday tasks such as opening and shutting doors, unloading the washing machine, picking up dropped items, pressing buttons and switches and getting help in an emergency. They also increase independence, confidence and self-esteem and bring companionship, a sense of security and increased social interaction.

Canine Partners receives no government funding and relies solely on public donations. For further information visit www.caninepartners.org.uk or phone 08456 580480.

Registered charity no: 803680 (England and Wales) and SC039050 (Scotland)